Nirode Kumar Barooah

India and the Official Germany
1886-1914

D1824483

With kindest regards
to Mr. J. B. Harrison
Nirode K. Barooah
Cologne April '77

Europäische Hochschulschriften

Publications Universitaires Européennes
European University Papers

Reihe III

Geschichte und ihre Hilfswissenschaften

Série III   Series III

Sciences historiques et sciences auxiliaires de l'histoire
History, paleography and numismatics

Bd./Vol. 77

Nirode Kumar Barooah

India and the Official Germany
1886-1914

Peter Lang Frankfurt/M.
Herbert Lang Bern
1977

Nirode Kumar Barooah

India and the Official Germany
1886–1914

Peter Lang Frankfurt/M.
Herbert Lang Bern
1977

ISBN 3 261 02102 0

©

Peter Lang GmbH, Frankfurt/M. (BRD)
Herbert Lang & Cie AG, Bern (Schweiz)
1977. Alle Rechte vorbehalten.

Druck: fotokop wilhelm weihert KG, Darmstadt

To Eli

who made it possible

CONTENTS

PART TWO

GERMAN ASSESSMENT OF BRITISH RULE IN INDIA
AND GERMAN ANTIPATHY TO INDIAN NATIONALISM
1886 - 1913

PART THREE

BERLIN'S RECONCILIATION WITH INDIAN NATIONALISM
AUGUST - DECEMBER 1914

ACKNOWLEDGEMENTS

This book grew out of my rethinking over the introductory portion of a work, India in Germany 1914 - 1939, on which I have been working for the past few years. I am very grateful to Professor Horst Lademacher, formerly of the University of Bonn but now of Free University, Amsterdam, whose encouragement made it possible for me to return, after a period of volo, non valeo, to the completion of the work and thereby add the finale to my studies in the University of Bonn. The work has been approved by that University as part fulfilment for the degree of Dr. phil. in history in January 1975.

I will soon have another occasion to thank other persons and institutions for very many help in my all-round research and studies in Germany, but I can not omit here to name Professor Theodor Schieder of the University of Cologne whom I owe a great debt of gratitude on many counts.

I thank Dr. Weinandy and his entire staff at the Political Archive of the Foreign Office, Bonn, for their friendly co-operation. The relevant manuscript resources of this Archive are the primary basis of this work. The India Office Library, London, also rendered valuable inter-library loan service and I am very thankful for that.

I have pleasure in recalling the encouragement and criticisms that I received from my uncle Mr. S. K. Borooah of Gauhati, Assam. My friend Dr. Peter J. V. Willis of London very lovingly went through the finished manuscript and made some invaluable suggestions for which I am deeply grateful.

Finally, I must say that my wife's contribution to the writing of this book is beyond what I can convey.

Cologne   N. K. B.
October 1975

INTRODUCTION

> "Would it be a possible thing for your Majesty to have
> prepared and framed a number of highly enlarged
> photographic likenesses of yourself, and possibly even
> to sign them with your own hand as a gift to the Princes
> concerned? The idea has occurred to the Viceroy, from
> having heard recently from a visitor to the Maharajah
> of Kashmir's Court at Jammu, that there was only in
> the Palace a bad chromo-lithographic likeness of your
> Majesty, while there was a fine autograph photograph
> of the German Emperor."

Lord Curzon to Queen Victoria
Lumding, Assam, 11 March 1900.

Without being controversial it can perhaps be said that the last
two decades of the nineteenth century and the years before the
First World War found the big powers of the time deliberately
following policies of expansive and aggressive imperialism. (1)
Acquirement of distant territories, extension of capital investments
abroad, competition for overseas markets, control of supplies,
employment of measures for promoting or consolidating a position
of world power - all these were typical features of the period.
The original economic ground for expansion was soon followed
by a diplomatic one and the whole movement of European imperialism began to be upheld by various theories of social evolution,
racialism and humanitarianism. The votaries of European imperialism
began to look upon it as "a policy forced upon a civilised nation
by the very fact of its civilisation."(2) Although in this attitude

---

1) It has, however, been convincingly shown by Gallagher and Robinson
   that in Great Britain the imperial expansion from mid-Victorian to
   late-Victorian period was a continuous one with no neglect of the
   Empire in the former period due to the influence of the Manchester
   School. But the same authors have also stressed on the successful
   exploitation of the Empire, both 'formal' and 'informal', for 'the
   deepest meaning of expansion at the end of the nineteenth century.'
   See J. Gallagher and R. Robinson, 'The Imperialism of Free Trade',
   as reprinted in G. H. Nadel and P. Curtis (ed.), Imperialism and
   Colonialism (New York 1964) pp. 97-111 from The Economic History
   Review, 2, VI, no. 1, August 1953.

2) A. P. Thornton, The Imperial Idea and Its Enemies (London 1959)
   p. 75. See also here the arguments of the imperialists against the
   doctrine of laissez-faire.

towards the inhabitants of the subjugated areas the imperialist powers were one, in the process of extending their national policies into active world policies - a stage that came to imperialism around 1900 (3) - they fell out with one another.

The resistance encountered by the imperialist powers from the natives of the subjugated or otherwise controlled areas was minimal. The real contest, where both sides feared each other's might, took place between the competing imperialist powers themselves. The powers that played the major roles in the conflicts and rivalries leading to the First World War were five European and one Asiatic powers: Great Britain, France, Russia, Germany, Austro-Hungary and Japan. The areas of their involvements were Africa, the Balkans, East Asia (the Far East), West Asia (the Middle East) and Central Asia. As each of these powers entered the age of 'new imperialism' with prior enmity, jealousy or mistrust towards one or more of the rest of the powers (4) and as the added divergent interests in the new age made it more and more difficult for any of them to carry out imperialist designs in complete disregard to, or without any helping hand from some of the other powers, such instruments of diplomacy as pressure tactics, threats, mutual give-and-take, arbitration, secret negotiations, and finally alliances - all these aiming at achieving the goal either by avoiding war or waging a successful one - came to play a bigger and bigger role in the relations between these contending powers. The fact that all these powers had their special areas of vital interests where they were most sensitive enabled their rivals with the aid of diplomacy to coerce them to concede elsewhere.

---

3) H. Gollwitzer, Europe in the Age of Imperialism 1880-1914 (London 1969) p. 10.

4) The traditional enmity and jealousy between Great Britain and France were carried over to the new age of expansive imperialism until 1904 as both powers contested in the new period in Africa and West Asia. Constantinople had been the traditional bone of contention between Russia and Great Britain. In the new age, the two powers confronted themselves in two other areas, Central and East Asia. Russia and Austria remained inimical to each other in the Balkan as before. Germany had been France's greatest enemy ever since 1870 and continued to remain so. Japan's motives were feared or suspected more or less by all the European powers but her interests clashed heavily with those of Russia in East Asia.

So far as Britain was concerned her most sensitive spot was India, the very nucleus of her Empire. India's position in the imperialist rivalries of the great powers was indeed a peculiar one. She was neither an area of open contest among the imperialist powers nor was she a field for the colonists. And yet she remained very much in the centre of British imperialism and kept Britain worried, all through the age of imperialism, lest India should slip out of her grip. By the 1880s, as pointed out by Robinson and Gallagher, India had become of first importance to the British economy. (5) The British power in India with its easily expandable military force secured and promoted British trade not only throughout India but also in South-East and East Asia. Moreover, the Indian army which included in it as many Europeans as half the British home army itself and which was free from British parliamentary control regarding its size, fought battles for the preservation of British interests everywhere round the globe without the British people having to pay anything for its upkeep. (6) It was no wonder therefore that all those concerned with the administration of India in the imperialist age, both in India and Britain, were one in their conviction that the loss of India would be a mortal blow to Britain's prosperity, prestige and power. (7)

---

5) See R. Robinson and J. Gallagher, Africa and the Victorians: The Official Mind of Imperialism (London 1961) pp. 9-13. Britain is said to have invested by then some £ 270 million in India, a fifth of her entire overseas investment. India had also become a valuable exporter and importer, taking about 19% of British exports. In addition, much of the regional trade with other parts of Asia fell into British hands because of her possession of India.

6) The following is a list of the places where Indian troops were most conspicuously moved to during the later half of the nineteenth century: Crimea 1854-56; Persia 1856-7; China 1856 and 1859; New Zealand 1860-61; Abyssinia 1867; Singapore 1867; Honkong 1868; Malaya 1875; Malta 1878; Afghanistan 1878-1881; Egypt 1882; the Sudan 1885; Burma 1885; Nyasa 1893; Mombasa 1896, the Sudan again 1896-99. See ibid., p. 12 and n. 2; Thornton, op. cit., p. 97.

7) J. A. S. Grenville, Lord Salisbury and Foreign Polic: The Close of the Nineteenth Century (London 1964) p. 296.

Britain feared danger to her Indian Empire from all her continental rivals and even from her Asiatic ally Japan at different
periods in the age of imperialsm. But it was the Russian expansion
towards India together with the supposed possibility of their
success due to the geographical situation and Indian antipathy to
British rule which gave Britain maximum anxiety until the first
decade of this century.(8) This fear of a Russian danger to India
conditioned British policy towards Russia in Europe. That India
held British foreign policy a captive (9) soon became common
knowledge among the big powers. So much so that on 2 November
1899 Tsar Nicholas II wrote to his sister, rather naively, that
it was in his power to change the course of the Boer war by
telegraphically ordering the whole Turkestan army to mobilise.
"The strongest fleets in the world can't prevent us from settling
our scores with England precisely at her most vulnerable point,"
he added.(10) This was of course an exaggerated notion of Russia's
advantages on the part of the Tsar, but what made the 'defence
of India' problem a major item in the diplomacy of imperialism
was that at no time until the Anglo-Russian Convention of 1907
did the British authorities at home and in India minimise the
capacity of Russia to harm British India in one way or the other.
Britain's Indian handicap had an important bearing on the policies
of the other powers, besides Russia, towards Britain, and vice
versa. The 'defence of India' problem, therefore, played a role
in the emergence of alliances and counter-alliances among the
big powers before the First World War.

So far as Germany was concerned, she was introduced to this
problem in the early part of the 'eighties when Bismarck's

---

8) The 1907 Convention, however, did not end Britain's
   Russian danger in India for ever. Even when all the
   threats from the other European powers subsided,
   towards the end of the First World War, it was Russia
   again - the new Bolshevik Russia this time - which by
   singling out India as ripe for revolution caused great
   concern for Britain in the early months of 1918. See
   R. H. Ullman, Intervention and the War (Princeton 1961)
   pp. 28-9.

9) Thornton, op. cit., p. 42.

10) Krasny Arkhiv, 1934, vol. 1 xiii, pp. 125-6 quoted in
    B. H. Sumner, Tsardom and Imperialism in the Far East
    and Middle East, 1880-1914 (2d ed. 1968) pp. 7-8.

helping hand in it was saught by Britain. The importance Germany attached to the Indian factors in formulating her policy towards Britain or judging Britain's diplomatic moves in world politics can be judged from the fact that ever since her establishment of consular relations with British India in 1886, Germany sent out to India only experienced men from the diplomatic cadre to fill the posts of the Consul General in Calcutta and his chief sub-ordinates there. These men and also the Consul at Bombay were mainly concerned with observing and reporting the political and diplomatic goings-on of the country (11) whilst another batch of specially trained men looked into the interests of German people, trade and commerce in India. Theoretically, the German Consul General in India was under the control of the German Ambassador in London, but in practice all the reports from India went straight to Berlin and it was from there only that some of these were redirected to London - in the later period often according to the wish of Kaiser Wilhelm II who took astoundingly great interest in British Indian activities.

The dominant thought that guided Berlin until 1907 was that Britain, considering the state of her relations with other powers, particularly Russia, and being faced with many problems affecting the security of her Indian Empire, would seek Germany's friendship and co-operate with her plans of economic expansion. Berlin was greatly influenced in this period by the reports it received from Calcutta, Vienna, St. Petersburg and Constantinople about the pessimism of the Anglo-Indians in tackling the two-pronged problem which threatened Indian possession then: the possibility of a Russian attack and the inevitable uprising of the Indians against the foreign rule in the event of such an attack. So great was the impact of the 'defence of India' problem on Berlin that when in 1907 the Anglo-Russian Convention solved the problem so far as it consisted of the fear of a Russian threat, Berlin was still not convinced that the external side - not to speak of the internal one - of the Indian security problem was eliminated thereby. In the Kaiser's thought even Japan was in a position to extend her sway over India if the native disaffection for the British was allowed to remain as it was. On the eve of the First World War, taking for granted that the Turkey oriented Islamic support in India was in her favour, Germany thought that even she could pose a threat to India.

---

11) The German Consul in Bombay, however, used to send a yearly report giving all the details about the Indian economic world which was published later in Berichte über Handel und Industrie of the Prussian Ministry of the Interior.

From what we have described about India's importance for Britain, it would seem natural if Berlin desired to profit from Britain's Indian problems. In some of the published pre-War German documents Berlin's hopes from Britain's external problem in India are revealed through certain diplomatic calculations of the Kaiser and his one-time Chancellor Bülow. From the hitherto unpublished sources we have here brought to light even more startling facts such as Kaiser Wilhelm II's interest in seeing the Indian Muslims being under Turkish influence as far back as 1897 (a year before his famous Damascus speech) and indirect contact maintained with the Indian revolutionists abroad by some influential non-official Germans, close to the German Foreign Office, as early as around 1909. These show how for the sake of Weltpolitik Berlin even desired the continuance of Britain's internal difficulties in India. Yet one of our main findings in this study is that the Germans, including the Kaiser, remained great well-wishers and admirers of the British Empire in India throughout the age of imperialism. Except one solitary remark from the last of the German Consul Generals in India in the middle of 1913, there never was even a thought among the official Germans throughout their pre-War connection with India, of entangling directly with Britain's Indian problems with a view to profit from them. Far from thinking in terms of destroying British sovereignty in India, the Kaiser and official Germany, in the pre-War years, were critical of the British for what they considered Britain's deviation from the path of absolute rule in India by granting liberal constitutional reforms which were bound to loosen their permanent hold there. Indeed, one of the official Germans in India went so far as to formulate a plan for Britain's everlasting presence in India. It is therefore no wonder that none of the pre-War official Germans in India either brainheaded or zealously supported Germany's War-time India programme. (12) The non-consideration of the

---

12) Indeed, a member of one of the many German Persian expeditions during the early years of the War, Griesinger, was to suggest court-martial for Reuß, the then German Minister at Tehran who had previously served as Consul General in India, for not zealously pursuing the cause of the expeditionists. See W. Griesinger, German Intrigues in Persia: The Diary of a German Agent (published by the British n.d.) pp. 22, 25, 29. Even among those Germans who took active part in these expeditions with the ultimate aim of bringing about anti-British revolution in India, there were some who, far from having any ill will

despatches of the pre-War German foreign service personnel in India has perpetuated hitherto the myth that Germany prepared for her War-time conspiracy against the British Empire in India long before the War. The fact, however, is that even after the outbreak of the War, it was not until the Indian revolutionists themselves took over the charge of the Berlin oriented War-time Indian programme towards the end of 1914, that the originally limited purpose (13) of this programme was enlarged to include measures towards the liberation of India.

The Germans in India were, of course, always under strict observation of the British Indian secret service and, as the quotation at the beginning of this introduction shows, (14) the British in India took no chance with even the remotest possibility of German influence in any sphere having to bear upon the question of 'defence of India'. But it was not this control - and not wholly either the India based official Germans' correct assessment of British strength in India (which was far more optimistic than that of the contemporary Anglo-Indians themselves) - which was the reason behind the absence of German ill-will towards the British Empire in India. The genuine German desire for the continuance of this Empire sprang from a variety of deep-seated

---

against the British rule in India in the pre-War years, were great admirers of it. For example, one of them, Dr. Erich Zugmayer, wrote about this rule as late as in 1912 thus: "India has never been ruled more peacefully, with more mildness, justice and freedom before coming under the British rule... The rule over India, however, must be preserved for the white race as long as it is possible... The nation that failed to hold with iron fists a possession like India would not be worth enough to exist further." E. Zugmayer, "Die nationalistische Bewegung in Indien" in Dr. Vosberg-Rekow (ed.), Asiatisches Jahrbuch (Berlin 1912) pp. 50-51.

13) to compell Britain to confine the bulk of her fighting men to India.

14) From a letter of Lord Curzon to Queen Victoria, Lumding, Assam, 11 March 1900. See G. E. Buckle (ed.), The Letters of Queen Victoria (hereafter Q. V. L.) (London 1932), 3, III, p. 511. Although there is no evidence that the German attraction to the Indian princely circle had any political bearing, Curzon rightly sensed the importance of the disaffected princes in any conspiracy against the British rule in India either from within or without.

ideological, temperamental and utilitarian sources. Even the high regard of the nationalist-minded Indians for Germany because of the enthusiams for indology in that country produced absolutely no sympathy among the official Germans for the political aspirations of the modern Indians.

The pre-War German attitude towards British imperialism in India being what we have described, a doubt about the depth of the change in this attitude, as occurered through German War-time co-operation with the Indian revolutionists, may very well be raised. Yet certain accidental factors put the Indians themselves in the control of Berlin's War-time policy of revolutionising India - an extraordinary event indeed.

In this study of the official Germany's relations with India during 1886-1914, the place of India in the diplomatic thinking of Imperial Germany from the last years of Bismarck to the year before the First World War is chronologically discussed in Part One. The attitudes of the official Germany towards the British rule in India and Indian nationalism during the same period are the subjects of Part Two. Chapter VII here should be taken more as an appendix to the whole Part rather than an independent chapter, for here we have been able to give not more than an outline of the German material interests in India from some published sources and accounts. Our requests for permission to consult the relevant primary colonial and trade-commercial records at the Potsdam Archive were unfortunately rejected by the authorities of the German Democratic Republic. Part Three with a single chapter describes how that extraordinary alliance between the Indian revolutionary nationalists and the German Foreign Office came about after all in 1914, at the outbreak of the World War. Being the climax of the pre-War terrorist movement, and being also connected with the growth of socialist and communist thoughts in India, the Berlin India Committee has often been referred to by scholars. However no authentic account of its formation (and also its four years of activities) has hitherto been attempted with due consultation of the original German documents. Although here we have dealt only with the formative phase of this organisation (a full study of this Committee is under preparation), we have, however, taken into consideration the nature and significance of all the activities during the whole period of its existence. As most of our conclusions appear in the chapters themselves, the concluding section of this study merely summarises the main events of the German-Indian relations during the period

of our study and tries to see the significance for the future of
the final event, i. e. the War-time co-operation between the
official Germany and the Indians.

PART ONE

INDIA IN IMPERIAL GERMANY'S DIPLOMATIC THINKING

1886 - 1913

I. BISMARCKIAN GERMANY STUDIES BRITAIN'S 'DEFENCE OF INDIA' PROBLEM 1885 - 87

> "Her easiness to pick up a quarrel with every sea power, the French interest in Egypt, the Russian policy in Asia, the entire Islam in India and the Levant, would so considerably increase her responsibilities that Britain would have reason to seek willy-nilly our support against all those existing and future opponents to her rule in the Orient."
>
> Bismarck to Prince Heinrich Reuß VII, 10 August 1882.

In 1886 Imperial Germany established her office of the Consulate General for British India and Ceylon in Calcutta. The earlier German commercial representations (Wahlkonsulate) in many parts of India (1) were, however, not hampered thereby; they continued to remain side by side, taking a major part of the strictly trade-commercial business from the Consul General and his higher subordinates both in Calcutta and Bombay and thereby allowing the latter to devote more time to observing and reporting the political and diplomatic goings-on of the country. No wonder therefore that almost without exception the pre-War German Consuls General to British India and their higher subordinates were career diplomats with experience. (2)

The time that Prince Bismarck chose for sending out diplomatic observers to India was very significant indeed. It was a time when Britain, due to French rivalry in Egypt (occupied by Britain with German encouragement in 1882) and West Africa on the one

---

1) See below chapter VII p. 158.

2) Three of these men later rose to the position of ambassadors in different countries and in the case of one, Baron Speck von Sternburg, the Consul General during 1901-1903, the immediate next assignment after India was ambassadorship in Washington. (As to their previous experiences, follow the careers given in footnotes where their names have first appeared in the text.) At the turn of the century Germany's sending of career diplomats to India for consular service was a matter of suspicion for at least one European country, Russia. (Radolin to Hohenlohe, St. Petersburg 16 May 1900 quoting Wesseliuki Boshedarovich's (Argus) article in Novoye Vremya.)

hand, and the evergrowing fear of a Russian threat to India from
Central Asia on the other, was looking to Bismarck as a saviour.
As compared to Britain's isolation in Europe at this time,
Bismarckian Germany was in a most commanding position among
the European powers. Austria and Italy were bound to her in
alliance since October 1879 and May 1882 respectively, and Russia,
too, was tied to her by the Three Emperors' League since June
1881. Germany was also in a position to show - as she had already done at the London conference on Egypt (June-August 1884) -
that she could bring about a united front of continental powers to
pressurise Britain if and when the need arose. (3) To this commanding position Britain had already given in in regards to German
colonial demands and by 1886 Germany acquired all that Bismarck
wanted to have in the colonial field. (4) No matter how unhappy the
British were at Germany's acquisition of colonies (5) and her
growing appearance as Britain's commercial rival (6) the British
governments had every reason to solicit Germany's friendship at
this time for the security of India.

In the summer of 1885, when Britain's Afghan boundary negotiations
with Russia broke down, Salisbury's Government thought that a war
with Russia would be inevitable. The Russians now at Penjdeh had
accepted the outgoing Liberal Government's proposal of arbitration

---

3) cf. W.H. Dawson, The German Empire 1867-1914 and the
    Unity Movement II (London 2d ed. 1966) pp.163-4.

4) The major German colonial possessions by this time were:
    The Cameroons (July 1884), German South-West Africa
    (August 1884), New Guinea (December 1884), German East
    Africa (May 1885). Thus except Samoa, added in 1899, the
    German acquisition of colonies was virtually the work of a
    single year. See A.J.P. Taylor, Germany's First Bid for
    Colonies 1884-1885... (2d ed. 1967) p.3.

5) At each of Germany's major colonial acquisitions there was
    British indignation. For the British press and public opinion
    see W.R. Louis, Great Britain and Germany's Lost Colonies
    1914-1919 (Oxford 1967) pp.19-20.

6) A Royal Commission was appointed in 1885 to investigate
    the causes of the 'depression of trade and industry',
    The Commission's report, published in 1886, showed
    Germany and the U.S.A. as the most serious competitors.

on the responsibility for the Penjdeh affair (7), but they refused
to accept the British case for Afghan control of the Zulficar Pass,
an approach to Herat. The British thought that knowing the strate-
gical importance of Herat the Russian generals would hardly stop
from advancing towards it. When Abdur Rahman, the Amir of
Afghanistan, found that he had a weak hold over the Penjdeh tribes-
men, Gladstone's Government had assured the Russian ambassador
of Britain's willingness to let Penjdeh go. But Herat was a fifferent
matter. A turning movement via Merv and Herat had been the traditional route for the conquest of India in the past as it bypassed the
formidable barrier of the Hindu Kush. (8) Hence Herat in the hands
of a hostile power was a much greater menace to the security of
India. Even the hitherto Russophile Liberals had agreed on this
and in April the Liberal Secretary of State Kimberley had accepted
the views of General Roberts and advocated that "India should have
a properly armed frontier such as exists between the great Continental States. "(9) So in June 1885 when Salisbury came to power
the position was that if Russia persisted on advancing to Herat a
clash between the Sepoys and the Cossacks would be inevitable.
This would lead to a general war because Britain would then consider it an absolute necessity to cut communications between Russia
and her central Asian possessions by forcing an entrance to the
Black Sea for British ships. For the latter course Salisbury, however, visualised the difficulties created by Britain's isolation in
Europe. He therefore tried to avoid a war and saught Germany's
help. Salisbury privately wrote to Prince Bismarck in July asking
whether the German Chancellor would agree to mediate between
Britain and Russia to restore good understanding between the two
countries, if not permanently then at least for a couple of years,
by the end of which Britain would be better prepared. (10)
Salisbury's emissary Sir Philip Currie, an Assistant Under Sec-

---

7) Early in March 1885 Giers had promised Gladstone that there
    would be no further Russian advance towards Afghanistan be-
    fore the delimitation commission got to work. Yet on 30 March
    there was a clash between the Russian and Afghan troops at
    Penjdeh.

8) As argued by Sir Henry Rawlinson, a senior member of the
    India Council. R. L. Greaves, Persia and the Defence of
    India 1884-1892: A study in the Foreign Policy of the third
    Marquis of Salisbury (London 1959) p. 57.

9) Minute by Kimberley 5 April 1885, ibid., p. 32.

10) Ibid., pp. 91-2.

retary of State, met in Germany Count Herbert Bismarck and Prince Bismarck for the same purpose. (11) So much did Britain desire German friendship that around the same time she also tried to win Germany as a joint guarantor of Persia's integrity by giving the whole 'settlement' in Persia, like the construction of railways and so on, into German hands. (12)

To all these overtures Bismarck's answer was a polite refusal. Britain was told that Germany did not wish to incur difficulties from Russia on her Eastern frontier; "the water is too hot" Herbert Bismarck told Currie, "for us to put our finger in. "(13) Fortunately for Britain the Russians suddenly changed their mind and on 10 September signed an agreement in St. Petersburg whereby they accepted the British case over Zulfikar pass giving preliminary definition to the boundary from there to the Oxus. If the motives behind this Russian volte face are not entirely clear (14) so also is incomplete the German argument for refusing a British alliance during this time. It is true that Bismarck had no faith in the English parliamentary system of government and he may well have been cautious about leaning strongly on Britain in 1885 not knowing the fate of an agreement with her in the event of change of government there. His dislike of Gladstone and the English Liberals - who actually came to power, although for a short while,

---

11) Sir Philip Currie's negotiations with Count Herbert and Prince Otto von Bismarck in autumn of 1885; ibid. , App. II pp. 237-254.

12) Count Wilhelm von Bismarck to Prince Bismarck, Pvt. London, 19 August 1885, J. Lepsius, A.M. Bartholdy and F. Thimme (ed.), Die Große Politik der europäischen Kabinette 1871-1917 (hereafter cited as G. P.) (Berlin 1922-27) IV, No. 784.

13) Currie to Salisbury, 4 August 1885, in Greaves, op. cit., p. 96.

14) It is supposed to be either because it was recognised in St. Petersburg that Salisbury would not cede what even Granville had refused or simply because, as Herbert Bismarck noted, that Russia was not yet prepared for a conflict in Asia. C. J. Lowe, The Reluctant Imperialists, British Foreign Policy 1878-1902 (London 1967) I, p. 91.

in February 1886 - may also have strengthened this suspicion. (15) But this point cannot be carried very far as when in 1889 Bismarck offered an alliance to Salisbury it was the same system of government in Britain. Nor did the memory of the recent colonial controversies, which arose out of what Bismarck regarded as inconsiderate treatment on the part of the British, constitute a sufficient bar to Bismarck's accepting the offered British alliance in 1885. It was his long conviction that Britain's national need to preserve India from dangerous neighbours would prompt her to seek a strong, peaceful continental power between Russia and France and only the joint peaceful policy of Germany and Austria could provide that. As early as 1880 Bismarck had analysed this in a letter to Prince Reuß, the German Ambassador in Vienna. He, however, added: "There might of course be great differences in the energy and choice of means of different English governments, and a redoubled vigilance is necessary in view of Gladstone's new experiments with the so-called principle of nationality."(16) In August 1882 in another letter to Reuß, Bismarck took up the same theme again. The easiness with which Britain could pick up a quarrel with every sea power; her unsettled question of Egypt with France; her concern about the Russian policy in Asia and 'the entire Islam in India and the Levant', would enhance her responsibility considerably and she would willy-nilly seek German support for her rule in the Orient. (17) The

---

15) Currie after meeting Prince Bismarck on 28 September 1885 noted that Bismarck's fear was that Gladstone might become P. M. again. Gladstone to him was a man who had no knowledge of foreign affairs and with whom it was impossible to do business, see Greaves, op. cit., p. 246; About Bismarck's dislike of Gladstone see also the letter that Bismarck wrote to Schweinitz, the German Ambassador at St. Petersburg on 26 February 1884 given in full in W. N. Medlicott, Bismarck, Gladstone and the Concert of Europe (London 1956) App. II, pp. 341-2.

16) Bismarck to Prince Heinrich Reuß VII, 23 April 1880, quoted in W. Windelband, Bismarck und die Europäischen Großmächte 1879-1885 (Essen 1940) p. 163; see also Medlicott, op. cit., p. 63. This Reuß should not be mistaken with Prince Heinrich Reuß XXXI of the same family but of different line who was the German Consul General in India during 1910-12.

17) Bismarck to Prince Heinrich Reuß, 10 August 1882, quoted in Windelband, op. cit., p. 407.

reasons behind Bismarck's reluctance to mediate over the Anglo-
Russian rivalry in Central Asia and to tie Germany with Britain
in 1885 seem to have been different from what has so far been
suggested. It was the disturbing information about the internal
insecurity of British India which the German Foreign Office had
been receiving from the sources then available which seems to
have played some role in it. It may have at least made Bismarck
cautious in 1885 lest he should back the wrong horse. This would
also explain the motive behind later sending out career diplomats
to India so as to get the proper picture of the British power position in India vis-a-vis Russia before he extended his hand to
Britain.

The so-called 'defence of India' problem arose, after all, as much
out of the jingoist 'forward' policy of the Anglo-Indians as from
the Russian advance across Central Asia after the Crimean War.
When in the later half of the eighteen eighties the Russian advance
from the Caspian towards Herat brought a new dimension to the
old problem of relations with Afghanistan by bringing the question
of Persia as well, it was political rather than military reasons
which were uppermost in the minds of the adherents of the 'forward' school. As Cross, the Secretary of State for India during
1886-92 was to describe later, the Russian Empire compared to
that of the British appeared as 'spreading power' and 'the people
worship only the rising sun'. In the eyes of General Roberts the
Indian princes were unreliable and it would be unwise to encourage
a high state of efficiency amongst the troops of the independent
states. Hence there was no question of defending India in India.
According to Salisbury, too, the Russian acquisition of territories
in Central Asia was gradually weakening respect for English arms
amongst the natives and this would in turn produce intrigues and
rebellions among the natives before the Russian arms met those
of the British on the Indian frontier. (18) To avoid all these difficulties and apprehensions it was proposed that the Cossacs were
to be met outside the frontiers of India. In other words, the problems of Britain's internal insecurity in India were to be solved
by gaining victories outside Indian frontiers.

The fact, however, was that the more the external danger from
the Russians was exaggerated to bolster up the cause of the
'scientific' frontierists, the more widespread became the knowledge of Britain's internal insecurity in India to the other European
Powers. The information that the German Foreign Office had already collected about India before the opening of the German Con-

---

18) See Greaves, op. cit., pp. 34, 67; Lowe, op. cit., pp. 76-77.

sulate General there gave a gloomy picture of Britain's strength and popularity in India. In the mid-eighties the chauvinistic English journals taking the view of the 'forward' school had deliberately published exaggerated news and articles about Britain's weakening position in India. They thereby tried to show the possibility there of a revolt, greater than that of 1857, in order to force the Home Government to strengthen its military position in India and suppress the educated Indians' demands for representative institutions. They exaggerated Indian discontentment with the alien rulers and advised the Government to suppress the native press, disband the forces of the native princes, and take a more serious attitude to the problem posed by the Russians. (19)

Compared to these, the information received by Berlin through other channels did not give such a bleak picture of the British position in India. Nevertheless they, too, revealed to the German Foreign Office that all was not too well with the British in India and an uprising among the Indians was not wholly unthinkable. In April 1885 it learnt from a report submitted by the Austrian Consul in Bombay to the Austro-Hungarian Foreign Minister Count Kálnoky that the preconceived notions and religious arrogance of the subject people on the one hand and the 'nigger' attitude on the part of the British on the other, kept the rulers and the ruled in India wide apart. (20) The Consul reported that most of the jobless educated or half-educated Indians took to journalistic professions expressing 'national' grievances which were on the rise since the time of the ill-fated Ilbert Bill + of Lord Ripon's

---

19) The earliest information of the German Foreign Office about the British Indian situation came from the following articles: 'Indian Dangers' in The St. James's Gazette 23 October 1884; 'The Garrisons of Revolt in India' in The St. James's Gazette 11 December 1884; 'India for the Indians' (reproduction of a letter from an Indian first published elsewhere) in Pall Mall Gazette 5 February 1883 (sic) Auswärtiges Amt, Bonn, Britische Besitzungen in Asien, 2, Britisch Indien (hereafter cited as AABI) 1.

20) Stockinger to Kálnoky, Bombay 25 February 1885, AABI 1.

+ Ilbert Bill (1883-4) sought to withdraw the privilege held by the British in India of being tried by judges of their own race. The Bill was defeated as a result of the rabid opposition of the European community.

liberal regime. Although the greater part of the Indian people
was well aware of the benefits of the British rule, this rule
was intensely if not openly hated by the princes, according
to the Austrian observer. The report also highlighted the
Muslim power in India; although only one fifth of the entire
population, the Muslims were said to be well-knit unlike the
Hindus and their solidarity was based on the ideas commonly
shared by all of them alike. They prayed daily for the Khalif
at Constantinople (although no one prayed for the Empress of
India) and lately at their request a Turkish Consulate General
had been established in Bombay. (21) In March 1886 a German
General Staff officer who had had earlier the opportunity of
observing British military manoeuvres in India reported to the
German Foreign Office that although the Indian princes were
by and large loyal to the British, it would not be difficult to
bring about an uprising in India and such an uprising would
definitely help any power threatening India. The officer further
mentioned that already in the summer of 1885 the agents from
Turkestan visited Lucknow and neighbouring areas and started
instigating the people against the British. (22)

Such news about Britain's internal difficulties in India kept on
coming throughout 1886 and it was through them that the German
Foreign Office tried to understand Britain's attitude to the
Bulgarian Crisis (1885-7). The Three Emperors League, visualising that the Union of Eastern Roumania and Bulgaria would
only encourage Serbia and Greece to stake out their claims and
would probably produce a general onslaught upon the Ottoman
Empire, decided to insist on a return to the status quo ante in
Bulgaria. This was against Salisbury's plan which aimed at
supporting the Union as he thought that an independent national
feeling might develop in Bulgaria which, combined with the
similar feeling that already existed in Roumania, might make
the Russian passage to Constantinople very difficult. (23) To
Friedrich von Holstein, an influential Senior Counsellor and a
private policy maker inside the German Foreign Office, a man
sincerely interested, at this time, in seeing Britain abandon her
isolation and involve in the affairs of Eastern Europe, it was
precisely the precarious Turkish influence over the Indian Muslim

---

21) Ibid.

22) Report of Baron von Hönningen, Berlin 15 March 1886, AABI 1.

23) Lowe, op. cit., p. 102.

which should lead Britain to do anything to prevent Turkey from coming under Russian control. In a memorandum of August 1886 which he arranged to send to the Queen of England through Crown Princess Victoria, Holstein argued that it was certain that the Russians would move against India at an opportune moment and that the British would then be forced - if no bold measure was taken in the meantime - to defend India under the worst possible circumstances after losing face to the Asiatics and without allies in Europe. (24) In September, while dwelling on the same theme - the lack of a bold British move to prevent the Sultan of Turkey falling under Russian control - Holstein saw how the destiny of the British rule in India depended on the 85 million of Indian Muslims. (25)

To others in the Foreign Office the reason for the British soft-pedalling with Russia was made clear by the recent happenings in India. In October 1886 Herbert Bismarck, now the German Foreign Secretary, explained to the Kaiser how Britain's policy in the Balkans was influenced by her insecure position in India. (26) He said that he had recently learnt from a very reliable source that a situation akin to the one created by the pork-beef-fat-alloyed cartridges at the time of the mutiny of 1857 recently occurred in Calcutta where the butter traders mixed in their products oleomargarin, a substance made out of pork and beef fat. The People were said to have been greatly upset and the Government immediately passed a law prohibiting the mixing of butter. The Foreign Secretary also attached great significance to Maharaja Dilip Singh's connection with the Russians and his antagonism to the British. This he found significant because the Sikhs, to which community Dilip Singh belonged, played the most important role in the Indian army along with the Gurkhas. Herbert Bismarck further mentioned that among the generals of the Indian

---

24) Holstein's point was that Britain could avoid this by acting at once to bolster the position of the Sultan and backing him against Russia. See. N. Rich, Friedrich von Holstein: Politics and Diplomacy in the Era of Bismarck and Wilhelm II, Vol. I (Cambridge 1965) p. 185.

25) Holstein to Radolinski, 13 September 1886, ibid., p. 178.

26) Herbert Bismarck to the German Emperor, Berlin 10 October 1886, AABI 1.

army the fear of an uprising in India was widespread. These generals, he added, blamed the former Viceroy Ripon who, with the support of Gladstone, had done all the harm with his liberalising measures - measures which brought the Indians to the stage of even adopting the programme of the British radicals, talking of public opinion and self-government and organising public meetings. (27)

A few days after Herbert Bismarck's memorandum Le Moniteur de Rome reporting on the internal situation of British India remarked that this rule, which had always been based on a moral prestige hammered on the minds of the natives with a great deal of fantasy and courage, was in a precarious and insecure position. The paper concluded that should there be a convulsion and foreign intervention, the British in India would find themselves in a desperate struggle from which they might come out victorious only by chance and through a great deal of heroism and no less cruelty. (28) This paper was considered by the German Foreign Office to be well informed about overseas conditions because of its link with the missions. (29) The news when read along with the recent report of the British Lords of the Admiralty about the poor cindition of the British fleet - a report which got publicity due to the indiscretion of the Pall Mall Gazette (30) - caused some concern in the German Foreign Office. Chancellor Bismarck asked for Le Moniteur de Rome article on India to be sent to the German ambassador in London for varification. (31) To cap the climax of bad news about Britain's position in India there came in early December 1886 a passage in a private letter to Herbert Bismarck from Bülow at St. Petersburg. Bülow, the future German Foreign Secretary and Chancellor, who was now posted as a Counsellor at the German Embassy in the Russian capital, wrote that according to information from his Russian friends the British rule in India was on shaky feet and that an

---

27) Herbert Bismarck to the German Emperor, 10 October 1886, ibid.

28) 'Indoustan', Le Moniteur de Rome 15 October 1886, AABI 1.

29) A. A. note on above, 17 October 1886, ibid.

30) Ibid.

31) A. A. A 12598, 20 October 1886, ibid.

uprising against this rule would take place in India before long. (32)

Thus till a year after Prince Bismarck's rejection of British requests for mediation and alliance the German Foreign Office remained convinced of Britain's insecurity in India. The result of this was Prince Bismarck's firm support of Russia in the Bulgarian crisis. As mentioned earlier the German Chancellor was, however, not against a permanent friendship with Britain. He had told Currie in September 1885 that he would be sending Hatzfeldt to replace Münster in London in order "to establish real and intimate relations with England. "(33) In December 1886 both Hatzfeldt (34) and Metternich (35) from London and Herman Gerlich (36), the first German Consul General in India form Calcutta, sent their reports on India. The proner and direct study of the Indian situation from the German official side began from this period.

The German Foreign Office personnel's own studies of the Indian situation in the next few years disproved many of the scare stories which had got currency through Russian and Austrian channels. Britain's fear of an Indian uprising was found to be greater than the actual chance of it. On 21 December Hatzfeldt sent a report from Metternich who had recently talked extensively with a British authority on Asian affairs about the Indian question. (37) According

---

32) Herbert Bismarck to Hatzfeldt at London, Berlin 16 December 1886, AABI 1.

33) Currie to Salisbury, Homburg 29 Sept. 1885, in Greaves, App. II, p. 253.

34) Paul, Count von Hatzfeldt-Wildenburg (1831-1901): 1874 Ambassador in Madrid; 1878 Ambassador in Constantinople; 1881-5 Secretary for Foreign Affairs; 1885-1901 Ambassador, London.

35) Paul Wolff, Count von Metternich (1853-1934): 1886-1901 Counsellor, Embassy London; 1901-12 Ambassador in London.

36) Dr. Hermann Gerlich (1844-1932): 1875 Vice-Consul, New York; 1877 Consul, Saint Louis; 1881-82 in Prussian Commercial Ministry; 1886 Consul General, Calcutta; 1891 German delegate at Dette Publique Ottomane, Constantinople; 1895 agricultural economic expert in German Embassy, London.

37) Metternich to Hatzfeldt, London 20 December 1886, AABI 1.

to Metternich's authority the British Indian troops would be
greatly outnumbered by those of the Russians and the best
of the Indian soldiers - the Sikhs and the Gurkhas - would
be no match to their Russian counterparts in the event of a
clash. Besides, Britain's problem would be whether in the
face of instigation from the Russians at Herat - if they were
to capture it - she would be able to rely on the loyalty of
the Indian people. The answer to this was no. Metternich was,
however, told that for the present there was no possibility of
an uprising among the Indian people even if a war with Russia
was to break out. The Amir of Afghanistan was also said to
be reliable for the time being as he very well knew that Britain
alone was his main supporter and Russia already had a successor
to this throne. Yet the Amir was not to be overestimated. Metternich was further informed that in case of a war with Russia it
would be waged on the Black Sea and there alone the struggle
for India would be decided. Locating the Russian war operations
in Europe would be Britain's policy in order to keep India safe.
This plan could, however, be implemented only when the Turkish
armies were bought off at the right moment and Britain got access
to the Dardanelles. (38)

In his covering letter enclosing Metternich's report Hatzfeldt
mentioned that he had learnt from a confidential talk with Lord
Salisbury that Britain could not rely on the loyalty of Afghanistan
although the Afghan loyalty question was not so important to him. (39)
Like Metternich Hatzfeldt, too, was informed of Britain's intention
to wage the battle for India on the Black Sea. Lord Randolph
Churchill was said to have particularly advocates this policy. (40)
This revealation seems to have puzzled the German Foreign Office:
"To do this the Porte must be Britain's friend," reacted the Ger-
man Foreign Office which also noted Britain's plan to win over
the Turkish army. (41)

Early in January 1887 arrived the first report from Gerlich in
India written in the first week of December. Gerlich who was
employed in the Prussian Ministry of Commerce before going
to India was an expert on agricultural economy. But neither his

---

38) Ibid.

39) Hatzfeldt to Bismarck, London 21 December 1886, AABI 1.

40) Ibid.

41) Marginal stress and comments on above.

special field of interest nor the general commercial character of a Consulate General could hide the fact that Bismarck had diplomatic purpose in sending him to India. Indeed, in this first report from India Gerlich wrote that British official circles were suspicious of him and everywhere the same question was in the air: "What could Prince Bismarck mean by sending Gerlich here?"(42) In India official circles believed at this time that Russia and Germany had already come to an agreement over Bulgaria to the disadvantage of Britain. Thus Gerlich was suspected as a political spy, and wrote that even the Viceroy, Lord Dufferin, was not free from this thought.(43)

As to the question of the Indian security problem Gerlich apparently did not see any immediate danger for the British, for he mentioned nothing about the brewing of an uprising. But Berlin was still informed by Vienna of the deteriorating situation of the British in India. In December 1886 Kálnoky told Remy, a member of the German Embassy in Vienna, about the latest reports he had received from his Consul in Bombay about people in general being in an agitated mood, defying the authority of the British civil servants and demanding from the Viceroy various reforms. The activities of the Russian agents in the native courts were also said to be continuing. The Consul visualised a serious crisis for the British in the future if all these various discontented elements were to be skillfully exploited by an outside power. Kálnoky of course said that his Consul was perhaps too pessimistic adding, however, that it would be unwise not to give attention to the Indian factors while considering British policy in Europe.(44)

---

42) Gerlich to Bismarck, Calcutta 6 December 1886, AABI 2.

43) Gerlich wrote that at the race course in Simla Lord Dufferin suddenly approached him and asked what was Germany's intention in Bulgaria. It appeared to Gerlich as if the Viceroy was trying to know Germany's mind about Russia. Gerlich leisurely answered that he had nothing to do with politics and that he would be the last person whom anyone would inform about the Bulgarian policy. He told the Viceroy that the latter was possibly better informed about German politics than he himself was. Gerlich, however, told Dufferin that Germany perhaps would not do anything more in the Bulgarian crisis than to leave the matter to those who were more closely participating in it. Duffering then told Gerlich that Britain was actually not interested either in Bulgaria or in Constantinople; the security of Egypt was her only interest. Ibid.

44) Remy to Bismarck, Vienna 29 December 1886, AABI 1.

In January 1887 Metternich checked with his expert on Asian affairs in London all the scare stories concerning British India which the German Foreign Office had lately received. Metternich was told that all the alarming rumours published in the British and foreign press were only minor details which should not be given any attention. (45) The recently circulated news that the alleged troop concentration of Russian cavalry (40,000 strong) between the Caspian and Merv caused a great stir among the Indian population was nothing but 'bazaar gossip' which could not be helped. It was, however, a fact, Metternich was told, that the Governor of Herat had recently been ordered to come to Kabul to justify before the Amir of Afghanistan his recent hostile behaviour towards the British, and this created a favourable impression in India. But this fact, too, should not be overestimated for it was impossible to count on the vague fluctuations of peoples' moods in India. There was actually no need to take that into account. Moreover, the Governor of Herat was called to Kabul not because of his pro-Russian attitude. This news was circulated from Ashkhabad, on the Russo-Persian border, and consequently was of Russian origin. According to the India Office the Governor was called just because Abdur Rahman, the Afghan Amir, wanted to do a favour to the British Government as in the previous year the Governor had behaved in a hostile way towards the British frontier commission out of his tendency to assert an independent position. (46)

About the internal matters of India Metternich learned that it was true that Lord Dufferin's latest tours in India did not receive the same ovation and popularity as those of his predecessor. It was because unlike Ripon, Dufferin did not approve of all those reforms which Ripon "in the spirit of the British radical school and wrong ideas of humanity and under the influence of Indian incense" had approved to help strengthen the Indians against the British. Hence in Agra and Bombay the municipal authorities, influenced by the English educated natives aspiring to local self-government, did not give the usual festive reception to the Viceroy. But such ommissions by no means symbolised the lessening of British influence in India, Metternich was told.

Metternich gathered that the rumours about the activities of the Russian agents in India were also similarly exaggerated. He came

---

45) Metternich to Hatzfeldt, London 28 January 1887, AABI 1.

46) Ibid.

to know that every year a few hundred traders went from Bukhara
to the north-west of India, mainly to Peshawar, to trade in dried
food in exchange for Indian tea. These people belonged mainly to
the tribes of Kokandis, Sartsans, and Uzbeks who were under
Russian rule. Some of them continued their journey further to
Lahore and Delhi and even to Bombay. They were, however,
very carefully watched by the Indian Government. In 1885-86 two
Russian travellers had entered India from the north and visited
the courts of the Indian princes, but due to their suspicious
behaviour both were arrested and expelled from the country. The
much circulated news of Russian agents at Indian courts was
therefore simply unfounded. Metternich was, however, told that
this did not mean that the Indian princes were free from indigenous
intriguers. Not just one or two but each had as many as thirty
intriguers. Every prince had his grievances; one had not got
enough salute, another was crying for a bigger guard of honour
and so on. The intriguers were fed by these grievances. (47)

Coming to the final part of the question i. e. the possibility of
an uprising in India, Metternich's authorative informer was frank.
No reasonable Britisher, he said, could have the least doubt about
the Indians' lack of love for England; they only feared and respected
British power. But this fear and respect were nevertheless effective
enough not to allow any uprising and no uprising would occur even
if the British were to be entangled with a foreign power. The situation
would, however, change, the expert added, in the event of a British
defeat in a war. The chances of an uprising would then rapidly
approach. But here again the variety of uncompromisable religions
and nationalities among the natives would keep the British going
for some time as there was no sign that the hatred prevailing
among the Indians themselves would suddenly be replaced by
reconciliation. Metternich was told that the greatest danger to
the British in India from inside was the spread of the British
educational system there. (48)

The information that Metternich collected about the external and
internal aspects of the 'defence of India' question gave a balanced
picture of the British position in India. To sum up this position,
neither a Russian invasion nor an Indian uprising was imminent
or easy but the possibility of their occurrence had by no means
ceased to be a concern for the British. Besides, an uprising

---

47) Metternich to Hatzfeldt, London 28 January 1887, AABI 1.

48) Ibid.

against the British in India was considered almost inevitable in the event of a British reverse in a foreign war although such an uprising might still be devoid of a complete success due to the inherent disunity among the Indian people. Firmly held by Berlin in the coming years, these basic propositions on the British Indian situation were to acquire special significance in the thoughts of Kaiser Wilhelm II all through the years leading up to the First World War.

II. INDIA IN KAISER WILHELM II's 'NEW COURSE'

> "In our opinion Germany, by no means, has any reason
> to let the general European interests and those of her
> own be bypassed by the Anglo-Indian interests."
>
> Bülow to the Kaiser, 29 August 1897.

During the Bulgarian cirsis some developments took place which
found Germany closer still to Russia. On 18 June 1887 the Reinsurance Treaty was signed between the two countries (1) and
on 3 February 1888 Bismarck went beyond the diplomatic support
given so far to Russia and approved the latter's policy in Bulgaria
in opposition to Austria-Hungary, Italy and Britain. Compared to
these actions of Bismarck's closing years of chancellorship Kaiser
Wilhelm II's earliest actions as emperor seemed drastically opposite.

With two of the earliest moves of the young Emperor India came
to be indirectly associated. First, by not renewing the Reinsurance
Treaty with Russia in March 1890 the Kaiser showed a desire for
friendly relations with Britain. Although in the summer of 1890
Anglo-German relations reached their 'high water mark of in-
timacy' (2) with the Heligoland-Zanzibar agreement in July, the
relations between the two countries did not develop into a close
friendship. In her desire either to gain Britain as ally if possible
or see her engaged with Russia in Central Asia in case an alliance
failed, Germany took a growing interest in Britain's 'defence of
India' problem. Secondly, the link that the Kaiser had established
with Turkey ever since his first visit to Constantinople in 1889 led
him to take an interest in the activities of the Indian Muslims so
far as they were geared to Turkey and in the pre-war period
Muslim politics in India were largely Turkey oriented.

------

1) By this treaty Russia was to remain neutral unless
    Germany attacked France and Germany was to remain
    neutral unless Russia attacked Austria-Hungary.

2) A. J. P. Taylor, The Struggle for Mastery in Europe
    1848-1918 (Oxford 1954) p. 329, see also note 3.

1. Germany fails to get Britain via 'Defence of India' 1890 - 94

In 1890 the new spirit of Anglo-German friendliness spread to India as well. The German Consul General in India of the time was Edmund Baron von Heyking. (3) Heyking and his literary wife whose grandmother had the honour of exchanging friendly letters with Goethe, (4) not only earned the friendship of Lord and Lady Lansdowne but also became very popular among British official circles in India in general. (5) German explorers and globe-trotters (6) poured in to India signifying not only the reign of a modern monarch who hobnobbed with scholars, industrialists, and scientists but also this new spirit of Anglo-German good-will. (7)

Wilhelm II's desire to bring England closer to Germany and her allies had however many hardships. The Heligoland-Zanzibar agreement had already annoyed Russia who turned to France in August 1891 and by

---

3) Edmund Baron von Heyking (1850-1915): 1889-93 Consul General, Calcutta; 1894 Consul General, Cairo; 1896 Minister, Peking; 1899 Minister, Mexico; 1904 Minister, Belgrad; 1906 Minister, Hamburg.

4) See Alfred Kantorowicz (ed.) Du wunderliches Kind: Aus dem Briefwechsel zwischen Goethe und Bettine von Arnim (Berlin 1950).

5) Mrs. Heyking's Indian diary is full of descriptions of the praise and popularity the Heykings received from the British in India. See Elisabeth von Heyking, Tagebücher aus vier Weltteilen 1886-1904 (2d ed. Leipzig 1926) pp. 57-123.

6) Some of these were: Baron Herrmann, Count Königsmarck, Count Spee, Prince Galitzin, the young couple Schwabach, and Otto E. Ehlers. Ibid. , pp. 67, 94-5, 106. The exploration report of Ehlers was even published by the Government of India (Report of a journey from Moulmein through the Laos and Shan States, to Tongking by Mr. Otto Ehlers).

7) The following is one clear expression of this goodwill: When in November 1890 the Kaiser learnt that Ehlers' (see n. 6 above) intention to visit Afghanistan was embarrassing to the Indian Government as they were unable to take responsibility for his safety in that country, the Kaiser at once asked the German Foreign Office to send the message that he would not like Ehlers to visit Afghanistan and thereby cause difficulties to the British. Heyking to Caprivi, Simla 19 Oct. 1890; A. A. message to Heyking 26 Nov. 1890, AABI 7.

August 1892 concluded a military convention with her - the be-
ginnings of the later Dual Alliance. Although Britain intended
to lean on the Triple Alliance she was afraid lest she got mixed
up with Berlin's policy: Germany might make her support to
Britain in Egypt conditional on Britain supporting her in Asia
Minor. Britain therefore did not want to bind herself prematuredly
to any side. This of course meant that the disappearance of the
Reinsurance Treaty took some of the importance from the Triple
Alliance. (8) In August 1892 Gladstone was also back in power
with an uneasy majority. His distrust of the Triple Alliance and
Austria-Hungary above all led him to think that reconciliation
with France was the best course for Britain. In this period of
dwindling prospects for his 'new course' the Kaiser seems to
have relied heavily on the continuance of Britain's problem of
Indian defence so as either to get Britain as partner of the Triple
Alliance powers or just to keep her - and also Russia - engaged
in the Central Asian field. From Heyking's reports of the period
the Kaiser drew his own conclusion that Britain was definitely
insecure in India.

In autumn 1890 Heyking first reported on Britain's problem in
constructing the strategic railways in the frontier area. (9) The
original British proposal was to push the railway into the Afghan
territory as far as Kandahar. The Amir, however, would not
allow this. He was angry that the British had already built their
railways too deep into his kingdom. He complained also about
Lansdowne's criticism of his brutal punishment of his subjects.
Heyking also reported that among British official circles opinion
differed as to the proper attitude to be taken towards the Amir. (10)
From his conversations with Sir Robert Sandeman, the forceful
commissioner of Baluchistan, Heyking learnt that the Government
was afraid of the Amir although Sandeman saw no reason for it.
Heyking, however, found no danger at this stage. Tackling the
question of Indian princes, one of the most important factors in
the event of an anti-British uprising, he wrote in a report admired

---

8)   H. Oncken, Die Sicherheit Indiens: Ein Jahrhundert eng-
     lischer Weltpolitik (Berlin 1937) p. 49.

9)   Heyking to Caprivi, Simla 8 Sept. 1890, AABI 7.

10) Heyking to Caprivi, Simla 1 Aug. 1890, ibid.

by the Kaiser (11) that the Indian rajahs did not possess even
the minimum cleverness required for a far-reaching traitorous
plan against the British. The rumours about the Russian agents
being in their courts were therefore unfounded. According to
Heyking they were circulated by those non-British foreign
travellers who either did not have sufficient knowledge or, what
was more probable, had 'certain envy of the success' of the
British policy in India.'(12)

Within two years, however, there came some changes to this
optimistic outlook of Heyking. There were difficulties in Britain's
forward policy in India. Towards the end of February 1892
Heyking reported the death of Sir Robert Sandeman whose activities on the North-West Frontier Berlin keenly followed. The
Indian Government considered it a public disaster. From Heyking's
tribute to Sandeman the Kaiser found it 'very interesting' to know
that he (Sandeman) had almost always disregarded the orders of
the Government at Simla or Calcutta in his forward policy and
the Government never had any alternative but to acknowledge a
successful fait accompli afterwards.(13) But still bigger problems
were awaiting around the Pamir crisis.(14) In 1891 Captain
Younghusband had been assigned from British India to delimitate
the frontier between Afghanistan and China. He was to occupy
the Pamirs and put a barrier between the Russians and the
Hindukush. The Russians were, however, vigilant about Younghusband's activities and were equally determined to occupy the
Pamirs. The German Foreign Office receiving the earliest information about a strong Russian expedition heading towards the
Pamirs informed the British Government of it.(15) Although the

---

11) Heyking to Caprivi, Simla 28 Sept. 1890, ibid. Kaiser's
    comment: 'very good.'

12) Ibid.

13) Heyking to Caprivi, Calcutta 28 Feb. 1892, AABI 9; In an
    earlier report Heyking had informed Berlin about his telling
    Sandeman how he was well known and admired in Germany.
    Heyking to Caprivi, Simla 1 Aug. 1890, AABI 7.

14) For the details of the first and the subsequent crises over
    the Pamirs see G.J. Alder, British India's Northern
    Frontier, 1865-1895 (London 1963) pp. 226-287.

15) In July Count Hatzfeldt passed the information originally
    acquired by chancellor Caprivi. Lord Salisbury thanked
    Hatzfeldt for the communication but doubted its correct-
    ness. Greaves. pp. 188-190 and n. 4 p. 188.

Russians denied the rumour on 13 August, Younghusband was actually told by a Russian party under Col. Ivanow that Russia had annexed the Upper Oxus territories and that Younghusband must withdraw. One of Younghusband's party, Lieutenant Davison, was temporarily taken prisoner for trespassing on Russian territory. These events caused great indignation in the British Foreign Office and The Times correspondent even described the Russian moves as equivalent to a declaration of war. (16)

Due to the strong stand - to a great extent a bluff - taken by the British Ambassador at St. Petersburg, the Russians came round to apologize for Ivanov's action and suggested a joint techno-geographical expedition to make the necessary preliminary enquiries before delimitation. Salisbury accepted this but by July 1892 the Russians declared the adjournment of the idea of a delimitation commission. When in the summer of 1892 Lord Salisbury's Government came to an end and the new Liberal ministry came into power, the situation on the North-West Frontier appeared in dark colours. There was, first of all, the vastly exaggerated report of large-sized Russian forces facing scattered detachments of the Amir and the Chinese. Again, the Chinese were not interested in what Britain wanted to bring as a Chinese claim. The British relations with Afghanistan were also getting worse. And the tribal belt between Afghanistan and British India was uneasy. The effect of all this was a sense of insecurity among the British in India. (17)

As the Russophobia increased and talk of war was in the air Heyking described how the situation would shape up if war broke out in reality. In the event of a war, he reported, the tasks of the British troops would be twofold: to fight the foreign aggressor outside the Indian border and suppress an internal uprising which in all probability would occur. This would be a situation different from that of 1857 when the British soldiers had only one task, i.e. to defend their position from inside. Would the British army be in a position now to fulfil both the tasks? Heyking asked the question of himself avoiding, however, a clear answer. But the Kaiser reading the report provided it: "I am afraid it will hardly

---

16) Alder, op. cit., pp. 226-6.

17) Alder, op. cit., pp. 245-7; Heyking to Caprivi, Simla 1 Oct. 1892, AABI 10.

be able to do that," he commented in the margin.(18) According to Heyking all the modern developments in communication which made the present situation different from that of 1857 should not be overemphasised as advantages for the British only. They would be open to use or abuse by the opposite side as well. To emphasise his point Heyking said that in a recent lecture in Simla on 'The Railway System in Times of War' all measures were taken to prevent any native hearing what was being discussed about the methods applied to destroy railways. But although the Indians in general were not given higher military training and the Muslims in particular were not much trusted, Heyking said that the soldiers of the native princes were lately getting better training and hence became a greater danger than in 1857.

Heyking was, however, sure that without a Russian war all the latent dangers would remain latent. Moreover, the Indians, too, did not doubt the superiority of their British masters, who in Indian eyes were always the greatest and the mightiest. Heyking personally did not think that a war would come, nevertheless, he informed Berlin how already the officers started thinking in terms of sending their families either to England or to some safer place in India. Heyking, too, was warned never to leave his family behind at any place where there was no garrison of English troops nearby. This made the Kaiser convinced of the British danger. He noted in the margin: "very reasonable but it shows."(19)

From now on until the era of 'Weltpolitik' Britain's India problem started playing hide-and-seek with the German Foreign Office making the Kaiser in particular intermittently happy and disappointed. In the midst of the second Pamir c ⁀ is a flicker of hope appeared of catching Britain for the Triple Alliance. In July 1893 a false report reached London that the French in Indo-China had ordered British warships to withdraw from Siamese waters. Siam being the buffer between French Indo-China and the British Indian Empire, Rosebery nearly panicced. Kaiser Wilhelm II happened to be in England at this time and he was asked for Germany's backing in the event of a war. Germany expected to expand the Triple into a Quadruple Alliance. This was, however, not fulfilled as the crisis subsided almost as quickly as it had arisen without developing into a danger. France

---

18) Heyking to Caprivi, Simla 1 Oct. 1892, ibid. When after the end of his Calcutta term Heyking met the Kaiser in Germany in May 1893 he got the impression that the Kaiser did not think much of the security of British rule in India. See E. von Heyking, Tagebücher, p. 127.

19) Heyking to Caprivi, ibid.

44

readily accepted the old bargain, a neutral buffer.(20) An Anglo-Indian paper arguing against Britain's joining the Triple Alliance was to comment later that it made no difference at all to India 'until we lose the command of the sea, for German, Austrian and Italian troops are not going to be sent round by the Black Sea and Caspian to fight on our frontiers at Gilgit and Kandahar.' (21)

The Siam crisis was succeeded by the success of Sir Mortimer Durand, the Foreign Secretary of the Government of India, in persuading Abdur Rahman, the Amir of Afghanistan to evacuate all the districts held by him to the north of the Oxus on the understanding that all the districts lying to the south of the stretch of the Oxus which formed his northern boundary should be handed over to him in exchange. The agreement which took place in November 1893 in Kabul was the prelude to the final settlement of the Pamir crisis with the Russians in March 1895.(22)

But the Indian danger, as often repeated here, had two sides. If there was constant endeavour for rapproachment on the external side there was no similar policy for resolving the internal tensions among the Indians, at least until the first decade of this century. The Kaiser was not alone in visualising British helplessness in the event of a coincidence of an outside aggression and an internal revolt in India. The British press and public were equally pessimistic. In fact some months before the final Pamir settlement with Russia a simple incedent in India caused a great deal of restlessness and apprehension among the British people at home. The official Germans both in England and India naturally took interest in the matter to probe into the question of British India's security from the internal point of view.

Early in May 1894 a report reached London that some Bihari sepoys of the 17th Bengal Infantry at Agra remonstrated against

---

20) See. G. P. VIII no. 1753, marginal note by Caprivi on Hatz-feldt to German Foreign Office, Cowes 31 July 1893; R. J. Sontag, Germany and England. Background of Conflict 1848-1894 (New York 1938) pp. 279-80; A. J. P. Taylor, Struggle for Mastery in Europe p. 343 and n. 1.

21) The Civil and Military Gazette, Lahore 8 Feb. 1894 in Schmidt-Ernsthausen to Caprivi, Calcutta 8 Feb. 1894, AABI 12.

22) See Alder, p. 275, and also App. II pp. 330-332 for the 'Relevant sections of the Duran Agreement' signed on 12 Nov. 1893 in Kabul.

the conduct of a British colonel. This incident soon got connected
with the smearing of some mangoe trees in some parts of Bihar
around the same time. (23) Tree smearing, rightly or wrongly,
was considered to be a sign of mutiny (24) and hence the incident
caused great alarm necessitating the participation of such leading
Anglo-Indian stallwarts as Lord Lansdowne, Lord Roberts, Sir
George Chesney, Sir Alfred Lyall, Sir Richard Temple, and
Colonel Malleson in the debate that soon followed about the prospects of British survival in India. (25)

Ultimately Sir Alfred Lyall had quietened down the climate by
pointing out in The Times that because the 'Mussalmans' and
'Hindoos' were quarrelling with each other they would not join
against the Europeans and The Saturday Review taking the same
view felt safe: "The ill feeling between Hindoo and Mahomedan,
which is our greatest safeguard, is stronger than ever."(26)
But although the detection of the wrong implication in the tree
smearing incident (27) removed the initial panic, it was soon

---

23) Hatzfeldt to Caprivi, London 12, 25, 28 May 1894, AABI 12
    and 13; see also The Spectator and The Saturday Review,
    12 May and The Times 25 and 28 May 1894.

24) William Beresford who had served as military secretary to
    three Viceroys of India and spent 18 years there told Hatz-
    feldt on 11 May 1894 that although he did not believe the
    present incident, the painting of the mangoe tree, as such,
    was a sign of discontentment which, if it were to take place
    in a warrior province like Punjab, could be dangerous.
    Hatzfeldt to Caprivi, London 12 May 1894, AABI 12.

25) Although most of these men discarded any need of pressimism
    regarding India the last named two took an apprehensive view
    together with the journal The Spectator, ibid.

26) The Times, 8 May, quoted in The Spectator, 12 May 1894;
    Saturday Review 12 May 1894. The Spectator was not fully
    convinced by Sir Alfred Lyall's argument. "They - the
    Mussalmans and Hindoos - have been quarelling for seven
    hundred years, and in 1857 sprang in perfect accord at our
    throats. The only Asiatics whom Mussalmans do not put up
    with are the Parsees, probably for some traditional reason."

27) For the origin of the tree smearing incident see A. Forbes,
    Commissioner of the Patna Division, in The Times of India,
    Bombay 9 June 1894 under 'The Religious Revival in Behar'.
    According to Forbes, tree-daubing had a local an recent
    origin connected with the Janakpur shrine in Nepal. Syburg
    to Caprivi, Bombay 9 June 1894, AABI 13; see also The Times
    4 June 1894 in Hatzfeldt to Caprivi, 4 June 1894, ibid.

evident that some real reasons were behind the alarm, the chief among which was the guilty conscience of the Anglo-Indians about the exemption of Manchester goods from the custom duties. (28) As The Times wrote in May: "Signs and warnings are indeed not wanting in India at this moment; signs not to be explained away, warnings wholly devoid of a humourous aspect. The Indian news-papers brought by each week's mail disclose a state of public feeling without example since the great catastrophe which trans-ferred the country from the company to the crown."(29)

There was, however, a quick effort on the part of the British in India to mitigate to some extent the most obvious grievance of the time: the exemption of Manchester goods from import duty. The great fear was, as The Times pointed out, "that every great movement in India tends to acquire a political or militant character."(30) The most patriotic British organs in India, the Englishman of Calcutta, the Pioneer of Allahabad, and the two leading daily papers in Madras and Bombay condemned the selfish policy of the Home Government in terms which The Times found "scarcely less servere than the denunciations of the native Press."(31) This, along with the boostering up of the morale of the British civil servants in India, as done by Sir Alfred Lyall in his lately published book Rise and Expansion of the British Dominion in India (32), and the internal communal disharmony among the Indians themselves as emphasised by Brodrick in his talk with Hatzfeldt in May (33), made clear to the official Germans in England that the chances of Britain's facing a revolt in India were becoming thinner. Theodor Rathsam, a member of the German consular staff in India, contradicting a report in the Kölnische Zeitung of 2 October strongly refuted

28) 'Indian Affairs', The Times, 28 May 1894. Hatzfeldt to Caprivi, London 28 May 1894, ibid.

29) Ibid.

30) 'Indian Affairs', The Times, 1 October 1894.

31) Ibid.

32) Ibid.

33) Brodrick, a Conservative M.P. and the future Secretary of State for India told Hatzfeldt that the chances were more for a big Hindu-Muslim communal riot than the both communities uniting in an uprising against the British. Hatzfeldt to Caprivi, London 19 May 1894, AABI 13.

that the increase in the self-assurance of the individual Indian
had already led to a danger for the British rule. "Such a danger, "
he wrote, "could arise only when the Indians would have a feeling
of nationality. But this will still take a long time; and until now
the only decisive feeling has been that of religious community. "(34)

The improbability of an uprising in India did not, however, automatically add any strength to the British in India to take a more
forceful attitude towards the Russians in Central Asia. In the
autumn of 1894 Germany to her disappointment found Britain in
the mood to compromise rather than confront Russia. The German
Consul General in Calcutta at the time, Baron von Gaertner (35)
reported to Berlin, with the Kaiser's full concurrence with his
views, that not being sure of how the Indians in the army would
fight against the Europeans, and the loyalty of the Indians being
dependent solely on who the winning side would be, the English
in India remained in perpetual fear of Russia.(36) Gaertner compared the undaunted and self-assured British in their home
country with their panic stricken counterparts in India who were
completely different from the archetypal John Bull. Not without
some truth, however, in the age of imperialism, Gaertner considered it nothing but Russophobia which prevented the British
in India from annexing Nepal and Afghanistan. "What else is the
theory of a buffer state" he asked, "if not the expression of fear
to face eye to eye an equal opponent. " He advised Berlin not to
ignore the fact that the mood of the British in India formed a
significant factor in Britain's entire foreign policy. The British
in India were, he said, hopefully looking for an outbreak of war
in Europe so as to get their problem with Russia in India solved
by someone else. As examples Gaertner referred to the Standard
articles regarding Russian troops concentration on Germany's

---

34) Rathsam to Caprivi, Simla 30 Oct.1894, ibid.; see also
'Die Finanzlage Indiens' in Kölnische Zeitung, 2 Oct.1894.

35) Günther Baron von Gaertner-Griebenow (1856-1898): 1881
joined diplomatic service; 1882 attached to German embassy
St. Petersburg; Legation Secretary, Bern; 1883 at Copen-
hagen; 1886 at Lisbon; 1888 II. Secretary, Paris; 1889
Legation Secretary, Stockholm; 1891 at The Hague; 1893
I. Secretary Madrid; 1894 Consul General, Calcutta; 1895
Minister, Teheran.

36) Gaertner to Caprivi, Simla 27 Aug.1894, ibid. The Kaiser
not only found the whole report "very well written" but
agreed with many of Gaertner's views.

western frontier and Indian Commander-in-Chief General White's showing great astonishment to him that the great war between Germany and Russia had not yet taken place. Only the news of the recent Russo-German trade agreement and the Reuter report on the articles of the Norddeutsche Allgemeine Zeitung in August in praise of the improved Franco-German relations braught some sobering effect on the Anglo-Indians, Gaertner wrote. He however remained puzzled why Baron Reuter, who normally cabled only British parliamentary debates, news on races and cricket, made an exception in regard to the article of Norddeutsche Allgemeine Zeitung. (37)

The German fear of a possible British reconciliation with Russia was not unfounded. In June 1895 Salisbury returned to power. Not having much faith in the ability of the Turkish empire to reform itself and being influenced by the campaign in England against the Armenian atrocities and also being disillusioned with Britain's former associates of the Mediterranean League, Salisbury thought in terms of partitioning Turkey and told Hatzfeldt that he was ready to let the Russians have Constantinople. (38) This of course upset the Germans greatly, but the fear was averted as Russia showed no interest in the partition plan. Germany's resentment of Britain at the time was expressed in the Krüger telegram (January 1896) which created a deep gap between the two countries. During this period of rift between the two countries there occurred in India anti-British unrest among the Muslims in 1897 which the Kaiser and the German Foreign Office keenly observed in the context of the British policy in Turkey at that time.

2. Turkey, Indian Muslims and the Kaiser in 1897

In the spring of 1897 the Greek organization Ethniké Hetairia having practically complete control of the Greek army, prepared for a war with Turkey making Thessaly the chief centre of operation. In view of this the Turks took precautionary measures and the Russians wanted the powers to intervene for the sake of the Concert of Europe. (39)

---

37) Ibid.

38) Hatzfeldt to Holstein, London 30, 31 July, Cowes 5. Aug. 1895, G. P. X no. 2371, 2381.

39) For a general survey of the whole question see Langer, op. cit., pp. 367-377.

Just at this time of Turkish preparations for defence Berlin
received news of growing sympathy for Turkey among the Indian
Muslims. Early in March Waldthausen (40), the German Consul
General in India at the time, wrote to Berlin that the Muslim
press in India was greatly agitated over the British Liberals'
earlier support for the Armenians and condemnation of the
Sultan. (41) This press asked the Muslims of India to collect
money to improve the Turkish army. Waldthausen came to know
from the Turkish Consul in Bombay that a large sum of money
had already been offered by some reputed Indian Muslims for
the purpose. Besides, prayers were held by Muslims for the
Sultan regularly in Aligarh. Waldthausen however observed that
although it was certain that the Indian Muslims would not like
Britain operating against the Khalif, their disappointment was
of no serious matter as such things had been occurring in India
for the last half century. The Kaiser however gave a great deal
of importance to the reaction of the Indian Muslims to the events
in Turkey. According to him "the results of Britain's secret
intrigues are turning up. "(42)

In April the Graeco-Turkish war finally broke out and the Greeks
were being defeated. Queen Victoria, not happy about this, appealed personally to Czar Nicholas and Kaiser Wilhelm to bring
about an armistice instead of waiting for the conclusion of the
war. The Kaiser however took a tough line, declaring that only
on the precondition that Greece accepted the longstanding proposal
by the powers for the autonomy of Crete, could negotiations for
peace start. He replied to his grandmother that the Greeks must

---

40) Julius von Waldthausen (1858-1935): 1888 Legation Secretary;
    1893 2d Secretary, St. Petersburg; 1895 Legation Secretary,
    Vatican; 1895 Consul General, Calcutta; 1904 Minister,
    Buenos Aires; Minister, Copenhagen; 1912 Minister, Bukarest.

41) Waldthausen to Hohenlohe, Calcutta 2 March 1897. AABI 15.
    The newspapers led by the Liberal Daily News and Daily
    Chronicle did acutally publish incredible, imaginary pictures
    of Turkish horror "which were accepted without question as
    gospel truth" in England. See Langer, op. cit., p. 327.

42) The Kaiser's comment on above.

'beg' for an armistice. (43) The Kaiser was consequently accused
in England of having encouraged the military party in the Turkish
capital. But as Russia also was not prepared to go with Britain,
abandoning Germany and Austria, Greece had to accept Germany's
terms and after yet another overwhelming victory by the Turks
at Domoskos negotiations for peace began.

In the negotiations that followed the Sultan insisted on having a
considerable part of Thessaly and indemnity. So far as the first
was concerned the powers agreed only to a slight rectification of
the frontier. On the question of indemnity the problem arose as
to how a bankrupt Greece could make it. Germany favoured a
loan and the institution of an international control of Greek finances
which the Greeks hotly rejected. As for Britain - as Bülow told
the Kaiser - after opposing this control at first she came round
to accept it by the end of July, provided that the control would
not bring any cost or responsibility on her. (44) But soon afterwards Britain's attitude changed again to that of rejection. (45)
Britain also insisted that strong methods be used to force the
Turks to accept the terms submitted to them by the powers. (46)

Both Bülow, since July the German Foreign Secretary, and the
Kaiser looked at the British attitude to the Graeco-Turkish
armistice negotiations at Constantinople in the light of the latest
happenings among the Muslims of India which we shall soon discuss. According to Bülow's analysis Britain was only trying to
use the Concert of Europe to subdue the Sultan so as to impress
upon her Muslim Asiatic subjects her wide power and influence
among the powers. Bülow opined that to allow Britain to achieve
her objectives in the current negotiations at Constantinople would
mean nothing but the European powers playing into the hands of
Britain. Bülow advised the Kaiser that Germany should by no
means allow her own interests and those of Europe to be bypassed by Britain's Anglo-Indian interests. Objection to British

---

43) Marschall to Tschirschky, Berlin 1 May 1897, G. P. XII no.
    3227; The Kaiser to Queen Victoria, Telgs. Berlin 8 May,
    and D'Urville 13 May 1897, Q. V. L. , 3, III, pp. 159-60, 162-3.

44) Bülow to the Kaiser, Berlin 29 Aug. 1897, AABI 15.

45) Ibid.

46) Langer, op. cit. , p. 377.

diplomatic advances on this issue, Bülow said, would not result in Britain's breaking away from the Concert since her enimies inside and outside Europe would consider it as weakness and in India particularly it would be an encouragement to revolt.(47)

The above memorandum of Bülow of 29 August was based on various reports of accelerating unrest among the Indian Muslims. The Turkish victory was an important event for the Muslims of India. The majority of the Indian Muslims, nearly one fifth of the entire Indian population, considered the Turkish Sultan as their religious head and they had been long discontent with Britain because she was no longer friendly to Turkey. When in spite of this Turkey won victory over Greece it was festively celebrated by the Muslims all over India not without creating some problems for law and order. Reporting Indian happenings in June Waldthausen, however, repeated his earlier observation that such incidents would create no danger to the British rule and that any Muslim uprising would be easily crushed by the British. Constantinople, after all, was far away from India, he wrote.(48)

This report of Waldthausen written in the first half of June did not reach Berlin until early August. Meanwhile Berlin had received news of many other happenings in British India in the later half of the month. On the basis of later happenings the Kaiser was again unconvinced that British India was not endangered by Britain's Turkish policy. If Constantinople was far away from India, the Kaiser commented, "London is still further away."(49)

With plague, famine, the after-effects of the great Assam earth-quake of 1896 and the tribal unrest on the north-west frontier the year 1897 was running not at all well in India by the time Queen Victoria's Diamond Jubilee celebrations approached in June. The latter half of the year was to be more disturbing alike to the Indians and Britons. The Government's anxious but un-cautious measures to stamp out plague (50) offended the privacy

---

47) Bülow to the Kaiser, 29 August 1897, AABI 15.

48) Waldthausen to Hohenlohe, Simla 12 June 1897, AABI 15; For the descriptions of victory celebrations see The Pioneer 30 May; Civil & Military Gazette 31 May and 3 June 1897.

49) The Kaiser's comment on above.

50) For the seriousness of the situation caused by plague and the preventive measures against it, see below p. 103.

and religious susceptibilities of both the Hindu and the Muslim communities and resulted in some of the severest criticism of the Government in the native press. In the neighbourhood of Calcutta open insults and attacks on Europeans occured. In June, during the festivities connected with the Victoria Jubilee, violences against individual Britons were committed both by Hindus and Muslims. At Peshawar on the north-west frontier a British officer was shot dead by an pan-Islamic fanatic and at Poona two British plague officers were similarly killed by two orthodox Hindu brothers, although the inspiration behind these two acts was totally different. (51) During the Muslim victory celebrations in Calcutta the Turkish victory was presented by the Muslim priests to the uneducated Muslim masses as the triumph of the true believer over the infidel and as an example of the powerlessness of the Christians. (52) During the same time Berlin was also informed by Radolin, the German Ambassador at St. Petersburg, of what he had heard to be the worsening condition of the British in India. (53) Radolin was informed by General Kuropatkin, the Russian Governor of Transcaspia, that in India the Hindus and the Muslims, who normally remained hostile to each other, had joined together in their common fight against the British and that an uprising was about to break out. The Kaiser who seems to have recollected at this time the earlier shooting incidents in India, agreed on this Hindu-Muslim unity against the British (he commented in the margin: "it is true") although there was no information from India that the Hindus and the Muslims were acting in a common cause. Radolin had even more ominous things to report. According to what he had heard from Kuropatkin the Amir of Afghanistan was bought off by the Russians and was only waiting for the Indian outbreak to take place so as to break away from the Pamir treaty and change over completely to the

---

51) Waldthausen to Hohenlohe, Simla 7 July; Biermann to Hohenlohe, Bombay 24 June and 2 July 1897; AABI 15. The Kaiser directed the former report to be sent to Stamboul, Cairo, Petersburg, and London.

52) Report of Wm. Bleeck, Calcutta 8 July, in Waldthausen to Hohenlohe, Simla 15 July 1897, ibid. Bleeck, too, did not believe it to be difficult for the British to suppress the Muslim unrest.

53) Radolin to Hohenlohe, Petersburg 21 June 1897, ibid.

Russians side. The Kaiser appreciated the news that the Russian rubles made the Amir incline towards Russia. "This would be very good," he remarked. (54)

The anti-British Muslim demonstrations and riots in Calcutta and its neighbourhood developed into an alarming situation which led to the death of hundreds of rioters in quelling the outbreak. In the middle of July, at a time when the Anglo-Indian press was beginning to urge that the time had come to remind the excited Indian Muslims that England was no Greece and that "We are in India and we mean to stay in India"(55), a fresh bout of Muslim unrest occurred among the tribes of the north-west frontier giving Berlin the impression that it was a gradual spread of anti-British sentiment from the Indian cities. Waldthausen reported that on 26 July the garrison on the Malakand pass was attacked by about 1000 local people under the leadership of a fanatical Muslim priest as a result of which some British officers were wounded and one killed. The attack on the Malakand pass had some connection with similar outbreaks on the north-west frontier which had occurred in the previous month in the newly acquired Tochi valley where on 10 June the political officer and his escort were attacked. (56) From there the revolt spread to Swat. Led by various fanatical mullahs, the Mahmands, the Orakzais and the Afridis revolted successively afterwards. As a result British troops had to march to these interior areas of the frontier. (57)

54) The Kaiser's comment on above.

55) Civil and Military Gazette 18 July, in Waldthausen to Hohenlohe, Simla 21 July 1897, ibid.

56) Waldthausen to Hohenlohe, Simla 27 July 1897, ibid.

57) Before the year 1897 ended, well-organised expeditionary forces finally brought the tribal insurrections to a halt. The German consul general took a great interest in these military operations - although so far as he was concerned, with full confidence in British power and victory - and sent elaborate reports of the British military strategy which the Kaiser ordered to be transmitted to the general staff. Later in April 1898 the consul general himself visited Malakand and the Swat valley. See Waldthausen to Hohenlohe, Simla 7 & 31 August, 13, 15 & 22 Sept., 13 Oct. 1897 and Calcutta 12 Jan., 20 March 1898; AABI 16, 17, 18, 20; Hatzfeldt to Hohenlohe, London 9 Feb. 1898 enclosing the printed Military Operations on the North West Frontier of India Vol. II (London 1898).

Even before getting any information as to whether any Turkish hand was involved directly in the affairs of the Indian Muslims the Kaiser was convinced that all the recent happenings in India were the result of Britain's wrong policy towards Turkey and in comparison he found German policy on the right path. He annotated a despatch from India expressing Britain's foolishness thus:

> "It is difficult to see which is greater - British blindness or the uneducated indifference to the coloured people whose spiritual life and religious development can bring enormous surprises. The British ambassador at Stamboul in particular does not even seem to foresee what danger for India and for England he provokes by his unqualified behaviour. Our attitude is excellently justified... Should it be possible to say about the British in India that quem deus perdere vult etc. "(58)

To deepen the Kaiser's belief that Britain was digging her own grave in India by her Turkish policy came in the second half of September various news about Turkey's hand in the recent Indian developments. Baron von Saurma, the German Ambassador in Constantinople reported on the Turkish pan-Islamic propaganda and the part played in it by two Turkish vernacular papers, Sabah and Malumat, which were later banned in India for their instigating articles on India.(59) From Bagdad also came the information that earlier the Sultan had sent a message to his brother-in-law, General Kasim Pasa at Bagdad, asking him to influence one Nakib Seyyed Sulaiman Effendi to prepare an uprising of the Sunnite Muslims of India against British rule. This Nakib was considered to be very influential in India and particularly with the Muslim press, and it was hoped that through the influential Muslim pilgrims from India who had visited his holy mosque he had done the job entrusted to him.(60) There were also rumours that one Sheikh Seyid Yahiya Efendi, an emissary of the Afghan Amir, was at the Sultan's court intriguing against British India.(61)

---

58) Kaiser's note in Waldthausen to Hohenlohe, Simla 12 June arrived in Berlin in August 1897; AABI 15.

59) Saurma to Hohenlohe, Therapia 8, 13, 29, 30 Sept. 1897; Gazette of India 21 Aug. 1897 in Waldthausen to Hohenlohe, Simla 22 Sept. 1897, AABI 16.

60) Richarz to Hohenlohe, Bagdad 17 Aug. 1897, ibid.

61) Saurma to Hohenlohe, Therapia 13 Sept. 1897, ibid.

By October it was however clear to Berlin that as far as the Afghan participation in the tribal uprisings was concerned the rumours were unfounded. The Kaiser to his disappointment learnt from Waldthausen's report that it was becoming more and more obvious that the Amir was openly taking the side of the British in their fight against the rebellious tribes. (62) The Amir publicly repudiated the complicity on himself or his officials in the frontier disturbance and blamed the mullahs for the uprisings. He also sent back the Afridi delegation which approached him for help and reiterated his friendship with the British. (63) Thus it was proved that fanaticism rather than Turkey was the predominant factor in the Muslim tribal insurrections. They were mainly the result of the British active forward policy pursued in the 'nineties'. (64) Waldthausen also reported the help rendered by the Indian princes of Kapurthala, Jhind, Gwalior and Jaipur with their troops for the frontier campaigns (65), thereby further disproving the earlier Kuropatkin-Radolin information that the Hindus and Muslims were uniting against the British.

Since the beginning of the Cretan crisis German policy in Graeco-Turkish affairs had been in the personal hands of the Kaiser (66) and this explains the great interest he took in the Muslim affairs of British India and her borderlands in 1897. But in his enthusiasm for his pro-Turkish role and the justice he attached to it, the Kaiser went beyond the information sent by the German representatives in India, to presume a steady growth of Muslim unrest both inside the settled provinces and the frontier areas of British India, due mainly to British injustice to Turkey. But as has been seen, the Kaiser was only exciting himself with a bogey of his own creation most of the time. At the same time it must however be pointed out that as Germany's diplomatic interest in India was

---

62) Waldthausen to Hohenlohe, Simla 15 Sept. 1897; Kaiser's marginal comment: "it is a great pity." Ibid.

63) Pioneer 8 Sept. 1897; 7, 9, 10 Oct. 1897 in Waldthausen to Hohenlohe, Simla 13 Oct. 1897, ibid.

64) C. C. Davies, The Problem of the North-West Frontier 1890-1908 (Cambridge 1932) pp. 94, 98.

65) Waldthausen to Hohenlohe, Simla 22 Sept. 1897, AABI 16.

66) Langer, op. cit., p. 363; M. Balfour, The Kaiser and His Times (London 1964) p. 200.

based on Britain's 'defence of India' problem, as reflected in her various international moves, her source of information about India was not India alone. In 1897, not unnaturally, the Kaiser and Bülow were influenced by Russian and Turkish sources. Moreover, it was not so much important what the British position in India actually was but what the British themselves thought it to be. Almost all official Germans personally observing the British Indian scene were more optimistic about the British strength than the British themselves and, as Gaertner wrote, (67) it was almost a fashion among the Anglo-Indians to minimise their strength. So, as it was not a policy towards India but a world policy which the German Foreign Office was busy formulating, there was every possibility of discrepancy in the final assessment of the Indian situation between Berlin and its accredited agents in India. The impulsive nature of the Kaiser made it more probable. This fact asserted itself more clearly when Germany formally entered the era of 'Weltpolitik'.

---

67) Gaertner to Caprivi, Simla 27 Aug. 1894, AABI 13.

III. INDIA AND 'WELTPOLITIK'

"The British should be aware that war with Germany
would mean the loss of India and thus the loss of
their world position."

Kaiser's comment on Metternich
to Bülow, 11 August 1908.

"Despite a desirable slow rapproachment between Germany
and Britain, for the time being we have no reason to make
it easier for the British to rule India."

Luxburg to Bethmann-Hollweg,
Simla 29 July 1913.

By the middle of 1897 the Kaiser and his new ministers (1)
decided to take the country along a new path, the path of 'Weltpolitik'. Although the new policy was not aimed against any nation,
enmity particularly with England was implicit in the two means
adopted to carry it out - imperialism and a navy. (2)

The basic presumption that went along with this new policy was
that Anglo-Russian differences were irreconcilable. The constant
Anglo-Indian fear of a Russian attack seems also to have enhanced
this presumption. Thus Berlin thought it could pursue its world
policy without committing herself for the time being, either to
Britain or to Russia and thereby gaining from the Anglo-Russian
antagonism until the time when Germany would be sufficiently
stronger than either of them. But in 1907 the external and more
frightening aspect of Britain's 'defence of India' problem came
to an end as a result of the Anglo-Russian Convention of that
year. In the immediate post-1907 period of 'encirclement' Germany
for a time still vaguely counted upon the internal insecurity of
the British in India as a factor in her favour in the event of a
clash with Britain. This vague hope became surer after 1912 when
the repercussions of the Balkan war on the Indian Muslims encouraged Berlin to formulate its own threat-to-India policy.

---

1) Bernhard von Bülow as Foreign Secretary, Admiral Tirpitz
as Naval Secretary and Count Posadowsky as the Secretary
for the Interior.

2) P.R. Anderson, The Background of Anti-English Feeling
in Germany 1890 - 1902 (Washington 1939) pp. 29-30

1. Curzon, the Anglo-Indians, and the German Economic Expansion 1900 - 1903

During the Boer war, which broke out in 1899, Berlin with its pro-English neutrality was expecting some rewards from Britain in the fields of colonies and overseas trade for its 'good behaviour'. (3) The fulfilment of some of Berlin's expectations depended on the good-will of the Anglo-Indians and particularly Lord Curzon, the Viceroy.

In the summer of 1900 Berlin had three good reasons for keeping the Anglo-Indians in good humour. First, Berlin feared that the prevailing Anglo-German mutual ill-feeling might result in British hindrance to German trade in India. Secondly, it was keen to get Indian immigrant labour for improving German East Africa which suffered from a labour shortage. A plan, which had earlier been formulated with the Aga Khan's co-operation, to recruit Indian agricultural families to settle in German East Africa, was pending for Curzon's final approval. (4) Thirdly, Berlin seemed also to have some anxiety as to how Curzon and the Anglo-Indians would react to their objective of the Baghdad Railway project in the Persian Gulf area.

Germany had been steadily extending her interests in the Ottoman empire for many years and in November 1899 obtained from the Porte a preliminary concession to extend the German-owned Anatolian railway from Konia to Baghdad and Basra. For the logical development of the railway line Germany was thinking in terms of a terminus on the shores of Kuweit harbour, and early in 1900 a German mission surveyed the area. (5) Curzon had already sensed possible Russian, French and German expansive and even conspiratorial designs in the Persian Gulf area (6) and

---

3) See Oncken, op. cit. , p. 68; Taylor, Mastery, p. 388.

4) For the details see ch. VII below, p. 154.

5) Lovat Fraser, India Under Curzon and After (London 1911) p. 93.

6) J. A. S. Grenville, Lord Salisbury and Foreign Policy: The Close of the Nineteenth Century (London 1964) p. 297, quoting Curzon to Hamilton, pvt. , 16 Feb. 1899, Hamilton Papers.

extracted a secret agreement from Mubarak, the Sheikh of Kuweit, almost as soon as he took office in India. The agreement precluded the cession of any portion of Mubarak's territory to any foreign power without the British Government's sanction. (7) Although this secret agreement was unknown in Germany, Berlin was well aware of the personality of Curzon, an imperialist of religious fervour, who recognised no buffer state policy in India and who considered the Persian Gulf as a close preserve of Britain. As early as 1892 Curzon declared: "I should regard the concession of a port upon the Persian Gulf to Russia by any power as a deliberate insult to Great Britain."(8) In February 1899 he forced the Sultan of Oman, under threat of bombardment, to cancel the lease of a coal depot at Muscat which he, the Sultan, had just given to France.(9) The good will of this man was therefore essential if the Kaiser and Imperial Germany were to proceed smoothly with their objectives in the Gulf area.

The circumstances were however not at all propitious for Germany to hope for any special favour from the British in India at the turn of the century; it would require a marvel of diplomacy for Berlin to change the prevailing anti-German sentiment among the Anglo-Indians without having any general agreement with Britain beforehand. First of all, besides his uncompromising view on the British rights over the Gulf, Curzon was not expected to be kind towards Germany and her Kaiser. In 1897 while in a position of lesser authority and status, Curzon had been rebuffed by the Kaiser who did not condescend to meet him.(10) As for the Anglo-

7) The agreement was signed on 23 January 1899. See G. P. Gooch and H. Temperley (ed.), British Documents on the Origins of the War (hereafter Br. Doc.) (London 1927) I, p. 333; Langer, op. cit., p. 642; Fraser, op. cit., p. 94.

8) G. N. Curzon, Persia and the Persian Question (London 1892) II, p. 465.

9) See Langer, op. cit., p. 643.

10) In 1896 Curzon, the young M. P., was rebuked by Sir William Harcourt, the leader of the Opposition, for making gratuitous and impolite references to Germany. Curzon denied having any ill will towards Germany and to prove this, in 1897 he took an assignment from Lord Salisbury for an unofficial mission to Berlin to curb the growing tension between the two countries by informal talks. The Kaiser, however, refused to see this young Parliamentary Under Secretary to the Ministry of Foreign Affairs. See K. Rose, Superior Person: A Portrait of Curzon and his Circles in Late Victorian England (London 1969) p. 312.

Indians in general, the situation was one of direct hostility towards Germany if the newspapers were any indication. The Kaiser and Germany rarely got a good press from the Anglo-Indians; the period of the Boer war and especially the opening months of 1900 were particularly bad as Germany at this time remained suspect in their eyes.

The Englishman, an organ of the English trading community in Calcutta, took the lead in attacking Germany ruthlessly during the early months of 1900. In January, when Bülow received in Berlin Dr. Leyds as accredited envoy of the Boer Republic, this paper announced it as Germany's violation of neutrality and a "shrewd and well planted blow at our continental prestige." The paper threatened that the British nation with grim determination would take note of it so as to repay with interest as soon as occasion offered. It also announced that despite the Kaiser's recent visit to England the feeling of indignation and distrust towards Germany which spontaneously sprang into being four years previously among Englishmen had not changed a hairsbreadth. (11) The German consul general in Calcutta, von Waldthausen, was not however upset at this point and considered the Englishman's outburst as a temporary outcome of the South African reverses. (12) Soon, however, it turned out to be a routine business of this paper to publish anti-German articles without even caring for the truth. Reading one of the baseless stories in Englishman the Kaiser once commented in English: "Where ignorance is bliss, 'T is folly to be wise. "(13) But the Kaiser could not completely ignore this tirade against Germany. When on 8 February the paper while reviewing 'German hostility and its causes' arrived at the conclusion that Germany "is our enemy, if words and deeds mean anything and there is not the slightest reason to suppose that

---

11) Englishman 29 Jan. 1900, 'India and the War.'

12) On the advice of Waldthausen a reply to the Anglo-Indian press was arranged by the German Foreign Office which was published in Münchener Allgemeine Zeitung 13 March 1900. Waldthausen to Hohenlohe, Calcutta 31 Jan. 1900, AABI 22.

13) 'A Boer or a German War', a letter in Englishman 3 Feb. 1900; Waldthausen to Hohenlohe, Calcutta 3 Feb. 1900, ibid.

her enmity will lessen in course of time" the Kaiser, who was accused at home for his pro-English policy, was naturally angry and suggested that Waldthausen should take the matter to Curzon who should not allow such things to continue further without punishment. (14)

The Englishman continued the theme of German-British antagonism for some more time considering Germany as "the most formidable antagonist with whom we have to reckon in the near future."(15) In the second half of February the paper concentrated on Germany's naval program and attacked Wilhelm II particularly for throwing a challenge to Britain. (16) The Kaiser was again irritated. (17) The semi-governmental Pioneer, too, was deeply concerned around this time about Germany's attitude towards Britain, with particular reference to Britain's diminished prestige in Europe. The recent writings of Professor Hans Delbrück, the historian, were high-lighted in this connection. (18) In March the Englishman went a step further in its usual invectives and threats and declared that the German expansion, whether territorial or commercial, was becoming an important factor "in the history of our time" and suggested that the British should face the problem straight on by resisting German encroachment "first of all very possibly by means of tariffs, but in the long run inevitably by force of arms."(19) The Kaiser's cup of anger seems to have been full. He commented in the margin of this passage in Waldthausen's report: "Well, well, as if big words alone would do it!!"(20)

---

14) Waldthausen to Hohenlohe, Calcutta 9 Feb. and A. A. to Waldthausen 17 March 1900, ibid.

15) Englishman 12 Feb. 1900; Waldthausen to Hohenlohe, Calcutta 12 Feb. 1900, ibid.

16) Englishman 17 Feb. 1900.

17) Waldthausen to Hohenlohe, Calcutta 17 Feb. 1900, ibid. The Kaiser commented: "The editor was perhaps under the spell of the dogdays."

18) Pioneer 12 Feb. 1900, in Waldthausen to Hohenlohe, Calcutta 16 Feb. 1900, ibid.

19) Englishman 1 March 1900, 'German Expansion vs British Possession.'

20) Waldthausen to Hohenlohe, Calcutta 1 March 1900, ibid.

If in private talks the Kaiser accepted the challenge of the Anglo-Indians, his immediate public action was far from being retaliatory. Quite the opposite was the case; he intended to curry favour with the Anglo-Indians. On 24 April the Daily Telegraph correspondent in Berlin reported that on the Kaiser's personal initiative a committee representing some big banking and commercial houses of the metropolis, such as Mendelsohns, Bleichröders, and Warschauers, had been raising funds for Indian famine relief.(21) A leading man on the committee said that businessmen in Berlin looked upon the Imperial request as "a matter of eminent political and commercial importance."(22) The immediate reaction to the Daily Telegraph report in Germany was one of distrust: the liberal Vossische Zeitung would simply not believe it and most Germans thought it to be a devise to shake people's confidence in the Kaiser by making him look like one serving the interests of Britain.(23) On 3 May the Kaiser himself disclosed the fact by his telegrams to the Viceroy of India and also to the Queen telling them about the collection of a sum of over half a million marks to be sent to India.(24) If the spokesman of the fund raising committtee had unfolded Berlin's motive rather indiscreetly the Kaiser tried to wrap it up again neatly with a sentence appealing to the sentiment of the Anglo-Indians: "Blood is thicker than water,"(25) he assured them.

That the Kaiser's motive was to please Curzon and the Anglo-Indians for Germany's benefit there could hardly be any doubt.

------

21) The Daily Telegraph 25 April; Metternich to Hohenlohe, London 26 April 1900, ibid.

22) Ibid.

23) The Daily Telegraph 27 April; Metternich to Hohenlohe, London 28 April 1900, ibid.; see also the Times 28 April 1900.

24) Wilhelm II to Viceroy of India and Queen Victoria. Tel. Berlin 3 May 1900, ibid.

25) The following is the full text of the Kaiser's telegram to the Viceroy of India: "Full of deepest sympathy for terrible distress in India, Berlin has with my approval realised a sum of over half a million marks. I have ordered it to be forwarded to Calcutta, to be placed at Your Excellency's disposal. May India feel in this action on the part of the Capital of the German Empire the deep sense of sympathetic love for India which prompted my people, and which emanates from the fact that 'Blood is thicker than Water'." Ibid.

Had the donation been a purely humanitarian gesture it should have taken place in 1897 or soon after when the famine first appeared. The blood relation sentence in the telegram sent to India clarified the real motive. Berlin felt urgent necessity to clear the Anglo-German mutual distrust and hatred at least from India. Not just the Anglo-Indian press but the tendentious articles published at this time in the German press as well about British India helped create unhealthy condition for German economic interests in India. (26) This, coupled with Curzon's known views on the Persian Gulf and his hurt vanity seemed to Berlin an insurmountable barrier in its expectation of rewards from Britain.

The Kaiser took great pains in giving elaborate publicity to his friendly gesture towards the English, (27) but it could hardly bring about any major change in British policy. Even among those in the British government who did not disapprove of Germany's presence in the Gulf region there was a deep-rooted distrust of the Kaiser and his traits. Only a couple of month after the Kaiser's donation, Lord Hamilton, the Secretary of State for India, was to remark about the Kaiser in a different context: "This august personage is one of the most ingenious blackmailers alive."(28) So it was impossible for anything to happen which was beyond what formal courtesy demanded. Victoria in a short message thanked the Kaiser for "the generous collections made in Germany for my poor suffering subjects in India."(29) Curzon, on the other hand, capitalised on the vital sentence in the Kaiser's telegram giving it wide publicity along

---

26) The article that was most damaging to German interest in India was the one published in Berliner Neueste Nachrichten in February 1900 throwing doubts on the loyalty of the Indian princes. In this article disparaging remarks were also made on Lumsden's Horse. For details see chapter VIII below, p. 162.

27) Besides the advanced publicity given by the Daily Telegraph about the collections and the Kaiser's two telegrams to Curzon and the Queen, the matter was a subject of another despatch of the Kaiser to the Queen giving details of his lead in it. See T.H. Sanderson (signed in the absence of the Marquis of Salisbury) to the Kaiser, 8 May 1900, AABI 23.

28) Hamilton to Curzon, 20 July 1900. Hamilton Papers (hereafter H.P.) C 126/2.

29) Tel. 5 May 1900, AABI 22.

with his own reply so as to impress upon the people of India
the good-will and respect the British and their empire in India
were still able to command in Europe despite the South African
war. In his reply to the Kaiser he wrote: "... it is indeed an
illustration of the binding force of kinship as testified by Your
Imperial Majesty that the German people should turn a kindly
thought to the work that is being done by the British Government
in this country..."(30) The Kaiser's gesture could not possibly
have created in Curzon any special warmth for Germany; it perhaps only enhanced his suspicion of the Kaiser's motives. The
care the German business circle in India itself took to be in
the good books of the Indian government and the general appreciation in India of the Kaiser's gesture saved German trade in
India from any damage.(31) But about the Indian immigration
labour question on which Berlin pinned high hopes Curzon refused
to show any such favour to Germany, saying frankly that he would
not like to see German East Africa as a paying concern - which
he declared had not been so hitherto - by means of Indian
labour.(32) So it was hardly to be expected that this man would
be so generous as to allow Germany far greater commercial
prosperity in the Persian Gulf, an area on whose strategic importance he held most uncompromising views along with his
colleagues in the Indian administration.

Early in January 1900 Curzon had written to Hamilton about his
concern at seeing the Germans in Asia Minor and about their
building a railway to Basra, although he was not hopeful of the
success of the German project as a whole without financial and

---

30) Curzon to the Kaiser; tel. 4 May 1900, ibid.; In January
1902, when the German man-of-war Thetis along with the
Austro-Hungarian man-of-war Aspern visited India Curzon,
while entertaining the officers of the ships formally recalled again the Kaiser's gesture to India in the summer
of 1900. See Pioneer 30. Jan. 1902.

31) From the general appreciation with which the governing
circle in India received the Kaiser's donation and message
Waldthausen inferred that antagonism created by the Boer
war and the press articles would soon be over. Waldthausen
to Hohenlohe, Simla 18 May 1900, AABI 23.

32) See below ch. VII p.

political help from England. (33) A month later however Curzon's concern increased. It looket to him as though Germany, who he claimed had never been heard of in the Persian Gulf three months before, was going to get the best port in the Gulf with no effort at all just because Britain was unable to oppose for fear of arousing a Continental combination against her. (34) It is quite likely that Curzon sensed a connection between the Kaiser's gesture and Germany's ambition in the Gulf, for in connection with the latter he was to say the following a year later:

> "Germany, to my mind, drives harder bargains than any continental Power. She gives us soft words and gentle speeches from the Kaiser. In return she exacts Kiao Chow, Zanzibar, Heligoland, Samoa, Asia Minor Railway, General Waldersee, and what not! In international politics never take your eye off the German Emperor. "(35)

It was largely due to Curzon's pressure that the British Government began to assert with increasing firmness its special rights over the Gulf in the early years of the twentieth century. In 1899 important members of the British Home Government concerned with the Indian administration could see no danger to British India in the event of either Russia acquiring a port on the Gulf or Germany getting a terminus there for her railway, provided the process of acquiring them was a gradual one. In June 1899 Sir Arthur Godley, under secretary of state for India, wrote to Curzon in connection with the Persian Gulf that "it is bad policy to annex or guarantee territory which you clearly have not the power of defending in case of war." Godley reminded Curzon how disregard of this principle had already got the British into a very awkward position with regard to Herat. (36) Hamilton, too, was conscious of Britain's present weakness in opposing Russia in the Gulf. He could not see how in the long run the British would be able to keep Russia out of the Persian

---

33) Curzon to Hamilton 4 January 1900, Curzon Papers (hereafter C. P.) F 111/159.

34) Curzon to Hamilton 15 Feb. 1900, ibid.

35) Curzon to Earl of Hardwicke, parly. under secretary of state for India, 11 July 1901, C. P. F 111/160.

36) Godley to Curzon 16 June 1899, C. P. F 111/158.

Gulf. He reminded Curzon in November of the same year that the present British policy of monopoly in the Gulf region was based upon conditions which had existed long before but which were steadily changing to Britain's disadvantage. (37)

The general distrust of Germany was greater than that of Russia by the British Government at this time (38) and yet Curzon's uncompromising views against Germany's desires in the Persian Gulf did not receive immediate general appreciation. Hamilton saw Curzon's agreement with the Sheikh of Kuweit with alarm. "I have never liked this arrangement," he wrote to Curzon adding that "by the attitude we have taken up in connection with this so-called Indian interest, we may accelerate an alliance and confederation against us in Europe, which unquestionably, if pursued to extremes, would imperil not only the safety of India but of the whole British empire. I think this is dangerous diplomacy...I have been an imperialist all my life, but I have noted with great alarm the spread-eagling ideas of the later and newer school of imperial expanse."(39) Hamilton declared that he frankly could not see how British interests could be harmed by Germany having a railway terminus in the Persian Gulf. (40) Moreover, he was quite sure of Turkey's stronger claim on Kuweit and he could also see the natural German interest in preventing that port from becoming a British protectorate, which was Curzon's objective. (41) Salisbury, too, could not fully agree with Curzon's policy with regard to the Persian Gulf. Referring to the Muscat affair he wrote to Curzon: "I have no wish to hinder your policy in the

---

37) Hamilton to Curzon 23 Nov. 1899, H.P. C 126/1.

38) Curiously enough Curzon considered the Germans at least better than the Russians if not 'pleasant bedfellows.' (See Curzon to Hamilton 4 Jan. 1900, C.P. F 111/159.) Salisbury once wrote to Curzon: "As to Germany I have less confidence than you. She will never...stand by us against Russia, but is always inclined to curry favour with Russia by throwing us over. I have no wish to quarrel with her: but my faith in her is infinitesimal." Salisbury to Curzon 17 Oct. 1900, C.P. F 111/159.

39) Hamilton to Curzon 26 Jan. 1900, H.P. C 126/2.

40) Hamilton to Curzon 2 Feb. 1900, ibid.

41) Hamilton to Curzon 13 June 1901, ibid.

Persian Gulf. I merely demur because I do not think your calculations are correct. "(42) Salisbury doubted if Curzon had
realised the exact position of France with her war party.

At the time when Curzon was insisting on the establishment of
a British protectorate over Kuweit and on overall strong posture
in Persia and the Gulf, British prestige on the Continent was
very low due to the South African war. Hamilton wondered whether
the Indian government had fully realised how weak the British
international position was. He found sufficient truth in the allegation
made by Germany that Britain, a signatory of the Treaty of Berlin
and one of the guarantors of the integrity of the Turkish empire,
had made a secret arrangement with a chief behind the back of
the sovereign of that empire purely for the exclusive advantage
of the British. In his view it was necessary for the British to
lie low for the time being. (43) But all this caution brought no
change in Curzon's line of thought. He told Godley, for example,
that the latter's remarks about the Persian Gulf excited nothing
but horror in his mind. (44) Curzon could not understand why the
British should accomodate any other power in the Gulf without a
prior understanding with them "What I cannot see" he wrote to
Hamilton, "is why we should allow these newcomers, who have
spent no money in the Gulf, who enjoy no trade there, have no
subjects there, possess no immediately contiguous territories,
and are drawn there solely by political ambition, to erode, fritter
away, and little by little destroy, the great body of interests which
we have built up there by a century of trade and domination. "(45)
If the British continental position did not allow any strong measures
Curzon insisted that at least a bargain be made with Germany by
showing her the British hand on Kuweit:

> "She [Germany] cannot build her big Asiatic Railway"
> Curzon wrote to Salisbury, "without our money. She
> cannot carry it to the sea without our consent. She
> ought, I think, to pay heavily for both advantages;
> and we should be able to exact from her pretty well

---

42) Salisbury to Curzon (no date) August 1900, C. P. F 111/159.

43) Hamilton to Curzon 13 June and 25 Sept. 1901, H. P. C 126/3.

44) Curzon to Godley 12 April 1899, C. P. F 111/158.

45) Curzon to Hamilton 15 Feb. 1900, C. P. F 111/159.

what agreement as regards free port, customs, railway
management, and also as regards the political future
of the Gulf - we desire. "(46)

As Curzon was not in favour of Britain joining the Triple Alliance,
which for him would mean habitual and incessant surrendering to
Germany on points where British commercial interests were concerned all over the world, (47) he argued that the establishment
of a protectorate over Kuweit would be an invaluable lever for
subsequent pressure upon, and accomodation with, Germany. (48)

It was under such pressure that in August 1901 a British warship
appeared in the Gulf off Kuweit to prevent the Turks setting foot
there and also to demonstrate Britain's right over the area. The
Germans of course protested against this proceeding as an 'unfriendly act' and the British had to withdraw the warship. The
British government declared that it had no intention of proclaiming
a protectorate over Kuweit and no objection to Kuweit being made
the terminus of the Baghdad Railway provided there was a previous
understanding on this point with Britain. (49) Curzon remained
unsatisfied with the status quo in Kuweit and kept insisting on
establishing a protectorate. (50) Before long the British Government veered round virtually completely to Curzon's way of thinking.

It was the frightening growth of the Russian military, strategic
and commercial influence in Persia during 1899 - 1901, about
which the British Minister at Tehran, Sir Mortimer Durand, had
been warning, that led the British Government to review its policy
towards Persia and the Gulf. Construction by Russia of the strategic
railway in Transcaspia and of a highway from Resht to Tehran
giving her commercial and military advantages; the appearance of
Russian agents in the central and coastal regions of Persia survey-

46) Curzon to Salisbury 7 June 1900, C.P. F 111/159.

47) According to Curzon Britain could get nothing in return
    from Germany as she would not require the German
    army and the German navy was not sufficiently strong to
    be of much value to Britain. See Curzon to Hamilton 15
    May 1901, C.P. F 111/160.

48) Curzon to Lansdowne, 15 June 1901, C.P. F 111/160.

49) Br. Doc. I, pp. 333-4; For German correspondences over
    the matter see G.P. XVIII nos. 5290-5314.

50) Curzon to Lansdowne 16 March 1902, C.P. F 111/161

ing potential harbours and establishing relations with local func-
tionaries; Persian insolvency problems leading to overtures for
loans from foreign powers on security of the customs of the
Gulf ports, were some of the developments which startled the
British. (51) Curzon was further worried about the subsidised
Russian steamers making their way into the Gulf which made
him think that "the artificial creation of trade will assuredly
be followed by the still more artificial generation of political
rights and claims. " Taking all this into consideration Curzon
had already written to Lord Lansdowne, the British foreign
secretary, on 5 April 1901 in a strongly worded 'private and
confidential' letter, that British prestige and influence had stood
never so low in the previous twenty-five years. He urged for a
definite British policy towards the Persian Gulf. (52)

Curzon's uncompromising attitude towards Russian advances into
Persia survived even the powerful British press campaign favouring
an Anglo-Russian entente. Between June and December 1901 various
anti-German articles by anonymous authors appeared mainly in the
National Review and Fortnightly Review recommending the Government to come to an early understanding with Russia for which a
port for her in the Persian Gulf was considered a sine qua non. (53)
The danger from Russia was taken too seriously by the Indian
Government and the latter's opinion during Curzon's viceroyalty
was too important to be bypassed easily by the Home Government.
Ultimately in May 1903 Lansdowne announced in the House of Lords
that the establishment of a naval base of fortified port in the Persian

---

51) See Langer, op. cit. , pp. 752-3; B. H. Sumner, Tsardom and
    Imperialism in the Far East and Middle East, 1880-1914
    (2d ed. 1968) pp. 23-24; R. Kumar, India and the Persian
    Gulf Region 1858-1907 (London 1965) pp. 218-223.

52) C. P. 111/160; also Lord Newton, Lord Lansdowne, A Bio-
    graphy (London 1929) pp. 230-32.

53) Most of the National Review articles appeared under the
    name of A. B. C. and were written by a number of persons.
    The Fortnightly Review articles were signed by 'Calchas'
    (J. L. Garvin). For a full summary of these articles, dis-
    cussions about them, and their impact on governmental
    policy see Langer, op. cit. , pp. 753-759.

Gulf by any other power would be looked upon as a grave menace to British interests. (54)

In the whole discussion about the possible Russian menace in Persia any understanding with Germany was considered impracticable as it was thought that Berlin would without fail claim Kuweit as a terminus for the Baghdad Railway. (55) The anti-German press campaign which followed Curzon's opposition further forced the British Government in 1903 to decline participation in the Baghdad Railway Company formed that year. Thus not only was Germany's hope of getting the Railway an easy access to the Gulf shattered, but she was also faced with the possibility of future British hindrance in the construction of any more line, even in other parts of the Ottoman empire. (56)

2. Towards the Disappearance of 'Pressure on India' 1903-1907

In 1903 Anglo-German relations were estranged by yet another rejection on the part of the British to get together with Germany. Just before her decision about the Baghdad Railway Britain also realised that her aggrement with Germany in the Venezuelan question might imperil her relations with the United States and

54) Lord Newton, op. cit. , p. 243.

55) Memorandum by St. John Broderick, under secretary of state for India, 4 Nov. 1902, cited in Kumar, op. cit. , p. 233.

56) One of the major fields of obstruction was the objection to the increase in Turkish custom duties, necessary for the project to be successfully financed. There were three clearly defined periods in the evolution of British policy regarding the Baghdad Railway question. 1) 1888-1903: Ready to participate in the internationalised Baghdad Railway in the beginning. But in spring 1903 misguided public opinion forced the government to retreat. 2) 1903-1911: Obstructing the Railway in every possible way first by asking for the control of the Baghdad-Gulf section and later by asking that two other Triple Entente members be consulted and satisfied by Germany before the British withdrew her opposition. 3) 1911-1914: Negotiations and settlement with economic, political, and strategic gains for the British. See M.K. Chapman, Great Britain and the Bagdad Railway (Northampton, Mss. 1948) p. 204.

she therefore preferred to go alone. British public opinion was strongly opposed to any association with Germany although, as Lansdowne was to express years later, "the Germans, upon the whole, ran straight as far as we were concerned."(57) The background to this state of affairs was the failure of the alliance negotiations between 1901-02. This aroused suspicion in Britain over Berlin's (Bülow, Holstein) interest in a British alliance in 1901 and of its naval programme at the time.

While Anglo-German relations further deteriorated in 1903, Britain's traditional fear of the Russian threat to India by no means decreased. The Committee of Imperial Defence, reorganised under the chairmanship of the Prime Minister, Balfour, came to the conclusion by the end of 1903 that it was in India that the Empire was most vulnerable. In December 1904 Balfour circulated a paper on the military needs of the Empire giving India the predominant place. (58) The Committee, however, concluded that any serious Russian challenge would be difficult to meet. It was therefore considered important not to provoke Russia, and more so after Britain's recent experience with her former partners in the Mediterranean Entente. In December 1902, Austria-Hungary, more anxious about Macedonian complications, had shown no interest in cooperating with Britain in protesting to Turkey about the recent passage of Russian warships through the Straits. Italy followed the Austro-Hungarian example to avoid offending Russia. (59) The question of a possible Japanese Alliance to help meet any possible Russian threat to India had also to be set aside by the Committee of Imperial Defence on the grounds of the increased commitments towards Japan which it might involve and because of the reluctance of the Indian government to have Japan involved in Indian defence. All this pointed

57) Lord Newton, op. cit. , p. 260. For the details of the Venezuelan question see also here pp. 255-261. About the British rejection of the Baghdad Railway also Lansdowne stated that he had been forced to yield to an ' insensate outcry.' He personally considered the rejection unwise. Ibid. , pp. 254, 249-255.

58) See G. Monger, The End of Isolation: British Foreign Policy 1900-1907 (London 1963) pp. 95-6. Balfour showed that the empire needed 209,000 soldiers: 27,000 for home defence, 30,000 for colonial garrisons, 52,000 for Indian garrisons and 100,000 to be immediately ready to reinforce India according to the earlier Indian government's demand.

59) P. J. V. Rolo, Entente Cordiale: The Origin and Negotiations of the Anglo-French Agreements of 8 April 1904 (London 1969) p. 143; Monger, op. cit. , pp. 86-7.

towards accomodation with Russia being the best policy. So one of the arguments used by Lansdowne in favour of an Anglo-French understanding was that it might lead to an improvement in Anglo-Russian relations. (60)

Although both Britain and France, her ally since spring 1904, hoped for a future Anglo-Russian understanding and although there was a change of attitude in this direction in Russia too, the Russo-Japanese war revived in Russia the old enmity against Britain. Some Russian counts had long been talking about the proverbial 'pressure on India' and after the Dogger Bank incident in October 1904 this was considered to be the easiest way to bring the British to reason. (61) Germany, which followed a pro-Russian neutrality in the war, and was also trying to strengthen her relations with Russia welcomed the opportunity when the Czar telegraphed the Kaiser to make an alliance. The Kaiser had read enough about British India's Russophobia for years and very lately Berlin had also been informed about the Indians' resentment at Curzon's Delhi durbar (62) and about Russia being considered by the Indians as their future saviour. (63) Influenced by these reports Berlin encouraged the Russians to make a military demonstration along the Persio-Afghan border. "Indian borders and Afghanistan were the only part of the Globe", the Kaiser wrote to the Czar in

---

60) See Rolo, op. cit. , pp. 201-2.

61) Hardinge to Lansdowne, November 1904, Lord Newton, op. cit. , pp. 317-18.

62) Voretzsch sent various criticisms of the durbar that appeared in vernacular papers which, although being loyal themselves, doubted the loyalty of the country to the British. In one of the passages of his report, marked heavily by the Kaiser, Voretzsch described the Mohamedan population and the visiting Muscat mission particularly, being deeply shocked at seeing the Viceroy's guests and other high Indian civil servants eating ham sandwiches and smoking at the pavilion built on the stairs of the great mosque of Delhi during Curzon's state entry. Voretzsch to Bülow, Calcutta 15 January 1903, AABI 27; Valentine Chirol, the director of The Times foreign department and a friend of Curzon, who was present at the durbar, later mentioned in his memoirs about the ham eating incident which created 'nearly an uproar.' See V. Chirol, Fifty Years in a Changing World (London 1927) p. 227.

63) Voretzsch to Bülow, Calcutta January 1904, AABI 29.

November 1904, "where the whole of her Battlefleets are of no avail to England and where their guns are powerless to meet [an] invader. The loss of India is the death stroke to Great Britain!"(64)

There was, however, no Russian march towards India. The Kaiser was also in the meantime told by the German General Staff that it was a good as impossible for a large army to undertake the invasion of India. At the request of the Kaiser the General Staff in November/December 1904 worked out a memorandum in which it was emphasised that preparations for an Indian march would take years and the march would last so long as to give Britain ample time to take all necessary counter measures. Even so, it was questionable whether the invading army would reach the frontier in a condition fit to attack. Contrary to his previous opinion the Kaiser now accepted the military judgement and came to the conclusion that as far as pressure upon India was concerned, this favourite catchword of diplomatic conversation was a complete illusion and therefore would have to be left out of the realm of sober Realpolitik. (65) When later the Kaiser and the Czar met on 24 July 1905 the Finish island of Björkoe to sign the ill-fated treaty, they naturally enough confined it to Europe only. To this Bülow, however, did not agree opining that one of the chief places where Germany would find Russian help valuable was in Asia. Bülow considered that the anxiety of the competent British quarter about India's security was proof that a Russian march against India would not be without prospects. (66)

---

64) Kaiser Wilhelm II to Czar Nicholas, Neues Palais 17 Nov. 1904, see Isaac Don Levin (ed.), Letters from the Kaiser to the Czar (New York 1920) pp. 135-6. The Kaiser wrote all his letters to the Czar in English.

65) Bülow to A. A. , Norderney 30 July 1905, G. P. XIX 2, no. 6229. The Kaiser first referred to this memorandum in his discussion with Bülow after Björkoe. The actual date of it is not clear; in March 1905, however, when the Kaiser read again about the resentments of the Indian princes at being asked to prepare for another occasion of pomp and show - for the visiting Prince and Princess of Wales - almost at the wake of the Delhi durbar, he commented: "what a beautiful opportunity the Russians missed through their war-weariness." Kaiser on Quadt to Bülow, Calcutta 27 Feb. 1905, AABI 30.

66) Ibid. , Bülow's reply to the Kaiser; Denkwürdigkeiten, II pp. 140-1.

The Björkoe treaty between Germany and Russia, by which Germany
planned to counteract Anglo-French anti-German policy, came to
naught anyway, as Nicholas II shuffled off the engagement as soon
as he was away from the Kaiser's personal influence. He agreed
with his Foreign Minister's objection to even the European clause
of the treaty which, according to the Minister, was breaking faith
with France. (67) Meanwhile England strengthened her Indian
security by renewing and extending her 1902 treaty with Japan.
In 1905 this treaty placed India under the protection of both the
allies and each side agreed on armed help in case the other was
being menaced by any great power. The defence of India was
further secured by the next move that Russia took in that direction.
Russia, which had recently abandoned her plans of Asiatic con-
quests, took a big step towards friendship with Britain. Count
Witte, the pro-German man at the Russian court, resigned in
April 1906. Besides, the new foreign minister Isvolski was pro-
English. Grey's endeavours to secure the safety of India against
an armed Russian attack or Russian intrigues were therefore
successful. The Anglo-Russian convention signed on August 31,
1907, among other things, guaranteed the security of India's
nothern frontier against Russian aggression and thereby eliminated
the external side of Britain's 'defence of India' problem. Its
international significance lay in the fact that to the Russians it
was a guarantee against an Anglo-German agreement whereas
Britain's gain was a guarantee against a Russo-German agreement. (68) In one of his early reports about the convention von
Miquel, the German charge d'affaires at St. Petersburg, wrote
in September 1907 that what impressed him most was that "the
meaning of the Anglo-Russian Agreement lay not so much in Asia,
but much more in Europe, where its consequences would be made
noticeable for a long time." The Kaiser agreeing to this also
remarked that Britain "will become still more unpleasant to us
in Europe than before."(69)

---

67) The treaty stipulated mutual military assistance to each
    other in Europe in case of attack on either side.

68) Oncken, op. cit., p. 126.

69) G. P. XXV, I, no. 8536 as quoted in R. P. Churchill, The
    Anglo-Russian Convention of 1907 (Iowa 1939) p. 318 n. j.

3. 'Encirclement' and Vague Reliance on Indian Uprising 1907-1910

In the orientation of the big powers in the post-1907 world Germany found herself in a situation which she called 'encirclement'. She was left with only Austria-Hungary as a friend and it appeared that the other big powers were determined to crush her 'world policy'.

One of the early signs of a change of attitude by the big powers towards Germany was the new argument advanced by the British opposition to the Baghdad Railway. In 1903 the main objection from the British point of view had been that in order to find money for the kilometric guarantee it would be necessary to raise the Turkish customs tariff and that this increase would react adversely upon British trade more than that of any other country. (70) In 1907 when negotiations for the Railway restarted with Britain, the latter attached military-strategic importance to the line and demanded British control over the final section from Baghdad to the Gulf. Lord Morley, the secretary of state for India pointed out that to have the line under a single foreign power allowed no guarantee either against British trade being driven out of the Persian Gulf by preferential tariff or against the line being used during war for military purposes to endanger India. Turkish troops, for example, could be sent to the Gulf region by this railway. (71)

The Russians were similarly apprehensive of the difficulties that Turkey with German backing might bring both to Britain and Russia by her Pan-Islamism. On 6 May 1908 Novoye Vremya opined that it was Pan-Islamism which instigated all the complications in Persia and India. The next day the democratic Rech holding the same opinion wrote that the unsatisfactory conditions along the Afghan borders could be explained through the conflict

---

70) Newton, op. cit., p. 251. About the British trade jealousy and rivalry behind the British opposition to the Baghdad railway see V. Chirol, The Middle Eastern Question or some Problems of Indian Defence (London 1903) p. 188; Ernst Jaeckh, 'Der deutsch-englische Kampf um die Bagdad-bahn' in Deutschland im Orient nach dem Balkankrieg (München 1913) pp. 34-43; R. J. S. Hoffman, Great Britain and the German Trade Rivalry 1875-1914 (New York 1964) p. 145.

71) Metternich to Bülow, Highcliffe, 19 Nov. 1907, G. P. XXV 1 no. 8670.

between Germany and Britain whereby Turkey had to play a role set upon her by Germany. (72)

The official Germans in India noticed the gradual growth of friendship between the Triple Entente powers in India both in political and non-political fields. In Calcutta a Russian consulate general was opened and in April 1910 even the wish of one Captain Polovtsov of the Russian General Staff to cross the Pamir and go via the strategic areas of the northern frontier to Russian Turkestan on and adventurous excursion was granted although not entirely without suspicion. (73) Then there were talks about a railway connecting Russia and India. In Simla, where according to the German Consul General hardly twenty persons spoke French well, a branch of the Alliance Francaise was opened with Education Member Butler as president and Foreign Secretary Sir Henry McMahon as vice-president. (74)

Against this friendly atmosphere among the Entente powers between 1907 and 1910 the Germans in India gradually noticed that the wind was turning against them. Even prior to the Anglo-Russian convention jocularly presented rumours appeared in the Anglo-Indian press about a German plot to assassinate the Afghan Amir in India with the cooperation of the Amir's brother's party. (75) Suspicion of the Germans was not confined to irresponsible quarters alone, for on 19 November 1906 von Keller (76), the Vice-Consul in Calcutta had complained to the government of India that an attaché of the German Consulate General, Waetjen,

---

72) Pourtalès to Bülow, St. Petersburg 7 May 1908, AABI 41.

73) Below to Bethmann-Hollweg, Simla 14 May 1910, AABI 45. When after three weeks of excursion Polovtsov returned to Kashmir, the Russian Consul General Arseniev went to meet him there. Later Arseniev told Dr. Remy, the German Vice-Consul that every one of his steps in Kashmir was watched by the secret agents of the Indian government. Remy to Bethmann-Hollweg, Simla 28 July 1910, ibid.

74) Reuß to Bethmann-Hollweg, Simla 16 Aug. 1911, ibid.

75) See The Statesman 12 Jan. 1907; Quadt to Bülow, Calcutta 13 Jan. 1907, AABI 37.

76) Dr. Friedrich von Keller (1873-1960): 1905-8 Vice-Consul, Calcutta; 1912 Senior Counsellor, Foreign Office; 1920 Chargé d'affaires, Belgrad; 1921 Minister, Belgrad; 1924 Minister, Brussels; 1928 Minister, Buenos Aires; August 1933 Representative of the German Reich in League of Nations; 1935 Ambassador, Ankara; 1938 retired.

was followed and his house searched in his absence by the detective police. (77) Although the government of India accepted the charge and regretted the incident, Count Quadt (78), the German Consul General remained unsatisfied. (79) In subsequent years along with the general deterioration of Anglo-German relations such suspicions increased. In October 1910 German Vice-Consul Remy informed Berlin of his suspicion that his mail was being checked by the Indian Government. (80) The official Germans in India were maligned even by their Russian colleagues. In August 1911 Prince Reuß (81) reported that the Russian Vice-Consul Reveliotty was not only intriguing in Simla against Germany but even claiming among other things that Reuß was working with spies. (82)

The growth of suspicion against Germany in India had, however, its parallel in Berlin's hopes of profit from Britain's Indian danger, inspite of the fact that the external and hitherto more frightening aspect of the problem was eliminated by the Anglo-

---

77) Keller to Sir Louis W. Dane, Secretary, Government of India, Foreign Department, 19 Nov. 1906, AABI 37.

78) Albert Count von Quadt to Wykradt and Isny (1864-1930): 1893 Legation Secretary, Tokyo; 1900 First Secretary, Washington; 1903 Consul General, Calcutta; 1908 Minister, Tehran; 1913 Minister, Athens.

79) Quadt to Sir Louis, 28 Dec. 1906. Quadt wrote that Waetjen of the 6th Thuringian Lancers had to undergo the unpleasant experience inspite of the fact that he had been in Quadt's staff for one year and therefore should have been well known to the detective force watching the foreigners.

80) Remy to Bethmann-Hollweg, Simla 13 Oct. 1910, AABI 46; Dr. Erwin Remy (1878-1925): 1909-12 Vice-Consul, Calcutta; 1913 Chargé d'affaires, Bangkok; 1923 Consul General, Canton.

81) Heinrich XXXI Prince Reuß (1868-1929): 1904 Counsellor; 1907 First Secretary, Brussels; 1909 First Secretary, Madrid; 1910 Consul General, Calcutta; 1912 Minister, Tehran; 1916 retired.

82) Reuß to Bethmann-Hollweg, Simla 16 Aug. 1911, AABI 47.

Russian convention. On Britain's demand for the final section of the Baghdad Railway the Kaiser had minuted in June 1907: "Impossible.' It must remain a German railway. If the most important end is left out, there is no point in the whole railway."(83) During his visit to Windsor in November, Haldane, the British War Minister, persuaded the Kaiser to give Britain the final section of the line which she considered the 'gate to India.'(84) But Bülow did not agree (85) to this and thus the situation reverted back to the Kaiser's earlier remark.

It appears that from the continuous reports of disaffection and unrest among the Indians, Berlin considered that the problem of Indian defence still existed for the British in a very real sense. Although Britain protected India from external danger by her treaties with Japan and Russia, the internal aspect of the 'defence of India' - the aspect which Salisbury had emphasised (86) - was far from losing its significance. As a matter

---

83) Kaiser's comment on Metternich to Bülow, London 17 June 1907, G. P. XXI 2, no. 7223.

84) Viscount Haldane, Before the War (London 1920) p. 48 ff.

85) Bülow to Schoen at Windsor, Berlin 14 Nov. 1907, G. P. XXV 1, no. 8667.

86) At the turn of the century Salisbury supported General Roberts' Seistan-India railway project not because he thought that the Russians had any serious plan to conquer India but because of the possible effect any Russian advance upon India might have on the internal situation in India. Such advance, he thought, could shatter British government in India and reduce India to anarchy. In this connection he regretted the presence of the 'damned nigger' element in British society in India and unfavourably compared British treatment of the natives with that of the Russians. See Salisbury to Northcote, then governor of Bombay, 8 June 1900, Salisbury Papers quoted in Grenville, op. cit., pp. 295-6. It should, however, be noted that some years previously Salisbury himself applied the words 'the black man' to Dadabhai Naoroji, the first Indian Member of the British Parliament.

of fact, due to the defeat of Russia by Japan and the growth of nationalism, this aspect was getting a dynamic character. The official Germans both in Berlin and in India did not, of course, appreciate Indian nationalism. (87) But both the political and non-political causes of Indian unrest seem to have given Berlin the conviction that in the final confrontation with Britain, Germany would be in a position to create a grave situation for the British in India. This conviction made Berlin very firm in not accepting British friendship on the precondition of reducing the strength of the German navy, which the German Ambassador in London, Count Metternich had been advising. Commenting on Metternich's reference to the friendly tone of the speeches by Asquith and Lloyd George about Germany, the Kaiser wrote in August 1908:

> "They all are completely without any significance since all of them aim at the reduction of our fleet as a pre-condition of their friendship. And this is exactly what we would not do. The British should be aware that war with Germany would mean the loss of India and thus the loss of their world position."(88)

Thus although Berlin did not approve of the Indian movement for self-rule in either its moderate or extremist developments, it continued to be well-informed about the activities of the Indian nationalists not only in India but also in various parts of the world. (89) Some influential pan-Germans, close to official circles, took an interest in the activities of the Indian revolutionary nationalists abroad. Professor Theodor Schiemann, the leading political commentator for the important right-wing conservative journal Kreuz-Zeitung and soon to become one of the Kaiser's

---

87) See chapter VI.

88) The Kaiser's marginal comment on Metternich to Bülow, London 11 Aug. 1908, G. P. XXIV no. 8228.

89) In October 1908 the German Foreign Office received that month's copy of The Free Hindusthan, a journal issued by the America based Indian revolutionaries. In July 1909 after the Curzon Wyllie murder in London it came to know about the London and Paris based Indian revolutionaries ('L'Empire des Indes' in L'Eclair 8 July 1909). About Indian revolutionaries in Japan see below ch. VIII.

intimates (90); Professor Ernst Jaeckh, an expert on Balkan and
Near Eastern problems, later to become an adviser to the foreign
office in 1912 (91), and Count Ernst zu Reventlow, the editor of
Alldeutsche Blätter and later to associate closely with Berlin
Indians and publish a book on the objectives of German political
and economic policies in India (92), were some of these men.

Professor Schiemann particularly had long been of the belief that
an understanding with England would be possible when she finally
saw that she could no longer ignore Germany's interests throughout
the world. He wrote that England "is still the state which has
least adjusted itself to the fact that Germany is the strongest
power on the continent, and that she is prepared, if necessary,
to compell this recognition."(93) One of the means adopted by
Schiemann to coerce Britain was to maintain contact with George
Freeman, the Irish Sinn Fein leader and publicist in America
who was then co-operating with the Indian revolutionaries in
Europe and America. In January 1909 Freeman gave this hope
to Schiemann: "Our news here of things in India is that no abate-
ment of the anti-English sentiment, but the reverse; (sic) also
that Mahrattas are organizing but making no outward show of
their feeling or designs. In Bengal there is an increase of anti-
English feeling but they are inclined to follow our advice from
here and elsewhere that premature action must be avoided, but
propaganda and popular organization should be widely and actively

---

90) It was the personal wish of the Kaiser that Professor
Schiemann should be appointed as 'ordentlicher Professor'
in History and Literature to the University of Berlin.
Tel. from Bülow to Willnowski, Kiel 27 June 1901, attach-
ed to the letter from George Freeman to Prof. Schiemann,
New York 17 Jan. 1909. See AABI 44.

91) See Fritz Fischer, Germany's Aims in the First World War
(New York 1967) p. 124. For Jaeckh's Indian activities see
below ch. VIII p. 172 n. 18, p. 201 and n. 124.

92) See Graf E. zu Reventlow, Indien: Seine Bedeutung für
Großbritannien, Deutschland und die Zukunft der Welt
(Berlin 1917).

93) Kreuz-Zeitung, 6. Jan. 1897 and Th. Schiemann, Deutschland
und die Große Politik I, II, p. 12 quoted in E. M. Carroll,
Germany and the Great Powers: 1866-1914: A Study in Public
Opinion and Foreign Policy (Hamden, Conn., 1966, 2d ed.)
p. 383.

carried on." Freeman then wrote about the Indian revolutionary activities in Canada and U.S.A. (94)

4. The German Crown Prince in India, December 1910 - February 1911

Whether Schiemann had any direct contact with the Indian revolutionary elements in America is not known. In 1910 there was, anyhow, a change of attitude among the pan-Germans; the death of King Edward VII in May that year was considered by them as the passing away of the leader of 'encirclement' conspiracy and they hoped that the year 1910 would mean the beginning of a new epoch for Germany. (95) Taking advantage of his friendly relations with the new King, George V (96) the Kaiser wrote to the latter in July 1910 about his decision to send his eldest son to the Far East and India for study and observation. George V welcomed the idea of the German Crown Prince's Indian visit most heartily: "Your wishes as to the visit being a purely private one, shall be carried out...but as German Crown Prince, his position must be recognised, especially in a country like India, where great importance is attached to all outward observances of rank and ceremony. "(97)

The German Crown Prince's proposed trip to the Far East fell through but on 14 December 1910 he and his party arrived at Bombay for the visit to India which lasted until the end of Febru-

---

94) G. Freeman to Prof. Schiemann, New York 17 Jan. 1909, AABI 44. From this letter it is very clear that Prof. Schiemann was in regular contact with Freeman. At one place Freeman writes: "I hope my last letters with the accompanying packages of papers duly came to your hands, and that they are on their way to their destination."

95) E.M. Carroll, op. cit., p.642.

96) See John Gore, King George V: A Personal Memoir (London 1941) pp.257, 286, 288, 308.

97) George V to the Kaiser, London 20 July 1910. Reise Sr. K.u.K. Hoheit des Kronprinzen nach Indien (hereafter cited as Preuss 1.) 1).

ary 1911. The Government of India did everything to make the visit extremely pleasant, spending a substantial amount despite the non-official character of the visit. (98) Pleased with the Indian government's efforts for his son's visit the Kaiser was to comment: "450,000 Marks were spent by the Indian Government for my son in India! What did the Germans do for his trip from the home end?"(99)

The German Crown Prince's programme in India was confined largely to pleasure trips, fun and sports. Von Treutler (100), the German Foreign Office's representative in the royal party was however conscious of the opportunities offered by the occasion to the Crown Prince to learn about all aspects of colonial administration and especially when he was so constantly surrounded by experts on those subjects. (101)

Reuß was also afraid that the appearance of the Crown Prince's visit merely as a pleasure trip both in the eyes of the British and of the Indians might be detrimental to Germany's interest. (102) For German political interests Reuß also favoured some expression of sympathy for India and the Indian people on the part of His Royal Highness while still proclaiming Anglo-German friendship. He found the moment psychologically ripe for conveying to the Indians that since Germany rejected the idea of conquering India by force she

---

98) Reuß to Bethmann-Hollweg, Calcutta 22 Dec. 1910, Preuss 1 (8); Sir Harold Stuart, who was accompanying the German Crwon Prince as the Government of India's representative, told Treutler that a number of Indian villages and towns would gratefully remember the Crown Prince's visit because of the essential communication improvements that came to them along with the visit. At Mathura, Treutler reported, a long standing wish by the farmers for a canal was fulfilled because of the need to water the polo ground prepared for the high dignitary. Treutler to the Kaiser, Mathura, 4 Jan. 1911, ibid.

99) The Kaiser on Reuß report above.

100) Karl Georg von Treutler (1858-1933): 1895 Legation Secretary, Tokyo; 1900 Minister, Brazil; 1907 Minister, Christiania; since 1908 followed the Kaiser in his travels as the Foreign Office's representative; 1911 Royal Prussian Minister, Munich.

101) Treutler regretted that the Crown Prince was more preoccupied with superficial things. Treutler to A.A., camp near Agra 29 Dec. 1910 draft telg. 'strictly confidential'; Treutler to A.A., 27 Jan. 1911, Preuss 1 (1).

102) Reuß to Bethmann-Hollweg, Calcutta 5. Jan. 1911, Preuss 1 (8).

was interested in the greater meeting of the two countries on 'moral and psychological' grounds. Such a message, he said, would dispel from the mind of the people the 'old fairy tale' that Germany was exclusively a military and police state. That the Crown Prince, by expressing sympathy for India and the Indians would be only sowing seeds on fertile soil, Reuß was very sure. The British by their 'German scare' alarm had only succeeded in raising the Germans in the estimation of the Indians. Besides, Reuß also came to know that Indians of higher class were impressed by Germany's selfless devotion to the study of Sanskrit. (103)

The German Crown Prince's visit did not, however, contribute anything politically to the relations between Germany and the Indians' India. Political Indians, at this time, were talking about democracy and self-rule and the more radical ones among them were against any kind of foreign domination. As will be seen in our next chapters, none of the official Germans, including Reuß and those in the Crown Prince's entourage, could appreciate the aspirations of the political Indians. In fact, they were very critical of them.

The British perhaps did not expect an improvement in general Anglo-German relations through the German Crown Prince's Indian visit. Lord Hardinge, an old Germanophob of the foreign office (104), had just been appointed Viceroy of India when the initial preparations for the German royal visit were made in London. (105) Arriving in India shortly before the German Crown Prince, it was he who made the rest of the arrangements until the end of the visit. Thus being connected with all the aspects of the visit, Hardinge wrote later in his memoirs that during the Crown Prince's visit he knew as an absolute certainty that there would be a war with Germany. (106) The British, however, tried and were successful in demonstrating their achievements in the governance of a vast and complicated country and in convincing the Germans of the trust and good will that Britain commanded from the Indians. The Germans were impressed.

---

103) Ibid. The Kaiser considered the whole report of Reuß as 'important'.

104) See Monger, op. cit. , pp. 100-3.

105) Hardinge to Metternich, Kent 9 Aug. 1910, Preuss 1 (1).

106) Lord Hardinge of Penshurst, My Indian Years 1910-1916 (London 1948) pp. 19-20.

Treutler considered British rule in India as one of the most outstanding works of the occidental culture (107), and the Crown Prince wrote to his father that all the rumours about a forthcoming uprising to detach India from the 'mother country' were absolute fairy tales. (108) The British praised the Crown Prince and the more so for his high tribute to the British Empire in India. (109) The Kaiser was so happy about this personal success of his son that in August 1911 he expressed his intention of sending a German warship to salute the British King on his arrival in Bomby for his forthcoming Indian visit. (110)

Thus in early 1911 it appeared for a while as though Berlin finally accepted the longstanding view of its representatives in India that there could be no uprising in India which the British would find difficult in suppressing. The Germans in India so far found nothing in the politics of the Indians which they could sympathise with. The Hindus who had dominated the scene hitherto appeared to them as backward rather than forward looking. (111) There was nothing for Germany to gain directly from Hindu politics. But suddenly towards the end of the year the Indian political scene appeared differently in the eyes of the

---

107) Treutler to the Kaiser, from Steamer Arabia, 28 Feb. 1911, Preuss 1 (10).

108) Crown Prince Wilhelm to the Kaiser on the way to Calcutta from Lucknow, 3 Feb. 1911, ibid. According to Treutler, a dangerous uprising in India would occur only should the 'mother country' be seriously endangered by a third force. Treutler in above.

109) See Pall Mall Gazette 25 Feb., Daily Mail 27 Feb., Times of India 27 Feb. 1911; Hardinge to the Kaiser 15 Feb. 1911, Preuss 1 (10). Years later Lord Hardinge, however, gave a disparaging account of the Crown Prince's character and skill in sports. See Lord Hardinge of Penshurst, op. cit., p. 19.

110) This offer was, however, politely rejected by the British foreign office pointing out that other countries would undoubtedly wish to follow the German example and there would be then an essemblage of foreign warships in Indian waters creating an embarassing situation. British foreign office to Metternich, London 5 Sept. 1911, AABI 47.

111) Luxburg to Bethmann-Hollweg, Simla 31 May 1913, AABI 50.

official Germans: in the reaction of the Indian Muslims to the
happenings in the Ottoman Empire they saw a new force of
international significance emerging in India.

5. Thoughts on a new 'India Policy' based on Pan-Islamism, 1913

Ever since the time of the Russo-Japanese war the Muslims of
India acquired a great significance in British imperial thinking.
The impact of pan-Islamism among the Indian Muslims was considered to be a danger in weakening the traditional Muslim loyalty
towards the British and the British imperial experts suggested that
deliberate attempts should be made to assure the Indian Muslims
of British friendship even at the cost of the Hindus and, if necessary, by rapproachment with Turkey.(112) In receiving a Muslim
deputation under the leadership of the Aga Khan by the viceroy
in 1906 and the Indian Government's subsequent sympathetic attitude towards the grievances of the Muslims a consciousness of
Muslim power was expressed.

The growth of political consciousness among the Indian Muslims
in both internal and extra-Indian spheres and the British attitude
towards it had been duly noticed from the start by the official
Germans in Simla, Cairo and Constantinople.(113) But never before, in this century, did the relations between the British and
the Indian Muslims enter as critical a stage as in the period following the Turco-Italian war. In 1911, besides various protest meetings
by the urban Indian Muslims over the Italian action in Tripoli, in
which British intervention on behalf of Turkey was urged, a committee named 'Aid to Ottoman Red Crescent Society' was formed to
collect funds for the support of those who suffered in the war in
Turkey. Reporting the events, Reuß wrote that sooner or later
the Indian question would force the British to appeal for peace.(114)

---

112) See V. Chirol, 'Pan Islamism', in Proceedings of the
Central Asian Society (London 1906) pp. 1-17 ff.

113) Quadt to Bülow, Simla 15 Sept.1906, AABI 36; Below to
Bülow, Simla 16 Sept. 1908, AABI 43; Oppenheim to Bülow,
Cairo, 20 Feb. and 16 May 1909, AABI 44; See also A. J.
Marder (ed.) Fear God and Dread Nought: The Correspondence of Admiral of the Fleet Lord Fisher of Kilber-
stone Vol. II, p.129 n., for Baron Marschall von Bieber-
stein's (German Ambassador at Constantinople 1897-1912)
knowledge of the subject.

114) Reuß to Bethmann-Hollweg, Simla 4 and 5 Oct. 1911,
AABI 47.

But the prerequisites of Britain's international diplomacy and her sympathies for the Indian Muslims did not go hand in hand. As The Times stated, "Indian Mahomedans may feel at times that British policy, with its manifold interests, is liable to overwork their sentiments and claims, but a deeper insight would assure them that British interests and theirs are inseparably intertwined."(115) In 1912 the onslaught on Turkey by the Balkan League with Russian inspiration and British connivance further agitated the minds of the Indian Muslims. They considered Prime Minister Asquith's Guildhall speech regarding the territorial readjustment after the Balkan war in November that year as Britain's lack of sympathy for Turkey and Islam.(116) The Red Crescent movement tended to become anti-British.(117)

The new German Consul General in India, Count von Luxburg (118) who arrived in India in November 1912, was at once struck by the great significance of the impact that the Turkish events had had on the Indian Muslims.(119) He was surprised, too, to see even the Hindus sympathising with the grievances of their Muslim brethren. However, it was the 'manly', 'proud' and 'action loving' Muslims rather than the visionary and merely 'thinking Hindus' who impressed Luxburg. In the context of the present Hindu-Muslim unity and the many channels of communication that were running now from India to Constantinople and noting also what the united Marathas had earlier achieved during the Mughal period, Luxburg saw in the sixty to seventy millions of Indian Muslims an emerging force capable of seriously endangering the peace of the country if guided from outside in a clever manner.

---

115) The Times, 16 March 1912.

116) Luxburg to Bethmann-Hollweg, Calcutta 30 Nov. 1912 and 2 Jan. 1913, AABI 49.

117) G. MacMunn, Turmoil and Tragedy in India: 1914 and After (London 1935) p. 67.

118) Karl-Ludwig Count von Luxburg (1872-?): 1909 First Secretary, Peking; 1912 Consul General, Calcutta; 1914 Chargé d'affaires, Buenos Aires; 1915 Minister, Buenos Aires; 1919 out of state service.

119) Luxburg to Bethmann-Hollweg, Simla 12 Nov. 1912, Tel., AABI 49.

He also wrote to Berlin that among those British civil servants
who like him saw the future of India as the future of the Indian
Muslims, the influence of Turkey was becoming an unbearable
experience. This was particularly so, he added, as in comparison
to the British plight, Germany had no friction in Asia. (120)

In the early months of 1913 Luxburg and Heyer (121), the German
Consul in Bombay, marked the growth of pan-Islamism along
with the growing enthusiasm for the Turkish fund. (122) What
impressed them was that even the poorest of the Indian Muslims
took part in the Turkish relief with their tiny contributions. By
early July 1913 Luxburg noted that some eight million rupees
had already been sent to Turkey through various channels. (123)

Observing the gradual transformation of pan-Islamism into an
anti-English movement Luxburg wrote that the anger of the
Indian Muslims against the British would not disappear easily.
This anger the Muslims expressed by even uniting with the
Hindus in demanding self-rule. (124) Against this Muslim loss
of faith in the British, Luxburg noticed the Indian Muslims' high
esteem for Germany because of her friendship with Turkey. The
anti-British Muslim views found expression in the Urdu journal
Zamindar of Lahore edited by Zafar Ali Khan, a noted firebrand.
In July 1913 Luxburg sent to Berlin the translation of an open
letter from a Muslim leader published in this journal posing the
question: "Should we look for England's help or Germany's?"
Here the author unfavourably compared British policy in Turkey
with that of Germany praising the latter's friendly attitude to
the Muslims inspite of the fact that she did not have as many

---

120) Luxburg to Bethmann-Hollweg, Calcutta 16 Jan. 1913, ibid.

121) Friedrich Heyer (1871-?): 1907 Vice-Consul, Constantinople;
    1909 Consul, Bombay; 1915 Consul, Glasgow.

122) Heyer to Bethmann-Hollweg, Bombay 14, 21 Feb. and 1 March
    1913; Luxburg in the same 12 March 1913. Luxburg on his
    visit to the Muslim College at Aligarh found it developing
    into a breeding-place of pan-Islamism to the great anxieties
    of the British, AABI 49.

123) Luxburg to Bethmann-Hollweg, Simla 31 May, 2 July 1913,
    AABI 50.

124) Ibid.

ties with Islam as the British had. (125) Referring to the anti-British Muslim riot in early August at Kanpur, a place not very far from Delhi, Luxburg wrote that although one of the expectations of the British while transferring the capital from Calcutta to Delhi was the loyal Muslim support in the latter, the Delhi bomb outrage of December 1912 and the present incidents in Kanpur had belied this hope. (126)

Luxburg saw that the Muslim disaffection was causing great concern even to the experienced Britons in India. What, then, should be the German policy in the light of such a state of affairs of the British in India and especially in view of the impending war between Germany and Britain? In the summer of 1913 Luxburg advised Berlin: "Despite a desirable slow rapproachment between Germany and Britain for the time being we have no reason to make it easier for the British to rule India."(127) Luxburg's advice was the first thing that the Kaiser and the German Foreign Office turned to when the war appeared imminent in July 1914.

---

125) Luxburg to Bethmann-Hollweg, Simla 17 July 1913, ibid. Open letter: Khwaja Sahib to the British Prime Minister; Articles with more emphatic Muslim support for Germany appeared in Barakatullah's journal of Islamic Fraternity in 1912. See J. C. Ker, Political Trouble in India (Calcutta 1917) p. 261. For some general details of the Pan-Islamic Movement see M. O'Dwyer, India as I knew it 1885-1925 (London, 1925) pp. 172-182.

126) Luxburg to Bethmann-Hollweg, Simla 7 Aug. 1913, ibid. The original cause of the Kanpur riot on 3 August was the Government's hindrance to the reconstruction of the outer part of a mosque in view of broadening a public road.

127) Luxburg to Bethmann-Hollweg, Simla 29 July 1913, ibid.

PART TWO

GERMAN ASSESSMENT OF BRITISH RULE IN INDIA

AND

GERMAN ANTIPATHY TO INDIAN NATIONALISM

IV. CONGRESS MOVEMENT TILL CURZON AND OFFICIAL
GERMANS

"The British who wish to educate this people [the Indians]
in European civilization and who describe it as their
prime duty, have now dissolved the old conditions and
created a half-educated, pretentious class of people who
have no longer any roots among their own people and who
at the same time nourish and spread discontentment with
the 'foreign' British administration. One day the British
will have to grapple with this discontentment."

Gerlich to Bismarck
Calcutta 6 Dec. 1886

As we have already seen, between 1886 and Curzon's viceroyalty (1899 - 1905) the German Foreign Service personnel
observing the Indian scene from London and India concentrated
mainly on the subjects which were directly connected with the
danger of a Russian attack on India. They were preoccupied
therefore with the events on the north-west frontier, the nature
and strength of the British army in India and the attitude of the
native princes towards the British rule in India and their would-
be reaction to an external attack on British India. The political
demands of the educated Indian middle class, being peacefully
presented by the moderate leaders with great respect for, and
high hopes in, the British government and people, did not constitute any danger to British rule at this stage and did not therefore receive any detailed discussion. However, the role of British Liberalism in the internal political problems of the British
in India was far too provocative a subject not to occupy the
minds of the official Germans in India at all. Besides, the new
acquisition of colonies by Germany during this period gave them
an additional interest in the relationship between the rulers and
the ruled in a colonial context.

The internal political problems of the British in India which we
are going to discuss here resulted out of a clash that had been
going on long before the commencement of our period, between
the British imperial interests and Indian national interests. This
was the clash that gave birth in 1885 to the Indian National
Congress which in turn set off a train of events leading eventually
to the emergence of Indian independence and the birth of Pakistan. (1)

<hr>

1) For the background of this clash until the emergence of the
Indian National Congress see Briton Martin Jr., New India;
1885: British Official Policy and the Emergence of the
Indian National Congress (Berkeley 1969).

Her world-wide imperial interests in the '80s of the last century made Britain look upon India as a highly valuable possession which she must continue to retain with an autocratic government and by keeping all important powers in the hands of Britons. The Indian educated middle class on the other hand, taking the Indian national and also their own interests in hand, demanded a share in all branches of government and began to look upon the foreign rule more and more critically. Some of the complaints of the educated Indians were: that the higher grade of the civil and military services were practically closed to them; that the native interests were unrepresented in the Legislative Councils; that the huge expense of the army was unnecessary; that the people were disarmed and 'demartialised'; that taxes left people on the margin of subsistence; that the land settlement was not made permanent and that visitations of famine were unchecked in their severity. (2)

While these and several other similar grievances kept on appearing in the resolutions of various organisations of the educated Indians, their main political campaign, now actively led by the Congress and its British supporters in England, centred round the demand for a gradual shift from autocratic to elected representative government, Indianisation of the Indian Civil Service and a drastic reduction in the 'Home Charges'. The Congress demanded that in the central and provincial Legislative Councils - i.e. the Viceroy's and provincial Governors' Executive Councils when they went into legislative session with added nominated members - half the members should be democratically elected by the people. The chief hindrance to Indianisation of the civil service was its entrance examinations which were held only in England. Congress therefore insisted on simultaneous examinations in India and England. The issue that with its high propaganda value helped the campaign to move gradually from an innocuous stage of mere pleas for reform to an anti-British movement for self-rule was the question of 'Home Charges' - i.e. the huge amount that India had to pay yearly in gold in London as expenditure on 'common interests between England and India.' The 'Home Charges' which totalled nearly sixteen millions sterlin in 1890-1 and absorbed well over a quarter of Indian revenue, habitually included such expenditure as the maintenance of the India Office in London, pensions and furlough

---

2) From an appeal to the British electorate by the Bombay Presidency Association, the Indian Association of Calcutta, and three other native political associations summarised in The Times, 13 Oct. 1885.

of the official Anglo-Indians, paying off capital investment and interest in London on Indian railways and the maintenance of military and diplomatic affairs in Aden and Persia.

In their demand for a share in the government of their country the educated Indians were supported not only by the fact that their English education made them fit enough to hold such posts but they could also show that their deprivation from such posts was contrary to the established law. By 1886 - the year in which Germany's consular-diplomatic connection with British India began - half a century had passed since English became the official language of India and the country acquired nearly thirty years of intellectual progress through English education (3) and as Macaulay, the father of that education had visualised in July 1833 in the British Parliament, the educated Indians arrived at the stage to demand European institutions. (4) Nor could they be held back legally, for the Charter Act of 1833 and the Queen's Proclamation of 1858 specifically recognised that no native of India may be denied any post or employment under the British Indian Government for reason of his birth, descent, creed or colour. The early leaders of the Indian National Congress and other Indian public bodies therefore never ceased to point out these two legal bases of their political rights and liberties. (5)

---

3) In 1835 Lord Bentinck's Government published a resolution "that the object of the British Government ought to be pro-motion of European literature and science among the natives of India and that all the funds appropriated for the purpose of education would be best employed on English education alone..." thus finally settling the old controversy whether to promote European or Oriental education. In 1857 the three presidential universities of Calcutta, Bombay and Madras were established.

4) The following is the most often-quoted passage from this speech of Macaulay: "It may be that the public mind of India may expand under our system until it has outgrown that system; that by good government we may educate our subjects into a capacity for better government, that, having become instructed in European knowledge, they may, in some future age, demand European institutions." Hansard, XIX (1833) p. 536.

5) See H. L. Singh, Problems and Policies of the British in India 1885-1898 (London 1963) p. 7; S. R. Mehrotra, India and the Commonwealth 1885-1929 (London 1965) pp. 22-23.

The official Germans in India were instinctively opposed to any democratic change in the existing political order in India. Any political power in Indian hands would, they believed, gradually weaken the strong hand of the British. In December 1886 in his first report to Berlin, Hermann Gerlich, the first German Consul General in Calcutta, wrote: "The civil quarters consist mainly of Gladstone's supporters who wish to make the country happy with their liberal and humanitarian ideas, but in so doing they are only slowly undermining the position of the British."(6) Gerlich criticised the British Government in India for being pre-occupied with suspicion of foreign enemies only and not handling firmly those native ones whom he called 'the half-educated pretentious class of people', 'a creation of Britain's own civilising mission', whose only job was to spread discontentment with their foreign rulers.(7)

Gerlich undoubtedly saw the India of his time against the background of the British Liberal attitude towards her and its impact on the current Indian administration and educated Indians in general. The history of this attitude went back to the 1870s when it was first expressed in a campaign involving support for the native press, an increase in the number of Indians in the civil service, opposition to the Bill creating Queen Victoria Empress of India, and support for Gladstone's basic proposition that the British title to India depended on it being profitable to the Indian people.(8) Under the viceroyalty of Liberal Lord Ripon (1880-84), during Gladstone's second Government (1880-85), an attempt was made to provide the Indians not merely with good administration of a benevolent despotism but also to raise them politically and socially, with the aim that one day they would be able to substitute a successful administration by foreigners with a complete self-government of their own.(9) Ripon liberalised internal administration, encouraged the progress of education, expanded the powers of local elected bodies, repealed the Vernacular Press Act of 1878 to give the local language newspapers freedom

---

6) Gerlich to Bismarck, Calcutta 6 Dec. 1886, AABI 2. For Gerlich's career see ch. I above, p. 33n. 36.

7) Ibid.

8) C. Bolt, Victorian Attitude to Race (London 1971) p. 180.

9) See H. L. Singh, op. cit., p. 2 and n.

equal to those in English, and tried through a bill, though un-successfully, to give Indian judges the same rights as European ones to handle the cases of European defendants. Ripon's Radical views on giving political education to the Indians as an answer to the growing spirit of progress were not shared by most Britons in India and Britain and his successor Dufferin (1884-88) had to placate the British community in India. However, in Dufferin's view too - which Gerlich apparently noticed - the objectives of even the most advanced natives were neither dangerous nor very extravagant.

Most Anglo-Indians, irrespective of their party affiliation, were convinced that secular education produced national self conscious-ness and hatred of Britain among the natives. Tories similarly argued that "only Liberals entertained the mistaken view that all men were alike, entitled to identical rights and fit to be governed identically, and that such beliefs, if applied to India, would lose it for Britain."(10) Gerlich's views thus tallied totally with the Anglo-Indian and Tory opinion.

This reaction to liberalism led other official Germans in India to be equally influenced by that section of the British conservative opinion which took an unfriendly attitude to Indian demands. Ever since its birth, the Indian National Congress had been treated with considerable misgivings and hostility by British conservative opinion. The most outspoken representative of that opinion was The Times. This newspaper objected to the reform of the Legis-lative Councils according to the Indians' demands on the ground that it would be tantamount to the introduction of Home Rule for India. Muslims were praised by the paper for having kept aloof from the Congress and the Hindus were warned that India was won by force and with force alone would she be held.(11) Appar-ently agreeing to such opinions Count Leyden, a member of the German embassy in London, wrote to Berlin in December 1888 that Congress by demanding expansion of the rights of the Legis-lative Council and Indian representation in it was influenced by the Irish Home Rule Movement and for this development Gladstone was partly to be blamed. Leyden reported the prevailing British opinion that the spreading of 'autonomous ideas' would be like playing with fire and that the introduction of franchise in India

---

10) See C. Bolt, op. cit., pp. 162, 180.

11) cf. Ram Gopal, Indian Muslims: A Political History (London 1959) pp. 63-4.

would lead to the concentration of power in the hands of the Hindus and the consequent suppression of Islamic and other elements and the likelihood of a civil war.(12)

A little more than a year later the second German Consul-General in Calcutta, Baron von Heyking, also seemed to have agreed with similar views expressed by the Anglo-Indian press of the time. In February 1890 he wrote that the prevailling official view was that religious and racial hostilities between the Hindus and the Muslims on the one hand and their common hostility towards the Christians on the other were such as to create anarchy in India if the representative institutions, with the usual fights for election, were to be introduced in India as demanded by the Indian National Congress in its recent Bombay session.(13) Heyking who with his wife maintained excellent relations with British governmental and social circles in India, was also influenced by Anglo-Indian opinion about the native press and Congress leaders. He reported that the Indian press did not express public opinion, for there could not be any opinion of the masses who lived without thinking and were pre-occupied with dire animal-like needs only. The native papers were, therefore, products of individual persons or of a clique whose profession it was to spread discontentment and bad feeling against the Government. They awoke in their readers the idea of protest against the established authority. To substantiate these charges against the native papers Heyking said that they had hardly any circulation to thrive on and they therefore blackmailed the native rajahs and other wealthy persons who always had something to hide from the public.(14)

In spite of the general Tory opposition to Indian reforms and Salisbury's own 'High Tory criticism'(15) the progressive

---

12) Leyden to Bismarck, London 30 Dec. 1888, AABI 4.

13) Heyking to Bismarck, Calcutta 1 Feb. 1890, AABI 6. About Heyking's career see above chapter I.

14) Heyking to Caprivi, Simla 23 June 1891, AABI 9.

15) Salisbury, a one-time Secretary of India himself, warned in the Lords on 15 Feb. 1892 against the application of occidental machinery, by which the British might bring into power the nationalists i. e. the artificial and weakly elements of Indian society, neglecting the natural, vigorous and effective ones represented by the fighting races. See S. Maccoby, English Radicalism 1886-1914 (London 1953) p. 425 and n.

opinion on India in the British Parliament and the need that Dufferin and his Liberal-Unionist successor Lord Lansdowne (1888-93) felt in India to placate the growing Congress movement by some harmless concessions, finally paved the way for the passing of the Indian Council Act of 1892 during Salisbury's second Government (1886-92), just before the general election in that year. The demand by the Congress for full democratic elections for at least half the seats in the Councils was however not realised; the Act only accepted in principle that the Legislative Councils should be enlarged and their members allowed to ask 'parliamentary questions' and discuss the budget. The fact that the Act was vague on the method of Council enlargement caused sufficient anxieties among the Anglo-Indians - and not unduely - lest its implementation took place under a Liberal regime. From Heyking's observations during the intervening period and after, his own mind about the ideal constitution of India is further made clear.

Heyking was not in favour of any constitutional reform that would restrict the autocratic powers of the Viceroy and as the Congress leaders, by demanding expansion of the Viceroy's Council and enlargement of its powers to control governmental finance, were striving for just that he had no sympathy for them. The fact that a few British Radicals and Gladstonian Liberals had been supporting the Indians' cause horrified Heyking. In July 1892, in a report on the successful contest of a leading Congressman Dadabhai Naoroji to the British Parliament on a Liberal ticket, Heyking put all these various feelings together aligning himself with the fears and forebodings of the Anglo-Indians of the time.

Heyking considered Naoroji 'a die-hard Radical'.(16) The greatest of the early Indian Congressmen, Naoroji (1825-1917) had, of course, been in close contact with the Radicals in England for a long time. During his first stay in England from 1855 until 1864 he played some part in helping such Radical 'Friends of India' as John Bright and Henry Fawcett to prepare the Indian briefs that they were to argue before Parliament. Back in England in 1867 he had busied himself with political pamphleteering on Indians' behalf and was an unsuccessful Gladstonian Parliamentary candidate in 1886. Presently he came to Parliament with Radical help. Heyking, however, did not draw his epithet for Naoroji from this background. For him the summing-up was simple: "for what else could an Indian be but Radical, if he dedicates himself to a par-

---

16) Heyking to Caprivi, Calcutta 11 July 1892, AABI 10, The Kaiser's general comment on the report: "well written".

liamentary profession, for in this Party alone he finds support for and approval of the natives' claims for political rights and participation in the rule of their country." Although there is some truth in the statement, as we have already noticed, Heyking in his dislike for parliamentary government in general and its introduction in India in particular, completely bypassed the moderation in Naoroji's political views. This moderation was best expressed in his presidential address to the second session of the Indian National Congress in 1886 when he called it the Indians' good fortune to be "under a rule which makes it possible for us to meet in this manner. It is under the civilising rule of the Queen and people of England that we meet here together, hindered by none, and are freely allowed to speak our minds without the least fear and without the least hesitation. Such a thing is possible under British rule and British rule only."

Heyking tried to visualise the effect of Naoroji's election on the political position of the Indians at the time of the inplementation of the latest reform. He knew that many of the built-in clauses of the Act would give a Conservative Viceroy every possibility to prevent far-reaching changes, but the same would not be the case if a man with Lord Ripon's mantle was to come as Viceroy in the event of a Liberal victory. This was the fear of most Anglo-Indians as well and the fact that in early July 1892 Heyking also learned personally from Lord Lansdowne of the likelihood of his resignation before the expiry of his term should the Gladstone Ministry come to power, made Heyking look pessimistically at the British position in India: "How can the dominant superiority of the Europeans be maintained in India, a country where the servility and subordinance of the natives make even the poorest white man a member of the aristocracy, when an Indian is placed on the same level as the most noble and most select ones in the mother-country!"(17)

The Viceregal Regulation on the new constitution of the Indian Councils did differ under Gladstone from those which Salisbury would have tried to make them. There were to be, of course, no straightforwerd elected representatives as such but the non-official members of the Provincial Councils were allowed to make recommendations for four seats in the Viceroy's Council and the select constituencies, such as the Municipalities, Universities, District Boards and Chambers of Commerce could

---

17) Ibid.; About the fear of the Anglo-Indians about the impending Gladstonian Liberal Government see also E. Heyking, op. cit., p.107.

make recommendations for eigth seats in the Provincial Councils. Thus although the elective principle was, in a way, introduced with reservations (18), this overcautious reform did not in fact give the Indians any effective voice in the councils of government.

Heyking would not like to see even the remotest possibility of undermining the authority of the Viceroy. There could be hardly any such fear since the four non-official members of the Viceroy's Council - like the other non-official members in the provinces - did not at all undermine the official majority. Moreover, the non-official members, although they got the right to discuss budgets and ask administrative questions, could not vote on them. Yet Heyking was still haunted by the bugbear of Radicalism. Reporting on the reformed Legislative Council of the Viceroy in February 1893, he said that according to the new regulations, newspaper correspondents would be permitted to report the Council's deliberations and the Radical journalists of England would therefore get a chance to attack the Government. He was, however, happy to see one positive contribution towards the enhancement of the Viceroy's strength vis-a-vis the Secretary for India. So far the members of the Viceroy's Council, being merely Government servants, could not assert their will powerfully against any measure imposed by the Secretary of State from London, but now the Viceroy would be emboldened, with the support of the elected representatives on his side, to reject any undesired imposition from London. (19)

In the last decade of the nineteenth century several happenings in the Indian world further influenced the official Germans in India against sympathy for the educated Indians' political aspirations. One of these which seems to have earned the Hindus a bad name was the controversy over the Age of Consent Bill of 1891. This bill sought to mitigate the evils of child marriage by providing that consummation of marriage should not take place before a wife reached the age of 12. Some of the Congressmen were opposed to the Bill on the principle that the foreign rulers had no right to encroach upon the social customs of the Indians. The division of opinion on such a reasonable and absolutely necessary measure among the Congress leaders seems to have

---

18) S. Maccoby, op. cit. , p. 427.

19) Heyking to Caprivi, Calcutta 7 Feb. 1893, AABI 10.

undermined them in the eyes of the Europeans. It led the wife
of a German diplomat to consider the Hindus 'atrocious'.(20)
Then came in August 1893 serious communal riots between the
Hindus and Muslims in Bombay and several places in north
and east India.

The Germans in India noticed that the British did not dislike the
prevailing animosity between the two major communities in India,
for it was a guarantee after all of their own survival (21) in a
country where the material for a rebellion was always present
and only a leader was not.(22) But it was not a happy situation
when a riot was to be counted upon as inevitable - as Elisabeth
Heyking experienced it - when the festivals of the two major
communities fell on one and the same day.(23) Then again, the
riots sometimes had their political overtones as well. Referring
to the Bombay riot, considered to be the biggest in the city since
the dispute between the Parsees and Muslims in 1874, the German
Consul in Bombay, Friedrich von Syburg (24), informed Berlin
that while the London press saw the hand of Congress in it, the
papers run by the Indians blamed the Government for instigating
it so as to keep the Muslims away from the Congress movement.
Syburg, however, found no direct political motive behind the Bombay
riot but he was of the opinion that Congress by its earlier 'anti-
cowkilling agitation' had tried to link politics with religion so as
to influence the silent millions of India to the Congress cause and
to that extent it was indirectly responsible for the growth of religious fanaticism. Syburg criticised Sir William Wedderburn (25),
one-time high officer in the Indian Civil Service and now a Liberal

---

20) E. Heyking, op. cit., note of 25 Feb. 1891, p. 86.

21) Gaertner to Caprivi, Simla 15 Sept. 1894, AABI 13.

22) E. Heyking, op. cit., p. 120.

23) Ibid.

24) Friedrich von Syburg (1854-1934): 1885 Vice-Consul in
    Shanghai; 1889 Consul in Bombay; 1895 Consul in Algier;
    1899 Consul General in Batavia; 1903 Consul General in
    Yokohama; 1912 Minister in Addis Ababa; 1920 retired.

25) William Wedderburn (1838-1918): 1860 entered Indian Civil
    Service; 1885 Judge, Bombay High Court; 1886-7 Officiating
    Chief Secretary, Bombay Government; 1887 retired; 1893-
    1900 Member of Parliament; 1889 and 1910 President of the
    Indian National Congress.

Member of Parliament, dubbing him as the 'apostle of freedom' for trying to defend Congress in the House of Commons on the question of cow protection agitation. (26)

During 1897 occurred certain other types of violence - violence against Europeans. During the festivities of the Jubilee of Queen Victoria in June a certain Mr. Ross, a government servant, was shot dead in Peshawar on the north-west frontier and on the following day, 22 June, shots were fired at two other British officers in Poona. Reporting the former incident which was suspected to have been caused by Muslim fanatics, the then German Consul General Julius von Waldthausen (27) wrote in detail about the history and seriousness of the anti-European Muslim religious fanaticism that had been going on for a long time in that frontier area. (28) The Poona incident in which the high-caste Hindus were involved was however a different story. In October 1896 bubonic plague was discovered in the slums of Bombay where it had previously been unknown. In Bombay some 20,000 people died and in spring of 1897 the disease spread to Poona. The chief plague officer there, W. C. Rand, went to excess in forcing sanitary measures violating the privacy of the conservative Hindu society. The result was that on 22 June 1897 while returning in their carriages from Governor Sandhurst's Jubilee reception Mr. Rand and his assistant Lt. C. E. Ayerst were shot and killed. Two high-caste Hindus were found to be entangled in the conspiracy. Congress leader Tilak severely criticised the excesses of the plague officers and in Parliament Wedderburn questioned again the necessity of employing European troops in enforcing sanitary measures in Poona. (29)

All these events showed the internal tension and disharmony amongst the Indian people themselves and their dislike of the Europeans. The German observers traditionally preferring strong centralised government and order came to see the demand for democracy by the educated Indians and their press only as a

---

26) Sÿburg to Caprivi, Bombay 18 Aug. 1893, AABI 11.

27) For the career of von Waldthausen see ch. II above p. 50 n. 40.

28) Waldthausen to Hohenlohe, Simla 7 July 1897, AABI 15.

29) Hatzfeldt to Hohenlohe, London 3 July 1897, AABI 15.
    Biemann to Hohenlohe, Bombay 2 July 1897, ibid.

further disturbing element and were convinced that strong foreign rule was the only salvation for India. Syburg, for instance, said in connection with the religious clashes between the various communities that these proved to the foreigners in India how much India needed the rule of the Europeans for her own peace.(30)

Against this background the official Germans in India considered the Congress movement neither useful nor significant. With their slogans at their annual sessions portraying the poverty and misery of the common people and condemning military burdens - all to enlist mass support - the Congress leaders appeared in the eyes of the German observers like their Social Democrats at home.(31) But lest Berlin mistook the Congress for an important organisation because of the honour lately bestowed upon Naoroji in Britain, the official Germans in India never ceased to emphasise the insignificance of Congress in relation to the general Indian condition and also its consequent failure to make any recent headway. Even Naoroji was mocked at and not considered to have done in his whole public career 'something really useful'.(32) The official Germans in India thought equally poorly of the British leaders of the Congress movement whom they considered nothing but merely disgruntled ex-Indian civil-servants trying to settle some personal grudges against the Indian Government by fomenting trouble for it. Like their Indian counterparts, they, too, were considered to be ignorant of the reality of the Indian situation.(33)

In the course of their decade long observation of the British rule in India the official Germans of course discovered much illogicality (34)

---

30) Syburg to Caprivi, Bombay 18 Aug. 1893, AABI 11.

31) Gaertner to Hohenlohe, Calcutta 26 Jan. 1895, reporting on the Madras session of the Congress Dec. 1894, AABI 13.

32) Syburg to Caprivi, Bombay 8 Dec. 1893, reporting on the arrival of the British M.P.s Wedderburn, Schwann, Paul and Naoroji for the ensuing Congress session. AABI 12.

33) Ibid.; Gaertner to Hohenlohe, Calcutta 26 Jan. 1895.

34) They are mainly in the area of social relations mentioned in some detail elsewhere in this work. But here is one illogicality described by Gaertner: He failed to understand how the British could consider a native incapable of holding a position of a lieutenant in the army, allowing him at the same time to prescribe laws to the British as a Member of Parliament. Gaertner to Hohenlohe, Lahore 4 Dec. 1894, AABI 13.

in the British attitude towards the Indians, but the disharmony in the native world and their own preference for authoritarian rule led the official Germans in India to think more about the good that Britain had already brought to India than the good that the Indians thought Britain had withheld from her. (35) They highlighted the beneficence of the British rule in giving stable peace to a country which had hardly ever known it before; eliminating internecine quarrels among the feudal lords and between the strong and weak princes; fixing just taxes; eradicating corruption by harsh punishment; checking dacoity; granting religious freedom; opening schools and universities; constructing railways, canals and irrigation projects and imparting justice with fair-mindedness in spite of their social contempt for the Indians. (36)

---

35) Heyking to Caprivi, Simla 30 Sept. 1890, AABI 7.

36) Voretzsch to Bülow, Calcutta Jan. 1904, AABI 29.

V. ASSESSMENT OF CURZON AND BRITISH RULE DURING HIS VICEROYALTY

> "If the power transferred to the Indian Governor-General-in-Council is used extensively and irrespective of any change of government in London - as it is being done now under the present Viceroy - India would enjoy the advantages which a more or less absolute rule under a wise ruler may offer."

Voretzsch to Bülow
Calcutta, January 1904

During the viceroyalty of Lord Curzon (1899-1905) a determined policy was undertaken to make clear, once and for all, the British purpose in India and the British attitude towards the educated Indians' demand for political rights. India to Curzon was the backbone of the British Empire and everything must be done to administer India efficiently. A good government must be provided and the key to this government must be centralisation and not autonomy or participation by the Indians in government. Indians should only be recipients of British beneficence. In short Curzon's programme concealed contempt for the Western educated Indians and brought in to the open hostility towards Indian nationalism.

Curzon attempted to take back all the advance that the Indians had already achieved in representation in local administration. In one measure after another he showed deep contempt for the elective principle and democratic decentralisation. (1) In April 1900 when there were not more than 20 Indians in the Indian Civil Service Curzon warned the Secretary of State of "the extreme danger of the system under which every year an increasing number of 900 and odd higher posts that were meant, and ought to have been exclusively and specifically reserved for Europeans, were being filched away by the superior wits of the natives in the English

---

1) In the very first year of his administration in 1899 Curzon attempted to reduce the elected members of the Calcutta Corporation to half of their original number and to vest its administration in a General Committee. This was followed by the officialisation of the universities, the curtailment of higher education, the abolition of open competitive tests for the Provincial Civil Services, and the enactment of the Civil Official Secrets Act.

examinations."(2) In November of the same year in another letter to the same person Curzon wrote that one of his greatest ambitions while in India was "to assist Congress to a peaceful demise."

In despising democracy and the political organisations of the educated Indians, Curzon argued that this minority of Indians acquired a political vocabulary only to dispute with the British rule, for their learning contributed nothing to help the masses; whereas his measures were directed to the good of the whole of India. Curzon's endeavour to expand technical education so as to employ Indians in the engineering field; his opening of new departments of commerce and industry and of archaeology; his promise to administer justice even-handedly; and above all, his drive for allround efficiency in administration undoubtedly brought a new era in Indo-British relations.

1. German Diplomats' Praise of Curzon

For a long time the complaint of the official Germans in India had been about the weakness of the British Government in India and its liberal attitude to the Western educated political Indians. The change that came with Curzon was therefore at once and heartily welcomed by them. Besides, in Curzon some of the official Germans seem to have found qualities dear to their hearts although Curzon himself had no sympathy for Germany. The urge to work, thoroughness, love of orderliness, aversion to formalism, self-willedness and romanticism are the generally accepted un-changeable properties of German character (3) and as Curzon in India showed these very traits in his public life, he was easily understood and appreciated by German diplomats so far as his administration of India was concerned. In June 1901 when Curzon had covered two and a half years of his term, the then German

---

2) Curzon to Hamilton, 23 April 1900, quoted in S.R. Mehrotra, op. cit., p.28; see also M. Edwardes, High Noon of Empire: India Under Curzon (Lond. 1965) p.252.

3) W. Hellpach, Der deutsche Charakter (Bonn 1954) p.171 quoted in Ralf Dahrendorf, Society and Democracy in Germany (New York 1967) p.23.

Consul General in India, Baron Speck von Sternburg (4) wrote to
Berlin that no one since Clive showed so much energy and eagerness in India and that any unprejudiced observer must admit that
Curzon's political acitvities in India were excellently successful. (5) Sternburg pointed out that Curzon's elderly predecessors
had regarded their job merely as one of maintenance and how
lethargy, routine and formalism crept into the administration
making it completely unfit for the needs of the time and serving
only the comforts of the British civil servants. In contrast to the
old order, the present youthful and intelligent Viceroy brought
new vitality by thorough reform and hard work. Sternburg saw in
Curzon a work-worshipping mentality: "Contrary to most of his
predecessors and other distinguished representatives of the British Empire he has a great feeling of responsibility which knows
only serious work and he allows entertainment only when the
spirit and body by all means require recreation. "(6)

Not just the internal policies, even the external policies of Lord
Curzon were appreciatively reported by Sternburg. The Kaiser
marked the passage in which Sternburg mentioned the Viceroy
telling him about his endeavour to strengthen Britain's interests
in the Persian Gulf and Arabia and to keep foreign influence away
from these two areas. Sternburg made no comment on this point
from his side and went on praising not only Curzon but his 'talented
and ambitious wife' as well. This unalloyed appreciation of Lord
Curzon from a German civil servant is noteworthy for in this
same report he also mentioned that he had been confidentially but
frequently informed by persons close to Curzon of the latter's
lack of sympathy for the Germans. (7)

Sternburg studied Curzon's personality not against an Indian background alone but also against the whole of British politics at the

---

4)   Hermann Freiherr Speck von Sternburg (1857-1908): 1891 Secretary
     of Legation, Peking; 1898 Counsellor, Embassy, Washington; 1899
     German member of the Supreme Commission for Samoa; 1900
     Consul General, Calcutta; 1903 Ambassador, Washington.

5)   Sternburg to Bülow, Simla 25 June 1901, AABI 24. The Kai-
     ser's general remark on the report: "very well written. "

6)   Ibid.

7)   Ibid.

time. In winter 1901-2 he had several discussions with Jan Malcolm, a friend of Curzon and a Member of Parliament and learned from him the image Curzon had in British political circles. Combining Malcolm's assessment with what he had already heard from other 'competent quarters' about Britain undergoing an 'abnormal political situation' threatening a 'national crisis', Sternburg let Berlin know the prevailing English opinion on Curzon's importance: "Looking in despair at her statesmen, Britain turns to Lord Curzon only with hope."(8)

In February 1912, nearly seven years after Curzon had left India and at a time when Curzon's 'partition of Bengal' was undone by the then Viceroy Lord Hardinge, the German Consul General in India at that time, Prince Reuß (9) also sent admiring reports on Curzon's personality and administration. Reuß, who had been in India in the winter of 1899-1900 and had also met Curzon a few times was simply overwhelmed by Curzon's personality. "I must admit," he said, "that seldom have I had the opportunity to talk with persons, especially with politicians, whose significance was so clearly written on their foreheads as in the case of Lord Curzon." Reuß then described Curzon's boundless factual knowledge about everything concerning India and how he replaced amateurism with professionalism in Indian administration. (10)

Towards the close of Curzon's viceroyalty, another German diplomat, Dr. Ernst Voretzsch (11), the Vice-Consul at Calcutta, also highly appreciated the centralised administration of Curzon. Unlike Sternburg and Reuß, Voretzsch was no uncritical admirer of Curzon's personality and he was also perhaps sceptical of the latter's character after the allegation that Curzon illegally accepted gifts

---

8) Sternburg to Bülow, Lucknow 29 Jan. 1902, AABI 26. The Kaiser particularly marked the words 'abnormal political situation' and 'national crisis' and commented in the margin: 'important'.

9) For the career of Reuß see ch. III. p. 79 n. 81.

10) Reuß to Bethmann-Hollweg, Calcutta 29 Feb. 1912, AABI 49.

11) Ernst-Arthur Voretzsch (1868-?): 1901 Vice-Consul, Calcutta; 1906 Consul, Hongkong; 1916 Consul, Hankau; 1920 Minister, Lissabon; 1928 Ambassador, Tokyo.

from the Maharaja of Banaras. (12) Nor did Voretzsch appreciate Curzon's constant preoccupation with pomp and show in order to impress upon the people British might and majesty. He agreed with the criticism of Curzon's Delhi Durbar of January 1903 as expressed privately by the Indian princes and publicly by the native press. (13) Nevertheless, he appreciated Curzon's insistence on having a greater voice with regard to Indian administration than the distant supreme authority at home, with its insufficient knowledge of local conditions and needs. Things like making India pay for the Indian contingency at the coronation, or the 'monstrous proposal of Mr. Brodrick' to make India share the expense for the contingency of troops meant for South Africa, were considered by Voretzsch as the result of the overpowering authority of the Secretary of State. Appreciating the balance of power between the home authority and the Indian Government during Curzon's forceful viceroyalty, which acquired greater independence from parliamentary or ministerial control, Voretzsch wrote: "If the power transferred to the Indian Governor-General-in-Council is used extensively and irrespective of any change of government in London - as it is being done now under the present Viceroy - India would enjoy the advantages which a more or less absolute rule under a wise ruler may offer. "(14)

2. Ernst Voretzsch and his Formula for British Permanency in India

While all the official Germans in India before and after Voretzsch were of the opinion that centralisation of government and efficiency

---

12) As Voretzsch reported Curzon came under heavy criticism even from the British circle for accepting a set of price-less old carved ivory furniture from the Maharaja of Banaras as gift. Although the transaction was shown by the Government as purchase, the clarification left many civil servants and even the pro-Government Pioneer unsatisfied in the context of the possible severe punishment a civil servant would have faced against such violation of the law in Curzon's regime. The Kaiser reading this report of Voretzsch made an ironical comment on Curzon's double standards. Voretzsch to Bülow, Calcutta 25 Oct. 1903, AABI 28.

13) Voretzsch to Bülow, Calcutta 15 Jan. 1903, AABI 27.

14) Voretzsch to Bülow, Calcutta ? Jan. 1904, AABI 29.

in administration - including improvement in the quality and character of the British civil servants in India - were the only ways to solve the grievances of the Indians and make them happy, Voretzsch, inspite of his admiration for the absolutism of the Viceroy, was of a different opinion. In January 1904 in a long report about the 'prospect of the British rule in India' for which he received 'full appreciation' from the Kaiser (15), Voretzsch discovered the fundamental weakness of British rule in India under the surface of its outward majesty. As it was the Western educated Indians who according to Voretzsch would create the greatest danger for the British in the future and as he was not in favour of granting this class the political powers they were demanding, it will be interesting to discuss Voretzsch's prognosis at some length.

Voretzsch's analysis of the British rule touched upon those economic and political spheres where the educated Indians had their grievances. Talking about the revenue and expenditure of the Indian Government Voretzsch mentioned that the Government spent abaut £ 20 million for civil and £ 18 million for military administration. It not only paid high salaries to the Britons but also sent each year some £ 2 million for civil and £ 2 1/4 million for military pensions to the mother-country. Besides, the Indian Government had to pay for various other expenditures which were only remotely associated with India - expenses such as those of an envoy staying in Tehran. Voretzsch said that despite this and also despite the public debt of £ 222 million the administration could be called a sound one. (16)

What added to the Indians' grievances, according to Voretzsch, was the Government's utter selfishness in looking for interests of Britain only. Taking examples from the trade-political field he pointed to the flooding of the Indian market with British products which threatened the growing indegenous industries. Cheap German salt, he said, was excluded not to enlarge the market for the Indian monopoly product but to make it easier for costly British salt to find a market. Voretzsch found that instead of giving India the opportunity which she had enjoyed hitherto to protect herself by her own tariff system against any country endangering her developing industries and to buy wherever she liked at reasonable

---

15) Ibid. Kaiser's comment on this report: "Excellently written. Give Voretzsch my full appreciation."

16) Ibid., p. 7.

cost, India was being taught 'imperialist patriotism' by Chamberlain's new tariff reform. (17)

In foreign policy too, Voretzsch observed that India was put to disadvantage in favour of Britain. Anglo-Russian antagonism made Britain maintain her position firmly in the Persian Gulf, in India and also in South-East Asia. Although Britain contributed to the cost of such maintenance some £ 257,000, this amount was nothing compared to the £ 18 million which was India's yearly expenditure on the army. From India's revenue again subsidies were paid to the Amir of Afghanistan, the Sultan of Maskat, the Sheikhs of the Gulf and the Khan of Kelat. In order to display Britain's high imperial majesty to Russia Curzon followed an expansive policy in the Persian Gulf, sent the Halmand Commission and the expedition to Tibet, and all these expenses would remain as long as Britain ruled India, for they were necessary for the maintenance of British interest. (18)

Surveying the social, economic and political position of the various sections of the Indian population, Voretzsch came to the conclusion that nowhere among the Indian people, except from the half-castes (19), was there any support for British rule. The princes, the nobility, the priests and various religious groups, all alike disliked their foreign rulers; they only failed to agitate against the contempt they received and the material loss they suffered from foreign rule. The educated Indians on the other hand - the scholars, the babus, the comparatively better placed people in the government, and the ones who generally read and thought - did not bear with the same equanimity the bad behaviour of the Europeans they encountered. Their representatives were often to be found in the offices of newspapers writing anti-Government articles or among the political writers, public orators and correspondents. Not always were they influenced by reason. None-the-less they wished, apparently honestly, to stand up for their people whom they considered suppressed, enslaved and unworthily treated. (20)

---

17) Ibid., p. 8.

18) Ibid.

19) The half-castes or the offspring of mixed Indian-European parentage were not, according to Voretzsch, the products of contact between better off or socially better placed persons of either side. Ibid., p. 22.

20) Ibid., pp. 11-19. Babus here meant the Indian clerks with a superficial English education.

Against this background of a general Indian dislike of foreign rule, the agitation by the educated Indians for higher employment in the government on the principle of equalitiy with the British was seen by Voretzsch as the most important of Indian political movements. He saw it as the logical outcome of past British liberalism, for the Indians were asking for jobs only because of their Western education. Nor did Voretzsch doubt the ability of the Indians to compete successfully with Britons in open examinations if such examinations were to be the chief criterion for selection for higher jobs. Voretzsch was convinced that Western education had come to stay in India and its growth was not going to stop. The half-castes, the scholars, the <u>babus</u> and the merchants would continue to be exposed to European ideas. The desire among the Indians of higher caste to hold their traditional high social position and honour would make them continually strive to reach an equality with the British in achieving high offices. Here lay according to Voretzsch, the greatest problem for the British, for this equality would lead to Indian predominance and this predominance would drive the rulers out. (21)

If such was the internal situation for the British in India, what was then the basis of British rule over a country which was as big as Europe from the Weichsel to Guadalquivir, with a population of about 300 million including 2 to 3 million fighting men and out of them again 500,000 trained soldiers? Voretzsch asked this question of himself and in his answer he was strinkingly close to Fitzjames Stephen, the former Law Member of India and political philosopher of the Indian Civil Service. Writing in 1883 Stephen had declared that the British Empire in India was an absolute government founded on military force and not on consent. One of its piers was military power and the other was justice. Voretzsch likewise mentioned that soldiers and the wisdom of the civil administration were the true bases of the British rule in India. "The 80,000 British soldiers stationed in India and 3,000 civil servants as well as the very few Europeans who help the Government - presumably less than the number of coloured people living in London - those are the two columns on which the British rule in India is based", he wrote, and emphasised that they were the only columns. (22)

---

21) Ibid., pp. 19-20.

22) Voretzsch, Jan. 1904, p. 22.

Stephen in general believed in vigorous government by the 'instructed few'. Even in Britain he was for checking the current of democracy: "I do not see" he wrote, "why as we go with the stream we need sing Hallelujah to the river god."(23) He believed that to assure Indians of good government it was necessary to continue permanently the British Empire and he rejected the view that Britain should train Indians for a democratic government.(24) Voretzsch was also of the same opinion but seeing the scene twenty years after Stehpen had seen it, he found the two existing pillars insufficient to keep Britain in India in the long run. The political education of the Indians, disclaimed by the earlier far-sighted imperialists, (25) had already taken deep roots. Now somewhere consent must be found amongst the subject people to assure British permanence. A representative system of government was obviously not the way to perpetuate foreign rule. Parliamentary democracy and decentralisation were naturally outside Voretzsch's line of thinking, for he was not concerned with Indian self-rule but with British permanence. He found that half castes in India were the only people with sympathy for the European rulers. At present they were insignificant in number and generally looked down upon by the Indians and the British alike. His suggestion was to deliberately create a respectable mixed race in India - a crossbreed between the whites and the high-caste Indians - so as to provide a strong permanent basis of support for British rule amongst the indigenous population itself. Not to make his suggestion appear revolting to the Europeans, Voretzsch argued: "We do by no means recommend an assimilation of the white and the unproductive, normally less worthy, negroe race, e.g. from Africa, but a mixed race of white people and a people which is related by blood and ideas to the Europeans seems to be very suitable for India as

---

23) Quoted in R.B. McDowell, British Conservatism 1832-1914 (London 1959) pp. 88-9.

24) See H.L. Singh, op. cit., p. 261.

25) Another British imperialist and administrative thinker, Sir John Strachey, wrote: "... There never was a country, and never will be, in which the government of foreigners is really popular. It will be the beginning of the end of our empire when we forget this elementary fact, and entrust the greater executive powers to the hands of Natives, on the assumption that they will always be faithful and strong supporters of our government." From Strachey's India (1888) quoted in M. Edwardes, A History of India (Mentor, London 1967) p. 283.

support for the European power. The same origin of both races, the undoubtedly high talents of the higher castes in India, should enable the products of such a mixture to develop into a strong support for the rulers with the right treatment and education."(26)

Voretzsch was no doubt conscious that his advocacy of miscegenation might appear repulsive to many. The Kaiser for one, who otherwise greatly appreciated Voretzsch's report as a whole, could not perhaps digest this, for on Voretzsch's statement that "in their maintenance of racial purity the British see the main, if not the only, guarantee for upholding their supremacy and rule", the Kaiser commented in the margin: "they are very right". To the polygenesists, who denied fertility to hybrids, Voretzsch's idea was bound to be most unpalatable. The polygenesists argued that where sexual relations took place between widely different races either the relationship proved barren or the offspring proved so in due course. Such mixing again, where successful, "led to the deterioration of the superior race and produced a vicious type of half-breed, useless alike to himself and the world."(27) Although Voretzsch did not bring in the scientific or pseudoscientific roots of racism at his time for discussion, from the context in which he referred to the negroe race in the passage quoted above and from the very problem that drove him to seek this mixed race formula, namely the building of European permanency in India on native consent rather than on mere military might, it appears that he was well aware of and influenced by the nineteenth-century English, French and German authorities on racism. Indeed, he could hardly escape such an influence, for it is said that from the 1870's into the 1920's and beyond, virtually every European concerned with imperial theory or imperial administration encountered the belief that the physical appearance of race was an outward sign of inborn propensities, inclinations, and abilities.(28) There were still to be found various confirmations of Knox's views on 'The Dark Races of Men' predicting the inevitability of a race war in which the whites would win all over the world outside the tropics. The obvious conclusion therefrom was that European supremacy in the tropics could only take the form of 'military masters lording it over a serf population' and keeping them in continual fear. All schemes of philanthrophy were useless under such circumstances. Nor could racial intermixture help, for it could benefit - so the experts said - only the primitive people and that if the gulf between the two intermingling races was not too wide. The Europeans - the

---

26) Voretzsch, Jan. 1904, pp. 25-26.

27) See C. Bolt, op. cit., ch. I p. 10 and passim.

28) P. D. Curtin (ed.), Imperialism op. cit., p. 1.

ruling race - were bound to lose their superiority in the process if it were tried. (29)

Voretzsch was obviously not daunted by such anti-mixed-breed notions especially as he did not consider the gulf between the Europeans and some of the Indians to be wide. He refuted the basis for the British belief that the survival of their reign in India depended mainly on the maintenance of their racial purity and considered it absurd on the part of the British to argue that all people who had earlier conquered India - the Greeks, Afghans, Mughals, Portuguese, and French - had maintained their Indian throne only so long as they did not mix with the Hindu blood. On the contrary, the most important Mughal emperors, he pointed out, were the sons of Rajput princesses. Voretzsch therefore defended his mixed-breed formula thus:

> "Everywhere in Europe we consider the age of the family and with it the striving for power and things higher, greater and better, which for centuries has been passed on from ancestors to their grandchildren, as a certain guarantee of the efficiency of the latter. In India where the Rajput and Brahmin families can trace back their pure genealogical trees not only to centuries but to milleniums, racial qualities in them have been preserved purer than anywhere else and the intellectual and physical advantages have developed to an unusual perfection. The claim that this [Indian] race is not capable of producing an efficient human being together with another closely related race is, therefore, illogical. "(30)

As a corollary to this change in the situation of the governed, Voretzsch also suggested a corresponding change in the ruling authority. Keeping men like Lord Curzon particularly in mind, he observed that every one of the Imperial representatives came to India with the intention of making his name immortal through some outstanding deed, but the glow achieved so quickly and which tended to fade out equally quickly was not what the Indian

---

29) See ibid., p. 12; Bolt refers in this context an article about Sir Richard Burton's travels in Brazil in Anthropo-logical Review (1896) which commented with dismay on the mixed breeds in that part of the world, opining that any Englishman helping to produce such hybrids should be severely punished.

30) Voretzsch, Jan. 1904, pp. 5-6.

sky required. It was necessary to give India herself a centre - a fixed, glorious star around which she should rotate. A viceroy, however brilliant he might be, could not achieve this. Voretzsch therefore suggested the other half of his formula: a king from the British royal house and dependent on Britain should start a dynasty in India with an army of civil servants who "would not strive to eat up their rich pensions in England" but settle in India, perhaps in a place like Kashmir on the Himalayan slopes with its European climate and beautiful landscapes. (31) Here of course the Kaiser quickly agreed with Voretzsch. He considered the suggestion of a separate British ruling line in India important. (32)

Voretzsch's extraordinary suggestion, partly of medieval Indian style, (33) was the furthest that any German diplomat went to incorporate the Indians in the government of their own country. It was his belief in European imperialism and monarchical absolutism rather than pure race prejudice which seem to have primarily guided his thoughts. He began his report by refuting the prevailing notion among Europeans to consider themselves as superior, more clever, stronger, and more moral than all the non-white peoples. According to him the application of this notion to the Indians was not justified. (34) Yet he found the qualities required for ruling among white races only - a racist angle to imperialism.

---

31) Ibid., p. 26.

32) The Kaiser's marginal remark, ibid.

33) During the medieval Muslim reign in India many - and at times most - high offices of state were occupied by foreign nobles from other Muslim countries who later settled in India.

34) Voretzsch, Jan. 1904, p. 1.

VI. POST-CURZON ERA OF UNREST AND REFORM AND THE GERMAN ATTITUDE

"Take a gathering of Indians. Remove their graceful, picturesque costumes, and clothe them in coat and trousers, wash the sun out of their skins, and then a stranger suddenly let down into the midst of them would have difficulty in saying whether he was in Manchester or Madras. This fact has a very important bearing upon the question of how far the Indian people can be trusted with the right of selfgovernment."

> J. Keir Hardie, India, Impressions and Suggestions (1909) p. 102

Report: "All Orientals in their heart of hearts cherish the hope that dispute between the great white nations might bring about the chance for the coloured people to liberate themselves."

The Kaiser: "This I know and therefore we shall not please them by doing this."

> In Kühlmann to Bethmann-Hollweg London 11 September 1910

In blocking the political aspirations of the educated Indians Curzon was only following an agreed policy of the Home Government to evade the principle of equality in practice. (1) But the forceful way in which he proceeded to hurt the sensibilities of the politically conscious Indians helped the growth of nationalism of radical character. The educated Indian was made to think that the political clock was set back for him for ever. It was however Curzon's last political act, the partition of Bengal in 1905, which broke the camel's back. The scheme being hatched in the dark and forced upon the people in the teeth of fierce opposition was enough to rouse the anger even of the moderate Congress leaders against Curzon's contempt for public opinion and his preference for bureaucracy over the interests of the governed. The younger

---

1) In May 1900 Hamilton, the Secretary of State wrote to Curzon: "One of the greatest mistakes that ever was made was the issue in the Proclamation annexing India of the principle that perfect equality was to exist, so far as all appointments were concerned, between European and Native."

generation of nationalists further believed that the objective of
the measure was to drive a wedge between the Hindus and Muslims
so as to divide the Indian people and kill their nationalism.

Several factors such as the recent religious reforms among the
Hindus, the growth of patriotic literature, the study of the growth
and development of nationalism in Europe, the victory of Japan
over Russia, the Sinn Fein movement in Ireland, the Young Turk
revolt, the revolutionary preparations in Russia and the achievement
of representative institutions by many former colonies of great
power such as the Philippines, the Transvaal and the Orange River
Colony, had already captured the imagination of the young intel-
ligentsia especially of Bengal and Maharashtra, infusing in them
a feeling of great patriotism, self-confidence and hope for self-
rule. When by the end of 1905 the Liberals came to power in
England the Indians naturally pinned high hopes on them for reversing
the partition of Bengal and allowing representative institutions. These
hopes were belied. The new Secretary of State, Lord Morley,
declared the partition a 'settled fact' and the Indians' demand for
English institutions 'a fantastic and ludicrous dream.' (2)

A few young nationalist leaders and their still younger groups of
followers - the product of the generation born around 1880 - with
their great self-confidence and self-reliance refused to put up with
the racial prejudice of the foreign rulers and they also lost faith
in the methods of the 'moderate' Congress leaders, denouncing
them as mere 'mendicancy'. Instead, the advocates of this 'new
nationalism' sought stronger measures to fight the reactionary
Government and a forceful means to achieve their goal. Indeed,
their patriotism made the feeling that had earlier inspired the
Congress seem a very bloodless thing. (3) Under such pressure,
in 1906 Congress had to propose the boycott of British goods
in favour of swadeshi (indigenous) goods, and the same year
for the first time it expressed its goal as the attainment of
'the system of government obtaining in the self-governing British colonies.'

The old Congress stalwarts 'were not men in a hurry' (4), but
the new nationalists were. In 1907 the extremist group drifted
further apart from Congress. Of the two categories of extremists,
the first consisted of those who desired autonomy and sought to
obtain it by such methods as passive resistance and the continual

---

2) See S.R. Mehrotra, op.cit., pp.36-37.

3) J.N. Farquhar, Modern Religious Movements in India
   (New York 1913), p.355.

4) K.R. Minogue, Nationalism (London 1967) p.93.

sapping of the foundations of loyalty to the British by means of attacks in the press (5) and on the platform, and the second consisted mostly of youths, still at school or college, who, were inspired by the revolutionary freedom movements of European nations and methods of conspiratorial terrorism adopted by the Russian Nihilists and other European underground groups. Their programme included assassination of generally unpopular officials, dacoitage to secure money, and fomenting mutinies in the army. Their main centres of activities were in Bengal, the Punjab, and Maharashtra. But the severity of governmental repression (6) drove some of the more resourceful ones to seek safer places outside India where they established centres of Indian revolutionary propaganda. The revolutionary nationalists were no politicians; they were preoccupied only with the demand of elementary rights and not with what would follow upon a self-ruling India. (7) Both groups of extremists considered foreign rule as utterly wrong and in their opinion nothing but complete self-rule would solve the nation's problems. Thus nationalism, in so far as it is a political movement depending on a feeling of collective grievance against foreigners (8) seemed to have come to stay. So quite

---

5) In Bengal particularly the vernicular press was most effective. The three important organs of the extremist circle of Bengal were the Bande Mataram, Sandhya and Jugantar - all these were banned by the Government in 1908. According to the Government report Jugantar first published in 1906 attained a circulation of 7,000 in 1907 and reached a wider range before it was banned. See Sedition Committee, 1918 Report (Calcutta 1918) p. 16.

6) The Seditious Meeting Act of 1907 restricted the right of holding public meetings; the Explosive Substance Act of 1908 laid down heavy penalties for possessing materials for manufacturing bombs or helping in the process in any way; the Newspaper (Incitement to Offence) Act of 1908 placed the existence of a newspaper virtually at the mercy of the Magistrate; the Criminal Law (Amendment) Act of 1908 changed the system of trial for facilitating conviction and armed the executive with almost limitless powers over individual persons and political organisations; the Indian Press Act of 1910 laid down heavy fines including for-feiture of the press for seditious publications which were defined in wide terms in favour of the Government.

7) See. R. MacDonald, The Awakening of India (London 1910) p. 186.

8) K. R. Minogue, op. cit., p. 29.

naturally the political climate of the post-Curzon era came to be described as 'Indian Unrest'.(9)

Britain realised that without some form of compromise with the moderate section of the educated Indians her rule was not safe. So along with repressive measures an instalment of constitutional reform was advanced. Known as the Morley-Minto Reforms and incorporated in the Council Act of 1909 they expanded and liberated the Legislative Councils in the centre and in the provinces. They accepted the elective principle and enlarged the rights of the members of the Councils to move resolutions on all matters of general public importance (subject to certain exceptions) and also on reduction or increase of expenditure. Furthermore, by admitting two Indians to the Council of the Secretary of State and one each to the Executive Councils of the Governor-General and Governors a gesture was shown that the British stood honestly by the Charter Act of 1833 and the Queen's Proclamation of 1858. Both Morley and Minto, however, dismissed the ideal of self-government entertained by the Indian nationalists as a mere dream. They could not conceive of the Government of India as anything but a benevolent despotism. (10)

The first of the political murders was committed on 30 April 1908 when a bomb thrown at a carriage that was thought to belong to the judge of Muzaffarpur (then in Bengal) mistakenly killed the wife and daughter of a British lawyer. Reporting this incident to Berlin, Baron von Richthofen (11), a member of the German General Consulate, wrote that the anarchist 'propaganda by deed' had lately found its followers amongst the discontented Indian elements and that the avowed object of the assailants was to liberate India. (12)

---

9) The phrase, first used by V. Chirol for his series of articles in The Times, later to come out in book form in the same year under the same title, has since been widely accepted. See V. Chirol, Indian Unrest (London 1910).

10) See S. R. Mehrotra, op. cit., pp. 51, 53.

11) Herbert Baron von Richthofen (1876-?1945): 1907 Legation Secretary; 1908 attached to the Consulate General, Calcutta; Secretary, Tokyo; 1930 Minister, Copenhagen; 1936 Minister, Brussels; 1939 Minister, Sofia; 1944 retired.

12) Richthofen to Bülow, Simla 7 May 1908, AABI 42. Richthofen, however, only confirmed the news which had already been published by Berlin papers. See Berliner Lokal-Anzeiger 3 May 1908, 'Eine Verschwörung gegen die Engländer in Kalkutta.'

The next year a District Magistrate, Mr. Jackson (of Nasik) in Bombay and an ex-Indian civil servant, Sir W. H. Curzon Wyllie in London fell victims to the violent methods of the revolutionary nationalists. These events led to continuous debates and discussions both in India and England about the Indian unrest. The German Embassy in London kept Berlin informed of all the news and views regarding the Indian situation from that end (13) while the official Germans in India sent their analysis from their direct observation.

1. The German Views on Indian Unrest and Reforms

The Kaiser and the official Germans traced the causes of the political unrest in India to the questionable social behaviour of the British towards the Indians. The gulf between the rulers and the ruled in India, they claimed, was the outcome of the decline of the Indian Civil Service.

In May 1906 the German Consul General in India, Count von Quadt (14), first reported to Berlin on the political significance of all kinds of British maltreatment of the Indians. He wrote that unlike the earlier British civil servants who had been self-controlled in their behaviour and had given the natives what they deserved, the new ones were uncultured and ill-tempered and fond only of sticks and abusive words while in dealing with the natives. Quadt predicted dire consequences for the British rule in India if the relations between the English and the Indians were to continue in this manner. (15)

Quadt's successor Claus von Below (16) also concerned himself with the subject of the Anglo-Indians' social misbehaviour towards the Indians. In August 1909, at a time when the Anglo-Indians press

---

13) Metternich to Bülow, London 3 July 1909 and to Bethmann-Hollweg, 16 August, 21 October 1910, AABI 44, 46; Metternich to Bethmann-Hollweg 3 September 1910, German Embassy London File (hereafter DBL) 360.

14) For Quadt's career see above chapter III, p. 79 n. 78.

15) Quadt to Bülow, Simla 11 May 1906, AABI 34. After reading the report thoroughly the Kaiser commented: "Well, then the Japanese would find it an easy game one day."

16) Claus von Below-Saleske (1866-1939): 1899 I Secretary, Peking; 1901 II Secretary, Vienna; 1907 I Secretary, Constantinople; 1908 Consul General, Calcutta; 1910 Minister, Sofia; 1913 Minister, Brussels.

was preoccupied with the Belgian atrocities towards the natives of
the Congo, Below reported some typical cases of British handling
of their own subject people in India, wondering why one living in
a glass house should throw stones at others. (17) Among Below's
examples was a story of a British major who, himself hardly an
educated man, forced two Indians, sons of a rajah, to leave their
first class railway compartment which the major was to share with
them. The railway authorities also forcefully intervened on behalf
of the major. In another case a carpet dealer was beaten up in
his shop by some Britons on the grounds of his not showing proper
obeisance to a British lady. On Below's enquiry as to how the guilt
of the dealer was ascertained, especially when the dealer spoke no
English and the lady no Hindusthani, he was told that it did not
matter whether the dealer was guilty; the beating was useful for
him all the same even if it was for nothing. Below however mentioned
that such cases were sharply condemned by many Britons themselves, particularly the older residents, although he did not believe
that such admonitions would make the younger civil servants res-
pectful even to the educated natives. He even found a man of Mr.
Sinha's standing - the newly appointed member of the Viceroy's
Executive Council and a man, he considered, of superior education
to many British civil servants - had to suffer tactless humiliation
at the hands of the Anglo-Indians. (18)

Pointing out further the plight of those charged with seditious
activities, Below wrote that the police did not shrink from applying
any means to get their desired confessions from arrested people.
Many even died in the custody of treatment received from the
police. The so-called 'punitive police', i.e. the temporary transfer
of a police detachment to a certain area, was nothing but a means
of making the inhabitants obedient to governmental demands. According to Below there were endless cases where the natives of all
classes were shamelessly treated by the higher civil servants and
other government officers. The Kaiser who seems to have read
the report line by line commented: "Well, this is really the truth!
Now the reason for the unrest in India can very well be explained. "(19)

---

17) Below to Bethmann-Hollweg, Simla 10 August 1909, AABI 44.

18) Ibid. For similar cases as Below's from an Englishman
    around the same period see J. Keir Hardie, India, Impres-
    sions and Suggestions (London 2d ed. 1909) pp. 97-100.
    Hardie also remarked: "I could fill a decent sized volume
    with cases which the reader would find it hard to believe,
    illustrating the way in which the colour line is drawn."

19) Ibid.

The official Germans in India found the root of such contemptuous behaviour by the British towards the Indians in recent developments in the Indian Civil Service depriving it of its pristine virtues. Successive German diplomats in India considered that the gradual reduction of the aristocratic element in the Indian Civil Service resulted in a consequent decrease in the strength and moral quality of rule. This, coupled with the academic qualifications and training among the younger generation of civil servants, lack of intellectual interests, their extreme indulgence in sports and club life, their frequent holidays at home, and lately also gains while in service in India led the Indian civil servants to do just their bare, official duties and remain completely ignorant and contemptuous of the India of the Indians. (20) According to German observers members of the non-wealthy middle class families, who now predominated in the Indian Civil Service and other colonial posts in the British Empire, looked at their jobs purely from a financial point of view. In their entire careers they were unable to cultivate any warm feelings for the subject people. Voretzsch had earlier explained this lack of a personal touch with an example. At home when he had been active in the government of Oppeln he came to know a subdivisional officer there who although hardly rich himself, bought from his own pocket a grass cutting machine for a poor co-operative which could not afford it from its own resources. Such an idea, Voretzsch said, would seem grotesque to an Indian civil servant. (21) Detecting a sense of demoralisation among the Indian civil servants which led them to take their 'white man's business' to rule lightly, Reuß commented that one should be more seriously concerned with the unrest among the European civil servants in India rather than the so-called 'Indian Unrest'. To the Kaiser's great astonishment - as his markings on the report show - Reuß mentioned that the less happy the Britons were in India, the more often they asked how much longer they were going to rule India. Not infrequently he was asked by the Britons whether he believed that Germany would take Britain's place in India. The public buildings in India, Reuß added, had

---

20) Voretzsch to Bülow, Calcutta January 1904; Quadt to Bülow, Simla 11 May 1906; Below to Bülow, Calcutta 6 Feb. 1909; Below to Bethmann-Hollweg, Simla 10 Aug. 1909; Reuß to Bethmann-Hollweg, Simla 5 July 1911; AABI 29, 34, 44, 47. In the earlier period as well the official Germans in India noted the ignorance of the Anglo-Indians about India. See E. Heyking, op. cit., p. 84.

21) Voretzsch in note 20 above. Oppeln, now in Poland, was then in former German Upper Silesia.

already begun to have the look of 'if we are going in ten years!' and so also the appearance of many applicants for the Indian Civil Service. (22)

Holding firmly to their view that the problem of Indian unrest was nothing but one caused by the unimaginative, insufficiently educated, indifferent, low born, unwealthy new comers to the Indian Civil Service, the official Germans could not appreciate the British Government's concessions in terms of constitutional reforms. In the summer of 1911, at a time when the Morley-Minto Reforms were being implemented and Chirol's book was being widely discussed, Prince Reuß questioned not only the use of the phrase 'Indian Unrest' for a few sporadic events of unrest in a country of 300 millions but also the sagacity of the British Government in granting far-reaching political reforms to the Indians. (23) The so-called Indian unrest, he said, was to be seen through the lowering of the prestige of the white race in various defeats since the eighteen nineties. He mentioned that India had also jealously watched the introduction of parliamentary government among the Asiatic countries first in Japan and then in China, Persia, and Turkey. (24) Reuß ignored the long movement for parliamentary democracy in India itself led by the moderate liberal leaders of Congress and also the accumulated disappointments of the educated Indians therefrom. Not having seen the Indian problem from this angle Reuß saw no logic in the Liberals' granting representative government. The great masses of India, he said, were least interested in parliamentary representation; only the Marathis and Bengalis in Bombay and Bengal, respectively, were stoking the fire of discontentment in their native press maintaining that the British had withheld that most significant of human rights from the Indian people. Neither the British Parliament's habitual interference with the absolutism of the Viceroy nor the present concession to the natives' clamour for democratic reforms were considered by Reuß as correct. According to him, by offering democratic reforms the British Government was relinquishing

---

22) Reuß in note 20.

23) Reuß to Bethmann-Hollweg, Simla 5 July 1911, AABI 47. Reuß, however, found Chirol's writings 'instructive and interesting.'

24) Ibid.

the power and authority of Parliament for a wrong cause, as this would not strengthen but weaken the Viceroy's position in his Council. With a significant question pregnant with the authoritarian's proverbial contempt for liberal democracy Reuß asked: "Will the British Parliament give up its prerogative to interfere in things about which it does not know anything at all, only to act - moved by wrong feelings of humanity - to please public opinion?"(25) By his stricture on parliamentary institutions and public opinion Reuß struck a familiar cord for the governing circle in Berlin. The Kaiser did not fail to put his remark on the margin of Reuß's lines: "Just like our Reichstag!"(26)

To Reuß the road to Indian reform lay not in the direction of parliamentary democracy and representative government but in the instalation of an energetic viceroy. (27) The old admirer of Lord Curzon did not find Lord Hardinge strong enough a viceroy to put an end to the encroachment of Parliament into Indian administration and also check the decline of the Civil Service. (28) Similarly he considered unjustified what he called Lord Morley's desire to give higher posts to the natives. (29) In April 1911 he met Sir John Hewett, the Lt. Governor of the United Province whom he had known since his earlier visit to India in 1899. Praising Hewett's 'almost princely' qualities and adding that he was probably the one person whom the Kaiser would like of all the Indian civil servants,

---

25) Ibid.

26) Ibid. The Kaiser's general remark on the report: "Very good."

27) Ibid.

28) Ibid.; Early in 1912 Reuß was unhappy that Curzon was not properly estimated in a recent news items about India in the German press. Referring to an article in Münchener Neueste Nachrichten of 20 January 1912, written by one Theodor Ling, Reuß took the writer to task for believing that Curzon had to resign because of his partition of Bengal. He also did not agree with the writer that the Bengalis roused the Indian national consciousness. Like most of Curzon's other measures Reuß admired the partition of Bengal and considered his talk with Sir Bomfylde Fuller, the first Governor of Eastern Bengal and Assam, a Curzon protegee and the most hated man among the Bengali nationalists in the unrest period, as one of great interest. Reuß to Bethmann-Hollweg, Calcutta 12 and 19 Feb. 1912, AABI 49.

29) Reuß to Bethmann-Hollweg, Simla 5 July 1911, AABI 47.

Reuß reported that in Hewett's opinion too, the Morley-Minto reforms were a political blunder. They were too far-reaching to be given to the Indians so soon. On Hewett's authority Reuß said that the Indians were more or less children who were to be guided firmly and fairly. Apart from exceptions, they were not mature enough to hold positions demanding initiative and determination. (30)

At the beginning of 1911 another official German, Treutler (31), showed a similar distrust of the educated Indians and their political aspirations. Treutler was then accompanying the German Crown Prince to the strategic North-West Frontier Province of India where he met the Chief Commissioner Sir George Roos-Koppel, an old-timer in India. Roos-Koppel was of the opinion that the natives should be given all political rights. Treutler found it not very objective a statement from otherwise so intelligent a person. Treutler presumed that it was the effect of long years of living with the natives. He said that he rather agreed with Sir Harold Stuart that every concession would merely whet the appetite of the natives for further concessions. (32)

The official Germans seem to have deliberately refused to see any intellectual reason behind the unrest. As Reuß did not understand British concession by way of constitutional reforms, so did also Berlin ignore the official British assessment of the extremist movement coming to it from a most reliable source. In the early spring of 1910 Count Kanitz (33), a conservative Deputy of the Reichstag, forwarded to the German Foreign Office a secret document of the Government of India which had been sent to him privately by a British civil servant as 'confidential information'. This was a copy of a circular letter from the Home Department of the Government of India to the governments of those provinces where the extremist movement found its roots, describing the nature and extent of the spirit of disaffection and suggesting some methods of checking its further growth. (34) Here the extremist movement was considered

---

30) Reuß to Bethmann-Hollweg, Simla 25 April 1911, ibid.

31) For Treutler's career see above ch. III p.

32) Treutler to Kaiser, Allahabad 16 Jan. 1911, Preuss 1 (9).
    Sir Harold Stuart then accompanied the German Crown Prince on his tour of India.

33) Count Hans Wilhelm von Kanitz-Podangen (1841-1913): 1889-1913 member, Reichstag.

34) Sir Harold Stuart, Secy., G.O.I., Home Dept., to Chief Secy., Govt. of Punjab, No. 348, Calcutta, 4 March 1910, AABI 45.

as intellectual and middle-class in origin, widely spread, and the party behind it to be "small in numbers but of considerable influence and inspired by convictions strongly and even fanatically held, who are opposed to the continuance of British rule."(35)

The main cause of unrest, according to this document, was the influence of Western education in the schools and colleges of India - the teaching of European history and modern economics particularly. Hence instructions were given to the district officers to win over various categories of people to the British point of view by persuation and discussion if possible but also by coersive means if the first line of action failed. The professors and schoolmasters were to be told that "mere abstention from seditious teaching can not be accepted as an adequate performance of duty on the part of those engaged in education." Lawyers maintaining anti-British views were to be told by the district judge "that hostility to the Government and all attempts to hamper the administration are incompatible with the position of a licensed pleader at the Courts of that Government." Those native public servants, who had children with extreme views about the Government were to be told "that their responsibility does not end with their own conduct but extends to that of their sons and of relatives over whom they have influence. If a father or guardian who is in public service has not done his best to check the seditious tendencies of his son or ward...he will incur severe penalty." The question of improper treatment of the natives by the Anglo-Indians was also touched upon by the document advising government servants to learn manners acceptable to the native gentlemen and thereby remove from their minds the misapprehensions regarding the character and results of the British rule.(36)

Thus it is clear that the Indian Government accepted the presence of the deep impact of nationalism and sought to eradicate it not by measured constitutional reforms and legally backed repressions alone, but also by persuasion. The official Germans, on the other hand, partly to deny any credit to liberal democracy and partly to justify imperialism on racial grounds, ignored the growth of nationalism in India altogether.

In their general hostility to liberal democracy the official Germans condemned all those British Liberals of radical or socialist hue who stood for the advent of democratic reforms in India. There is of course no denying the fact that since 1886 constant criticism of the Government in the House of Commons by men like W.S. Caine, W.T. Stead, Alfred Webb, W. Wedderburn, Samuel Smith,

---

35) Ibid., para 2.

36) Ibid., paras 3, 4, 6, 10.

Henry Cotton, Keir Hardie and others on such Indian questions as
the Indianisation of the Indian Civil Service, the dispute on cotton
duties, suppression of the opium trade, the curtailment of Indian
expenditure and 'Home Charges', vices in the Indian army and
generally, the autocratic and irresponsible nature of the Indian
Government, augmented reforms and encouraged the Indian movement. (37) If these Members of Parliament had little success in
creating a direct effect on the British public because of 'the nearly
empty House in which Indian business was normally conducted' their
fact-finding tours of India helped the Indian leaders build Indian
public opinion around democracy and the rights of man. It was
this aspect that led Reuß to be sarcastic about 'the wrong feeling
of humanity' and public opinion. The Tories had been charging
such visiting MPs in the same way for years, for exalting the
Indian to 'a sense of rights he never possessed, which he has
not earned, to wrongs he has not suffered...' (38)

The Anglo-Indians were of course most irritated by such visiting
MPs - 'travelled idiots', in Kipling's phrase (39) - and the official
Germans could not appreciate this Anglo-Indian opinion more. In
1908 Richthofen wrote that the discovery of a Russian anarchists'
connection with the educated Bengali revolutionists, who studied in
Oxford and Cambridge, would, as hoped by the British circles in
India, silence those 'babblers' in the House of Commons like Sir
Henry Cotton and others who on the basis of an entertainment trip
through India acted as defenders of the Indian people in Britain. (40)
Another official German, a visitor himself, Treutler, wrote in the
same vein to the Kaiser in January 1911 that considerable demage
was done both to the British Home Government and to India by the
pressure of Britain's 'ultraliberal elements'. He added that compared
to the past and present mistakes of certain Members of Parliament
and the radical press of Britain, all the mistakes committed, often
with the best of intentions, by the Anglo-Indians in the internal administration of India were insignificant. Treutler opined that the

---

37) See Maccoby, op. cit., pp. 425-447.

38) Arnold White, English Democracy, Its Promises and Perils
    (1894) quoted in S. Maccoby, op. cit., p. 423, see also p. 428 n.

39) See 'Pagett, M. P.' in R. Kipling. Departmental Ditties etc.
    (London & New York 1925[ed]) p. 84. See also R. MacDonald,
    op. cit., p. 205 for one of those visiting MPs accounts of how
    the Anglo-Indians were "sadly mesmerised by the jingle of
    'Pagett, M. P.'".

40) Richthofen to Bülow, Simla 7 May 1908, AABI 42.

works of men like Keir Hardie, who only made 'propaganda trips' to India, could justly be called high treason. (41)

The terrorist acts of the revolutionary nationalists further distanced the official Germans from the Indian movement, for terrorism indeed was - and is - a ghastly affront to German faith in Rechtsstaat (42) so respectfully upheld in Imperial Germany as it is today. The loose use that the British made of the term 'anarchists' (43) for the Indian terrorists may also have made any connection between them and the British socialists the more revolting in the eyes of the official Germans. The two important Labour Members of Parliament who visited India during the unrest period, James Keir Hardie and Ramsey Mc Donald, did not go very far beyond wishing the British Government in India to be a calm, patient, judicious, farsighted and responsible ruler (44) although the former, through the highly distorted British press reports during his India visit (45), and his earlier effort to

---

41) Treutler to Kaiser from the ship 'Arabia' 28 Feb. 1911, Preuss 1 (10); Keir Hardie (1856-1915): A British Labour leader and the first to lead the Labour Party in the House of Commons in 1906. A dedicated socialist and pacifist, he was also a critic of British policies towards India in the House of Commons. He visited the post-Curzon Indian and published his Impressions in book form first in 1907.

42) Rechtsstaat (the rule of law) is, however, "not the same as democratic institutions, and insistence on it is as such no testimony to the basic attitude of modern liberalism". It existed in Imperial Germany without much civil equality. It simply means that "everything, including the actions of those in power, should be done in accordance with codified rules, or at least be limited by these". See R. Dahrendorf, op. cit., pp. 66-7, 197.

43) There have never been doctrinaire anarchists as such in India although the modern political scientists may call men like Mahatma Gandhi, Vinoba Bhave and, more recently, Jayaprakash Narayan 'gentle anarchists'. The revolutionary nationalists always objected to this misuse of the term for them. See below pp. 179-80.

44) See J. Keir Hardie, op. cit., pp. 70-79; R. MacDonald, op. cit., pp. 208-9.

45) During Hardie's visit to India he was much maligned and ridiculed by the British press at home and his words were utterly distorted. He was charged for promising to assist in making India a self-governing colony whereas on his own

make the Government of India legally responsible to the House of
Commons (46), could not have earned anything but contempt from
official Germans. However, it was the more radical H. M. Hyndman
and his Social Democratic Federation with its strong denunciation
of British rule in India and direct encouragement to the Indian extremists, who aroused in the Kaiser his predictable anger against the
socialists.

Hyndman had of course been connected with the London group of
the Indian revolutionary nationalists ever since the formation of
the 'India Home Rule Society' by Shyamaji Krishnavarma in 1905.(47)
In September 1910 Richard von Kühlmann (48), Counsellor in the
German Embassy at London informed Berlin about a recent appeal
by the Executive Committee of the British Social Democratic Federation to the British public published in their organ Justice.(49)
The appeal accused the 'Liberal and Radical Government of Britain'
of arresting Indian patriots without charge and deporting them without trial; of outraging the right of asylum; of denying political
prisoners the right of defence by counsel; of suborning perjured
witnesses; of putting down public meetings; and of suppressing the
freedom of the press. It was because of these, the journal argued,

----

    claim he said nothing of the sort. The Times and Punch
    charged him for fostering sedition in India. See E. Hughes,
    Keir Hardie (London 1956) pp. 149-158 ff.

46) The Government of India was not only not responsible to
    Indian opinion, it was not even responsible in practice to
    the House of Commons, for the salary of the Secretary
    for India was not upon the British estimates and hence he
    was not subject to the House of Commons. In July 1906
    Hardie, in order to erase this anomaly, moved that in
    future this change be effected. This was supported by a
    large number of Liberal and Radical members and the
    Government was saved from defeat only by Tory votes.
    See S. Maccoby, op. cit., p. 447.

47) For Hyndman's sympathy for the cause of the Indian revolu-
    tionary nationalists, see I. Yajnik, Shyamaji Krishnavarma:
    Life and Times of an Indian Revolutionary (Bombay 1950)
    pp. 124-5.

48) Richard von Kühlmann (1873-1948): 1905-06 Chargé d'Affaires,
    Tangier; 1909-14 Counsellor, London; 1914-15 Counsellor,
    Constantinople; 1915-16 Minister, The Hague; 1916-17 Am-
    bassador, Constantinople; July 1917 - June 18 Minister for
    Foreign Affairs.

49) Kühlmann to Bethmann-Hollweg, London 7 Sept. 1910, AABI 46.

that disaffection, secret conspiracy and open assassination had
become the only means of protest in India. The journal sympathised
with the Indians struggling to be free from 'monstrous' British
domination.(50) Reading the summary of this appeal in Kühlmann's
report along with the news of the British socialists' contact with
the Indian revolutionaries, recently unearthed by the Indian police,
the Kaiser, whose hatred for the socialists, whether they be home-
brand or of foreign breed, could even the bloodthirsty (51), observed:
"Socialism after all is revolution! And so it stays under international
connection and international influence." He considered the British
socialists' connections with the Indian freedom movement as 'high
treason'.(52) When in December the same year, while presiding
over a lecture by the Indian nationalist leader Bipin Chandra Pal
at Caxton Hall, Westminster, Hyndman reiterated his criticism of
Lord Morley and warmly welcomed the nationalist movement in
Indie, the Kaiser as before deplored such lack of patriotism in
Britons.(53)

It is clear that, not wishing the end of British rule in India even
in the distant future, the Germans found Britain's granting of
democratic institutions to the Indians suicidal - running away from
the white man's business to rule.

2. Germany, Indian Nationalism and White Man's Supremacy

As has been seen, it was the growth of nationalism and hatred for
foreign rule which Curzon's actions aroused in Bengal that primarily
caused the political unrest of the post-Curzon India and not merely
the misconduct of the Anglo-Indians, as the German observers were
suggesting. However, when one sees the whole problem against the
ideological background of the age of expansive imperialism, the
question of racial harmony does appear relevant in so far as the
concept of the white man's supremacy encouraged aggressiveness on
the part of the imperialist rulers and aggravated counter-offensives
on the part of the ruled - as shown by Indian terrorism.

---

50) Ibid. See also Justice, 27 August 1910, 'Infamies of Liberal Rule in India.'

51) Cf. B. Bülow, Denkwürdigkeiten, II (Berlin 1930) p.198.

52) In Kühlmann's report in n.49.

53) In Kühlmann to Bethmann-Hollweg, London 23 December 1910,
AABI 46.

But could a European power adhering to the idea of the white man's supremacy really think in terms of social harmony between the rulers and the ruled in a colonial context? In close analysis German criticism of Anglo-Indian behaviour turns out to be touching merely the superficial and not the substantial aspects of the issue. Being themselves not free from racial prejudices the official Germans found themselves on inconsistent ground while trying to connect political unrest with the decline in the qualities of Indian civil servants. For example, one of the basic arguments of the German diplomats in India had been that the older civil servants in India, having lived there for a longer period, understood India better and were more efficient and better behaved compared with the younger ones. Yet when Treutler was told by Roos-Koppel that the natives should be given all political rights Treutler thought it to be the bad influence of living too long with the Indians. Similarly Voretzsch found among the educated Indians the calibre for attaining higher government jobs but he would withhold such jobs from them purely for the sake of European permanency. Yet Voretzsch blamed the British for their contempt for the Indians and for their racial pride. The German attitude to the punishment of the 9th Lancers by Curzon will illustrate this dichotomy best.

Curzon endeavoured to check the gross partiality in the administration of justice in India. In the spring of 1902 he found an occasion to exhibit this in a case where two troopers were involved of a famous British Army cavalry regiment - the 9th Lancers. These soldiers who had come from South Africa for a spell of Indian duty had beaten a native cook to death. The military authority made no attempt at first to investigate the crime or punish the culprits. Curzon however influenced the Commander-in-Chief into giving an exemplary punishment: the leave of all the officers of the regiment in India was stopped for a period. Such a severe and collective punishment created considerable agitation in European circles and Curzon was charged even by responsible people with lowering the prestige of the army and of white men in general.[54] We have mentioned before how Curzon's administrative efficiency was praised by the official Germans. Curzon's adherence to the principle of equality before the law was, however, seen by them in a different light. Even Sternburg considered that Curzon had gone rather too far with this principle.[55] During the Delhi Durbar which followed the incident

---

54) M. Edwardes, High Noon of Empire: India Under Curzon, p. 167.

55) Sternburg to Bülow, Simla 22 May 1902, AABI 26.

the European community found an occasion to publicly demonstrate
their dislike of Curzon's treatment of the 9th Lancers. Voretzsch
reported that every time the 9th Lancers passed by the tribunes
in the vicinity of which Curzon sat, there was thundering applause
with endless shouts of 'Bravo the 9th.' This ovation, Voretzsch
wrote, had the sole purpose of offending Curzon and it really led
Lady Curzon to tears after the show was over. The Kaiser under-
lined this passage on Curzon's plight and left a remark in English:
'alright'. (56) The Kaiser's satisfaction at the insult suffered by
Curzon was perhaps due more to his dislike of Curzon for his anti-
German feelings and the special importance the Kaiser attached to
things military. He may not have cared to know Curzon's lofty
defence to his measure which was to preserve the morality and
'righteousness in administration'. (57) But Sternburg and Voretzsch
were admirers of Curzon's administration. In any case it would
have been only logical for those who criticised the contempt of
the British towards the Indians to appreciate Curzon's endeavours
to achieve at least equality before the law.

The fact was however, that the concept of the moral superiority of
Europeans as rulers was too vital for most imperialists to admit
any failings before the subject people. As Curzon did just that by
punishing the European soldiers he was equally to blame with all
the Liberals and their humanitarian ideals. To many theorists and
votaries of imperial expansion the white man was, irrespective of
his social behaviour or education, a born ruler and the idea of the
subject people having any political rights was simply revolting.
Jules Harmand, the French imperial theorist, wrote in 1910 that
"Governments of India have already overstepped reasonable liberalism
in making Englishmen submit to the judgements of Hindu magistrates
and admitting their native subjects to certain executive posts."
According to him "The Hindu, demoralized by an assimilative education ill-suited to his type of mind and overexcited by the Japanese
victories - which were not so much victories against the Russians
as against the whites and against their Anglo-Saxon allies themselves - takes every concession as the sign for a further retreat
by his masters and a new crack in the edifice of the beneficent
authority."(58) The comments of a Berlin professor, Georg Wegener,

---

56) Voretzsch to Bülow, Calcutta 15 January 1903, AABI 27; For
the 'Bravo the 9th' incident see also V. Chirol, Fifty Years
in a Changing World; op. cit., p. 227.

57) M. Edwardes, High Noon etc. p. 167.

58) Jules Harmand, Domination et Colonisation (Paris 1910);
excerpts incorporated in P. D. Curtin (ed.) Imperialism
(New York 1971) see p. 306.

in 1911, seem also to be relevant here. Wegener who visited India three times, in 1898, 1906 and 1910 - the last time as a member of the German Crown Prince's official entourage - met Surendranath Banerjea (59), the prominent leader of the Indian National Congress, in Calcutta during his 1906 visit. Banerjea was alleged to have shown his great surprise to Wegener at so many uneducated and even stupid Britons ruling India. On this Wegener later reflected: "This man had not understood at all that not the intellectual but the moral qualities of the British and the ethics and will power of the white man, all of which an Indian lacks, are the reasons for this rule."(60) Explaining further about white supremacy Wegener wrote that Britain's loss of India would be a great setback not only to Germany but to the white race as a whole. He therefore said that

> "all white nationals must stand united if victory is to be
> on their side in the struggle in Asia," and "India is that
> part of the earth where supremacy of the white race over
> the coloured is most evident. Should the Asiatics succeed
> in destroying British sovereignty the position of the whole
> white race on the globe, our own not excluded, would
> suffer a fatal blow."(61)

When men like Gerlich and Heyking, Syburg and Richthofen, Reuß and Treutler detested the influence of British Liberalism in India which resulted in the political awekening of the Indians, it was the same undercurrent of racialism which was acting.

So far as the Kaiser was concerned he never minced his words on the white man's supremacy. In September 1910 he read a report from London mentioning among other things an article in the Daily Graphic on the Indian situation. The author's thesis was that the prestige of the white race, including the British, suffered greatly by Japan's victory over Russia. The Kaiser commented: "as if I had written this myself." The author, des-

---

59) Surendranath Banerjea (1848-1925): 1871 entered Indian Civil
    Service; 1874 dismissed from I.C.S.; 1895 and 1902 President,
    Indian National Congress; 1921-23 Minister in Bengal Govern-
    ment; Founder of the journal Bengalee.

60) G. Wegener, Das Heutige Indien (Berlin 1912), originally
    a lecture delivered to the Geographical Society of Berlin
    in July 1911, p. 43; Banerjea, however, promptly repudia-
    ted the remarks attributed to him by Wegener. See The
    Bombay Chronicle 26 Mai 1913.

61) Ibid., p. 49.

cribing the condition of post-1907 India, said that in India the
revolutionaries were happily waiting for a war between Germany
and England and that all Orientals in their heart of hearts cher-
ished the hope that the dispute between the big white nations
might bring an opportunity for the 'coloured men'. This statement led the Kaiser to make a significant comment: "This I know
and therefore we shall not please them by doing this."(62)

3. Kaiser Wilhelm II, Japan and Indian Nationalism

For Kaiser Wilhelm II India was the test case for white supremacy
in a very special way. There was every reason for him to want a
firm hold by the British over their Indian empire for otherwise the
Indian unrest would augment Japanese imperialism which, in his
opinion, had already become a threat to Christian power.

Kaiser Wilhelm II's self-imposed guardianship of Christian honour
and his emphasis on Christian interest are well known. In 1895 he
presented to Czar Nicholas that famous allegorical painting, based
on his own rough sketch, of himself as Saint George at the head of
the Western nations marching against a distant Buddha, the symbol
of the 'yellow peril'.(63)

In June 1904 the Kaiser got a shock while reading a report from
Simla about the Indians' enthusiasm at the Japanese successes in
their war against the Russians. Consul General Quadt wrote that
the official Japanese in Bombay confirmed receiving some 65,000
rupees from India for the support of the widows and orphans of
the Japanese killed in the war. From the names of the donors

---

62) Kühlmann to Bethmann-Hollweg, 11 Sept. 1910, AABI 46; In
his conversation with Sir Edward Goschen, the British
Ambassador in Berlin, the Kaiser is alleged to have told
the Ambassador thus: "I am all for the white man against
the black, whether they be Chinese, Japanese, Niggers and
Slav." Quoted in N. Mansergh, The Coming of the First
World War; A Study in the European Balance 1878-1914
(London 1948) p.147.

63) See E.M. Carroll, op. cit., p.358. In his memoirs an American dentist, Arthur N. Davis, mentioned Wilhelm II telling
him in 1907 that he (Wilhelm) originated the phrase 'yellow
peril'. Professor Gollwitzer's research shows that the Kaiser's
painting did not contain the phrase 'yellow peril' nor did he
use it himself before 1900. According to Gollwitzer the phrase
originated in 1895 west of the Rhine and got circulated from
there. See H. Gollwitzer, Die Gelbe Gefahr (Göttingen 1962) p.42.

Quadt easily determined that except the very tiny percentage of Britons most of them were Indians. The enthusiasm among the Indians at the Japanese victory was so great that, Quadt wrote, it made many old time Britishers in India worried. Even the Afghan Amir did not fail to use the opportunity to remind his people of the virtues of a united people. The Kaiser exclaimed: "cela promet! The awakening of the Asian peoples! People of Europe?"(64) In March 1906 a similar situation evoked from the Kaiser a similar remark. An Indian paper in the Urdu language, Watan, of Lahore, let it be known that the British monthly The Review of Religion would soon be distributed in large numbers cost free in Japan to make propaganda for Islam. The Waten appealed to all Muslims to support the venture. Reading Quadt's report on the matter the Kaiser commented: "And where do we Christians stand?"(65) When in December 1905 Quadt recalled what Lord Kitchener had earlier told him about his being super-fluous in India after the defence of India had been assured through the Japanese alliance, the Kaiser commented in the margin: "very optimistic! by this India is really handed over to the Japs! the result may be a nice awakening!" On Quadt's remark that with the departure of Lord Kitchener his innovations would fade away and there would hardly be a successor of similar energy and drive, the Kaiser further commented: "This the Japanese will do."(66)

Not that the British in India did not mark the dangerous effect the rise of Japan had on the growth of Indian nationalism. On 1 January 1906 Quadt at Calcutta met Lord Kitchener at a dinner given by Viceroy Minto in honour of the visiting Prince of Wales. In the course of the discussion the General, who had a talkative nature, entertained all kinds of questions put to him by Quadt and said that the alliance with Japan was only a 'great bluff' for he was of the opinion that Japan would follow her own interest only and there was certainly a motive in her coming to an agreement to support Britain in defending India. The Kaiser seems to have agreed on that.(67) But Quadt dit not fail to appreciate Kitchener's unspoken meaning. As mentioned earlier, Kitchener had earlier

---

64) Quadt to Bülow, Simla 30 May 1904, AABI 29.

65) Quadt to Bülow, Calcutta 5 March 1906, AABI 33.

66) Quadt to Bülow, Calcutta 28 December 1905, ibid.

67) Quadt to Bülow, Calcutta 2 January 1906, ibid. The Kaiser wrote on the margin in this connection: "Important!"

told him at a reception given by the Germans that the defence of India being secured by the Japanese alliance, his presence in India was superfluous. (68) The reason for Kitchener's new stand in minimising the importance of the Japanese alliance was therefore based on an important psychological point. Quadt argued that the British alliance with Japan for Indian defence profoundly affected British prestige in India, for the Indians were now happy to know that Britain admitted her own weakness. (69) Hence, according to Quadt, Kitchener's remark was nothing but a device to counteract the harmful effect of such a situation at a time when thoughtful Britons in India and elsewhere began to realise sadly the true value of their Japanese alliance. (70)

In March 1906 the German Foreign Office was further informed about Japanese expansionist designs. One Dr. Karminiski, an Austrian officer, after touring East Asia on a government assign-ment informed Quadt in Calcutta that Japan was working on her expansion greedily. Dutch East India would be her next objective. Dr. Karminiski said that the Japanese there were trying to transform some 150,000 Chinese living in Dutch India into Japanese, to start mixing with the Dutch Indians with the ultimate aim of finding a pretext to annex it. Karminiski was alleged to have said that until this should happen the Japanese would go on behaving reservedly toward the British despite the alliance. (71) To the Kaiser such news was ominous. He seems to have thought that Japan's appetite would naturally direct her to India. In June 1906 he read with much interest a report from Quadt on the Anglo-Indian civil servants' disagreeable treatment of the natives, in which Quadt concluded that if things continued to develop as they were, the mutual discontentment and

---

68) Quadt to Bülow, Simla 28 October and Calcutta 28 December 1905, AABI 32.

69) Same as in 67.

70) In March 1906 Dr. Karminiski, an Austrian Foreign Service man, after travelling in East Asia arrived at Calcutta and informed Quadt that everywhere on his trip, especially in Singapore, he noticed among the British a deep dislike of the alliance with Japan. Dr. Karminiski was alleged to have said that the British in Japan, when they got the news of the signing of the alliance, were shocked at putting Britain on an equal footing with an inferior race. Quadt to Bülow, Calcutta 7 March 1906, AABI 33.

71) Ibid.

distrust between the rulers and the ruled would lead to serious consequences. To the Kaiser at least one consequence was clear: "Well then the Japanese will have an easy game one day."(72) In October the same year while reading another report from Quadt in which he mentioned about the masses of political leaflets printed in America being distributed in West India, the Kaiser wondered whether the place of origin was not Japan. Underlining the word 'America' he commented in the margin: "Tokyo? I have read it in translation. It comes from Japan."(73)

Japan's attitude towards India was closely watched by Germany. In late 1907 Dr. Mumm von Schwarzenstein, German Ambassador in Tokyo, informed the Foreign Office in Berlin of Count Okuma's support for the Indian national movement.(74) Okuma, the leader of the Progressive Party, delivered a speech at the Kobe Chamber of Commerce mentioning that 300 million Indians who suffered under the European yoke were looking for Japan's support. The Count said that there would soon be a movement in India boycotting European goods and Japan should not lose the opportunity thereby disappointing the Indians. This speech was much commented upon in the European press. Sharpest criticism naturally came from the English. Okuma, however, retreated from the pressure of public criticism. Taking the opportunity of a banquet speech at the Indo-Japanese Society in Tokyo on 4 March 1908, tactfully he first mentioned India from whence Japan, via China and Korea, got the seed of her civilisation in the fields of art, literature and religion, and then added: "Presently India is ruled by the Government of King Emperor Edward VII, the outstanding supporter of freedom and justice. If at present India does not enjoy full freedom then this is not Britain's fault, but that of the Indians themselves who have not yet made sufficient progress in the field of education and morale."(75) The Kaiser was not impressed. To him all these were "lies and hypocracy". "The true opinion" he said, "was the one given previously when Okuma talked about the sufferance of the 300 million Indians under British yoke."(76)

In November 1908, giving all the recent developments in the Japanese press and politics, Schwarzenstein informed Berlin of the true nature of Indo-Japanese relations.(77) He wrote that the widely held view

---

72) Quadt to Bülow, Simla 11 May 1906, AABI 34.

73) Quadt to Bülow, Simla 26 September 1906, AABI 36.

74) Schwarzenstein to Bülow, Tokyo 13 April 1908, AABI 41.

75) Ibid.

76) The Kaiser's marginal remark on above.

77) Schwarzenstein to Bülow, Tokyo 3 November 1908, AABI 43.

that Japan by her victory over a big European power infused the idea of freedom among the Indian people was unpleasing to the Japanese themselves from the beginning. More than once the leading Japanese press organs had stated emphatically that Japan had got nothing to do, neither directly nor indirectly, with the Indian freedom movement. Some even went to the extent of blaming the Indians for being ungrateful to the British. Schwarzenstein observed that Japan's disinclination to have anything to do with India did not merely stem from her alliance with Britain. Arrogance being the outstanding national character of the Japanese, he wrote, Japan really did not want to be compared in any sense with a suppressed people. As a big power Japan considered herself standing at the same level as Britain. She did not want to be equated with the other Asian people - not even as primus inter pares. (78) Schwarzenstein however mentioned that Japan could not at the same time be entirely unsympathetic towards the Indian movement. Newspapers did publish news about the Indian movement in the form of letters or short articles. Japan was also not totally unconcerned about the profit to be derived from the boycott of British goods in India. Japanese exports to India which before the Russo-Japanese war amounted to approximately 16 million marks increased to 27.5 million marks in 1907, and this trade was all the more important for Japan because the goods exported to India were mainly manufactured products, namely silk textiles (100 million marks), cotton textiles (1 million marks), cotton tricot textiles (6 million marks), matches (1 3/4 million marks) etc. which gave a market to Japan's rising industry. On the other hand, the importation of Indian raw products by Japan was also large - in 1907 raw cotton (121 million marks) and rice (27 million marks). Thus for economic reasons alone the maintenance of good relations with the nationalist India was essential. (79)

So far as Japan's possible bid for expansion towards Britain's Indian Empire - the fear of the Kaiser - Schwarzenstein said that for the time being it was impossible for Japan to have any intentions in India other than economic. In his opinion the idea that should the British call Japan to defend India the Japanese would come with the intention of grasping India for themselves was just a phantasy. "I am convinced" he wrote, "that here one does not see the slightest possibility of such a thought. "(80) Schwarzenstein depicted Japan as terribly self-centred and practical and this, he said, was just what

---

78) Ibid.

79) Ibid.

80) Ibid.

disappointed the nationalist Indians. The latter came to realise towards the end of the first decade of this century that the hopes they laid on Japan as the saviour of Asia were useless. Their slogan of solidarity of the Asian peoples did not find an echo in Japan and their proud political dreams could not be brought into line with Japan's Realpolitik. Nationalist India demanded an Asia with newly strengthened Oriental ideals; Japan was striving for hegemony of a Western pattern. It was therefore no wonder, Schwarzenstein said, that Calcutta's Modern Review (Satis Chandra Basu) accused Japan of treason for ruining the joint Asian cause. (81)

The Kaiser, however, still continued to think in terms of a Japanese expansive policy towards India. In August 1910 while reading one of Count Metternich's despatches from London dealing with the current British press on the anti-British movement in India (82) the Kaiser came across the comment from the Morning Post that the movement was exclusively confined to the Hindus. Refuting this he hinted that the Japanese were behind the Hindu movement. (83) In October of the same year the newly appointed Viceroy, Lord Hardinge, gave a speech at a dinner given by the County of Kent before his departure for India. Hardinge talked about his ensuing plans for India in the direction of extending the era of reforms which had already begun. Reading this in another report from Metternich, the Kaiser commented "Well, if the Japanese allow it. "(84)

4. Indian Attitude towards Germany

Before summing up the German attitude towards the political move-ments of the educated Indians it is perhaps necessary, at this point, to note also the educated Indians' attitude towards Germany in the period of their political awakening.

---

81) Ibid.; Schwarzenstein wrote that Indian disappointment found its expression in the abrupt reduction in Indian students in Japan. Shortly after the Russian War the number of Indian students abruptly increased to 80 and towards the end of 1908 the number was hardly half that much according to the Japan Daily Mail. The sudden reduction in their number led to the conclusion that the Indian students had political motives. The same motives had operated when their numer increased after Japan's victory over Russia.

82) Metternich to Bethmann-Hollweg, London 16 Aug. 1910, AABI 46.

83) Ibid.; The Kaiser's comment.

84) Metternich to Bethmann-Hollweg, London 21 Oct. 1910, ibid.

From the foregoing account of official Germany's contact with
British India since the early years of the Indian National Congress
we have seen that the educated Indians never got any sympathy for
their political aspirations from the official Germans throughout the
pre-War period. Nor did the official Germans show any enthusiasm
or appreciation for things Indian. The German diplomats in India
being down-to-earth practical men of business had nothing to do
with ancient Indian history and culture. One does not find in their
reports a mention of indology and its impact in Germany. As for
their experience of the natural surroundings and culture, one of
them (Below) found India completely devoid of scenic beauty. (85)
Another (Gerlich) stated that the only thing among the native population in northern India having a sparkle of culture was Mohammeda-
nism. (86) And many, of course, found some of the Hindu customs
simply revolting.

The scientific study of Sanskrit and Hindu scriptures (87) need not
necessarily produce any love for India or the Indians either on the
part of the scholars themselves or their fellow-countrymen. The
impact of Indian ideas on some German scholars, poets and philosophers, engendered eulogistic enthusiasm in some of them. Particularly through the researches, writings, lectures, and contacts
(with Indian scholars and socio-religious reformers) of that famous
Oxford professor of German origin, F. Max Müller (1823 - 1900)

---

85) Below to Bülow, Simla 20 June 1909, AABI 44.

86) Gerlich to Bismarck, Calcutta 6 December 1886, AABI 2.

87) There had been great enthusiasm for ancient Indian languages,
literature and culture in Germany ever since the last decade
of the eighteenth century. In May 1791 the Germans translation
of Shakuntala was published and the same year also saw Goethe's
quatrain on it. In the following years until the founding of a
chair in Sanskrit at the University of Bonn in 1818 either
translation of or treatises on various Indian works were
published including the Laws of Manu (1797), Gita-Govinda
(1802), and F. Schlegel's Über die Sprache und Weisheit der
Inder (1808). The following is a list of universities offering
courses of indology in the pre-War Germany: Bonn (1818),
Leipzig (1848), Tübingen (1856), Göttingen (1862), Munich
(1867), Marburg (1869), Hamburg (1914). For some details
on these see W. Nölle, Impact of Indian Thought on German
Poets & Philosophers (Aliganj, 1963) pp. 10-22; W. Leifer,
India and the Germans. 500 years of Indo-German Contact
(Bombay 1971) pp. 118-150.

who was active in the heyday of Victorian imperialism, the Indians
seemed mistakenly to have found a connection between the study
of indology and a love for India. Like Johann Gottfried Herder
(1744 - 1803) before him, Max Müller, who never visited India,
but was lifelong preoccupied with the Sacred Books of that land,
called India 'the very paradise on earth'. (88) Such appreciation,
coming from Europeans themselves contributed much to the self-
confidence of the Indians and hence to their nationalism.

The impact of Indian ideas on the West was not, however, always
favourable to the Indians - at least in the case of the 'Aryan race'
concept it was not. The comments and discussions on Aryan languages
among European scholars brought frequent references to a highly
civilised Aryan race who spoke these languages - and Max Müller
was one of the first to equate the two. (89) The Indian Aryans as
a race did not fair well. The Western racial theorists tended to
confirm the earlier view of the French racialist historian Arthur
de Gobineau (1816-82) that the 'Indo-Aryans' had long lost their
pristine Aryan virtues because of their intermingling with other
inferior races and failure to preserve the purity of their blood.
Soon the French, British and Germans, each according to their
own claim, became the true descendants of the original Aryans
leaving the Indians far behind. The racial theories of neneteenth
century imperialism had, as we have already seen, convinced the
Westerners, including the Germans, that Indians required white
rulers for their own survival.

Such unfavourable interpretations by the West did not, however,
much disturb the Aryan-minded among the Hindus who remained
elated nevertheless by the fact that modern materially advanced
nations of the West were beginning to accept the greatness of the
Aryan culture which had once flourished in India and had continued
to inspire her ever since. It is interesting to note that even when
the claim of pure Aryanism was most ominously advanced by Nazi
Germany, a section of the Hindus, drunk with the ancient glories
of the Aryan Hindus and erroneously believing that the Nazis had
a special regard for the Hindu heritage, found no fault with the
Nazi programme and policies. As late as March 1939 the Secretary
of the All-India Hindu Mahasabha let 'the people of Germany and
the Führer's Government' know that Germany's solemn idea of
revival of the Aryan culture and the glorification of Swastika

88) See F. Max Müller, India: What Can It Teach Us? (London
    1883) and Biographical Essays (London 1884).

89) G. L. Gomme, Ethnology in Folklore (London, 1892) quoted
    in C. Bolt, op. cit., p. 13.

were welcomed by 'the religious and sensible Hindus of India with jubilant hope.' (90)

It must, however, be pointed out that the majority of the active Hindu nationalists and certainly the most significant of them, who in their politics used religion or were otherwise inspired by it, were not concerned with the Aryan race theory and their attraction to Germany, wherever it occured, did not derive from this source. (91) It was purely because of the utilitarian motives on both sides that the Kaiser and Hitler got groups of Indian revolutionary nationalists to make common cause against the British. However, there could hardly be any doubt that in both periods there existed an undercurrent of love for Germany among the Indians including the nationalists - although to some of the militant nationalists the attitude of the official Germans towards them was not unknown. (92) The use of 'made in Germany' products and the award of business to German firms - even printing of seditious colour paintings (93) - were perhaps due more to the high regard the Indians had for German efficiency and workmanship. But a different sort of love and regard for Germany also existed as exhibited by Raja Shyama Kumar Tagore of Bengal for example, when he donated a valuable collection of old Indian artefacts to the Berlin Museum in 1911 to mark the visit of the German Crown Prince to India. (94) Two further examples would show the nationalists' soft spot for Germany.

---

90) Report of German Consul General in India to A. A. 25 March 1939 incorporating the statement of Padamraj Jain, Hon. Secy. All-India Hindu Mahasabha. The statement also assured the Germans that "Only a few socialists headed by Pandit Jawaharlal Nehru have created a bubble of resentment against the present Government of Germany but their activities are far from having any significance in India. " The statement similarly bypassed Mahatma Gandhi's criticism of Nazi ruthlessness as utterances of "a man who has betrayed and confused the country with affected mysticism. "

91) In fact Lala Lajpat Rai, an extremist leader with Arya Samajist background, refused to join hands with Germany during the First World War even for the sake of Indian freedom.

92) In a letter (in French) to a high dignitary in the German Foreign Office Har Dayal was to write in May 1915: "Most of your diplomats know very little about our movement. Your consuls in India estranged themselves from the Indians and shared the life and views of the British. "

93) See below ch. VII pp. 163-4.

94) See Reuß to A. A. Telg. Calcutta 9 Feb. 1911, AABI 47.

We have mentioned earlier the contents of the telegrams exchanged
between Kaiser Wilhelm II and Lord Curzon at the time of the
Kaiser's famine relief donation to India in the summer of 1900. (95)
The Indians kept quiet about the Kaiser's sentence on blood relations
with the British but took Curzon to task for expounding it further.
The nationalist Hindu of Madras commented: "...Viceroy happily
observes... 'it is indeed an illustration of the binding force of
kinship...' But on a platform much higher than this are we prepared to recognize this act of noble charity and trace its motives
to that sympathetic love of the German people for India whose
ancient literature and history the savants of that country have
studied and interpreted as those of no other country have done."(96)
Similarly, when in 1913 The Nineteenth Century and After reprinted
Wegener's 1911 lecture on India, which also we have mentioned
earlier, (97) it is again the objective of the English journal in pub-
lishing the 'ill informed views and ignorant deductions' of the
German gentleman, which came more under suspicion and criticism
from the Indian nationalist press than Germany as such. In The
Bombay Chronicle's reply to Wegener the educated Indians' unflinching dedication to democratic institutions was best expressed. The
paper wrote:

> "...perhaps even Dr. Wegener may live long enough to
> see much wider development of those representative
> institutions, which he seems to regard with misgivings"
> and that "the safety of Germany's colonies might be
> better guaranteed by an imitation of British methods
> in this respect."(98)

To sum up, the Indian movement for democratic institutions which
later turned into a movement for self-rule was not at all appreciated
by the official Germans and they blamed the British for first, arousing
among the Indians such useless ideals through their liberalism, and
then not suppressing the Indian movement with a stronger and more
efficient government. As the clamour for a democratic institution and
self-rule was confined only to what they called a tiny, misguided,

---

95) See above ch. II p. 64 and n. 25, p. 66.

96) The Hindu (Madras) 7 May 1900.

97) See above p. 150.

98) See 'A German on India', The Bombay Chronicle 26 May 1913.

Western educated minority in a vast country of teeming millions,
the official Germans were convinced that it could easily be
suppressed and the country very well governed by a British ruling
class of high-born, well-mannered and efficient civil servants,
subordinated to a more or less absolute Viceroy, who himself
would be free from any parliamentary control either at home or
in India.

In fact the Germans had their own political system in mind while
thinking of a better political system for India and hence their
appreciation of Curzon in India, who most nearly approached the
German model in revising the Indian constitution. The constitution
of Imperial Germany has been defined by a prominent German
Liberal and sociologist as 'the authoritarian welfare state'. (99)
It was a state where leadership undisputedly rested on 'a stratum
generally legitimated by tradition.' Those in power were not subject
to any decisive control by representative institutions and they prevented political participation by the majority. Although it did not
need the participation of the governed, the authoritarian state of
Imperial Germany was not a totalitarian or terror state. It was
a mixture of severity and benevolence and it concerned itself
seriously with the welfare of its subjects. It was even enlightened.
However, there was to be found no concern here for the individual
and his rights, or autonomy of social groups or liberalism. (100)

Conditioned by this home background and having a built-in handicap
as representatives of the aristocracy or upper middle class in
understanding any mentality other than their own, whether their
compatriots' or foreigners', (101) the official Germans in India
continuously ignored the intellectual development of the middle
class, educated Indians and the roots of their political aspirations.
Through British contact the Indians came to believe that democracy
was itself a good and superior form of government and that its

99) See R. Dahrendorf, op. cit., pp. 58-60.

100) Ibid., pp. 58, 39. A prominent German historian-cum-politi-
cal scientist sees the political structure of Imperial Germany
as 'pseudo-constitutional, semi-absolute, feudal, military
and bureaucratic state'. See K. D. Bracher, 'Kaiser Wilhelm's
Germany' in J. M. Roberts (ed.), Europe in the 20th Century,
Vol. 1, 1900-14 (London 1970) p. 79.

101) See R. H. Lowie, Toward Understanding Germany (Chicago
1954) p. 109.

adoption carried with it an assertion of equality. Their faith in parliamentary democracy on the part of the Indian nationalists sprang also from their belief that the working of this system would disprove the assumption of inferiority which they hated. (102) Despotism, however benevolent or however close its association with India's past history might be, was clearly incompatible with current Indian nationalist thinking. (103)

---

102) See R. Emerson, <u>From Empire to Nation: The Rise of Self-Assertion of Asian and African Peoples</u> (Cambridge, Mass. 1960) p. 228.

103) The following quotation from one of the Indian national-ist leaders, G. K. Gokhale, addressing the Europeans is very significant in this respect: "We feel you have con-tempt for us because we submit to personal and despotic government, and so we feel that it is not compatible with self-respect to acquiesce in it. You would disdain to be governed in that way yourselves, and so you despise those who submit to it." Quoted in above.

VII. PRE-WAR GERMAN INTERESTS IN INDIA

"We consider the maintenance of British rule in India as
great luck not only for Britain but also for all other
people including Germany whose imports from there
amounted to 407 million marks in 1907 and whose exports
to that country amounted to 105 million marks."

Vossische Zeitung, 24 July 1908.

"Various events during the past five years must have sadly
reduced the numbers of the optimists who declared that con-
sanguineous races like the German and the British could
never in the nature of things come to blows in the struggle
for existence... The mere fact that Germany has become a
colonising and manufacturing power is enough to bring about
a collision."

Englishman ·(Calcutta), 1 March 1900,
'German Expansion Vs British
Possession'.

It has been clear from the foregoing chapters that in the pre-War
years of Indo-German relations official Germany avoided being
directly involved in any act against the British Empire in India.
There were occasions, however, as we have seen in different
periods of Anglo-German estrangement, when the Kaiser, Bülow
and the last of the pre-War German Consul Generals in India,
Count Luxburg, either showed little sympathy for or were exalted
by the British predicament in India. The Indian Empire, being
considered the basis of Britain's world power, did naturally
arouse some feelings of jealousy on the part of the rival imperial
power; but such feelings were never translated into direct inimical
deeds. Since it was thought that nothing less than defeat of Britain
in a major war could possibly deprive her of that precious Indian
possession, only the forfeiture of the advantages derived by Germany
from that Empire could result out of any luckless German venture
against it. Inspite of all the rumours about Russian threats and the
possibility of Indian revolt for nearly two decades, none of the pre-
War German officials on-the-spot - except perhaps Luxburg on the
eve of the great War - considered the British Indian Empire to be
in really insurmountable danger at any time. Nor did the official
Germans take a favourable attitude to the Indian movement for self-
rule which according to them could at best bring anarchy. These
factors therefore led official Germany to support Britain's hold on

India so long as Germany herself was not in a position to derive any greater gain there by way of change in the existing power situation.

There were two major fields of German material interest in the British Indian Empire. First, Germany hoped to get some help from the British Indian Government in the smooth running of her own colonies. Secondly, pre-War Germany had ever growing trade-commercial relations with India. Expectations in both these fields depended on strong and stable British rule which the German official and business circles in India supported all along.

1. British India as a Help to German Colonial Rule

Although the official Germans were critical of the arrogance of the British in India in their relations with the Indians, they were great admirers of British rule in India, considering it - to use the words of Treutler - "one of the most outstanding works of occidental culture." The official and semi-official Germans in India in the pre-War years never failed to emphasise the significance for Germany of good relations with British India. Thus in 1904 Voretzsch wrote to the German Foreign Office: "Should there be any intention of sending young colonial civil servants to an old colonial power for education then there could hardly be any better place than India."(1) In 1911 Professor Wegener said in the same vein: "Whatever attitude one may have towards the British, one cannot deny that they are the most experienced and most successful colonising people in the entire world... and we as colonial beginners have yet to learn. But nowhere better than here [in India] can all the great and difficult questions connected with the administration and development of colonies be better studied."(2) Wegener therefore pleaded for continued good relationships between Germany and Britain. Keeping Indian nationalism in mind he warned his countrymen and all other white nations not to harbour ill will against Britain's Empire in India by siding with the Asiatics. Yet another person who visited India and studied the Indian administrative system with an eye to its significance for German colonies was Hans Zache, who was attached to the Kolonialinstitut of Hamburg. (3)

---

1) Voretzsch to Bülow, Calcutta January 1904, AABI 25.

2) G. Wegener, op. cit., p. 6.

3) See Hans Zache, Die Ausbildung der Kolonialbeamten (Berlin 1912) pp. 9-12. Zache, too, was a member of the German Crown Prince's Indian entourage and he later wrote a book on the visit called Mit dem Kronprinzen durch Indien (1913).

The Germans were struck by the fact that with very little man-power Britain was able to govern such a vast country as India successfully. This achievement, they were convinced, could not be explained just by the negative reason that the masses lacked political interest. According to them a great deal depended on many positive factors the foremost of which was the skilful use of the principle of divide et impera with which the British played people against people, religion against religion, caste against caste and prince against prince, so as to make all the subject people realise the necessity of a strong foreign rule. The studied aloofness on the part of the British from interfering in the religious life of the people; their great instinctive talent for administration, which prompted them to keep the Indian Empire entirely autocratic; their specially trained, well paid and exceptionally able civil servants; and their maintenance of a smart army in India - all these were considered the basic factors of British success. (4) When he sent his eldest son to India for study and observation the Kaiser expressed to King George his admiration of India where "the British adminis-tration has done so much for the development of the country and the successful establishment of law and order. "(5)

Not just civilians the military personnel as well were aware of the opportunities for learning the problems and perfection of colonial rule from British India although most German military experts did not think too highly of the Indian army. (6) One of the many military experts who made study tours in India was Count Hans von Königs-marck, a Major of the German General Staff who after several visits to the East (7) turned into an enthusiastic admirer of the Brit-ish method of ruling the Asiatic people. (8) During the campaign against the Afridis and Arakzais on India's north-west frontier in

---

4) Ibid., pp. 28-34.

5) The Kaiser to King George V, 29 October 1910, Preuss 1 (6).

6) See 'A Fallen Idol', Pioneer 20 April 1904, wherein a retired Indian army officer refutes the German criticism of the Indian army.

.7) His first visit to India was in 1892. See E. Heyking, op. cit., p. 94.

8) Königsmarck's eulogistical remarks on the British society in India, although published in the Anglo-Indian press as opinions of 'an eminent military expert' (Statesman 6 Feb. 1909) were however not accepted by all official Germans in India. Below to Bülow, Calcutta 6 Feb. 1909, AABI 44.

1897-98 one Capt. Gedner, an officer of the Prussian Infantry
Regiment was taken by General Sir William Lockhurst with him
so as to acquaint him with the organisation and field action of
the British Indian army. The Kaiser was particularly pleased to
hear of Lockhurst's willingness to take Gedner along again or
any other German military officer on similar occasions. (9) In
September 1910 another officer, von Berger, of the German
East African colonial force also made an elaborate study of the
Indian military system. (10) These are, however, only a few
particular instances of the German military personnel's endeavours
to profit from British experiences in colonial administration; they
can by no means be compared with the detailed studies and data
collections made by regular official German observers on the
Indian army. (11) Kaiser Wilhelm II himself took special interest
in all aspects of the Indian army (12) and was a regular reader
of Indian army bulletins.

German's greatest hope of profiting from British India in the
colonial field was that of developing German East Africa with
Indian immigrant labour. German East Africa, the most
important of the German protectorates in Africa, came under
German influence through the individual initiative of Dr. Karl
Peters in 1884. In 1891 the Imperial Government took over the
administrative responsibility from the German East African Company. The total area of the protectorate was about 385,000 square
miles, almost twice the size of the German Empire. (13) Germany
sought to develop a plantation type economy in the area giving
emphasis to rubber, sisal, cotton and coffee. However, due to

---

9) Waldthausen to Hohenlohe, Calcutta 3 Feb., Simla 30 May
   1898, AABI 17, 19; the Kaiser's remarks in both.

10) Remy to Bethmann-Hollweg, Simla 5 Oct. 1910, AABI 46.

11) For details see AABI Militaria Vols. 1-18.

12) For example in 1899, in response to the Kaiser's special
    wish, Waldthausen sent to Berlin an album of photographs
    entitled 'Types of the Indian Army' along with various oil
    paintings showing Gurkhas, the Viceroy's body guard, an
    Afridi, a cavalry officer of the Patiala army, and a lancer
    of the Jodhpore Maharaja. Bülow to the Kaiser, Berlin
    9 December 1899, AABI 21.

13) A Handbook of German East Africa (London 1920) pp. 7-8,
    16.

the great reduction of the African population in the colonial wars and massacres, there was a great shortage of man-power. The plantation owners and construction firms of German East Africa were therefore interested in recruiting foreign workers. Following the example of the French who had been using Indian labour since the second half of the nineteenth century in the Antilles, Réunion, and Guiana (14), the German colonial exploiters also thought in terms of importing Indian labourers. The Usambare Coffee Plantation Company, supported by similar other firms, proposed in 1894 solving their labour problem permanently by bringing Indian families as settlers to German East Africa. G. Meinicke, the chairman of the Usambara Coffee Plantation Company, informed the German Foreign Office in February 1894 that he had got the support of von Schwarze, the director of the Leipzig Mission in India, in getting Tamil Christian settlers. The details of the plan foresaw giving the would-be immigrants a higher status than the natives.(15) This plan however did not materialise as the Indian Emigration Act of 1883 came in its way. Prior licence from the Government of India and binding contracts between the parties were essential under this Act before immigrant labour could be procured.(16) The British were not willing to help the Germans. Towards the end of 1896 The Times in London and the Pioneer in India pubslished articles against possible German exploitation of the Indian labour force, 'so valuable a class of British subjects'.(17)

---

14) Louis Vignon, L'exploitation de notre empire colonial (Paris 1900): excerpts in Philip D. Curtin, Imperialism (New York 1971) pp. 172-73.

15) See I. Werner, 'Zur Indienpolitik des deutschen Imperialismus seit dem Ende des 19. Jahrhunderts bis zum Ausbruch des ersten Weltkrieges', Zeitschrift für Geschichtswissenschaft, Sonderheft IX (East Berlin 1961) pp. 294-295.

16) According to one account the British concern was over a clause in German regulations permitting flogging as a punishment for Asiatic labourers. See L.W. Hollingsworth, Asians of East Africa (London 1960) p. 62. See also J.S. Mangat, History of the Asians in East Africa, c. 1885 to 1945 (Oxford 1969) p. 31; R.G. Gregory, India and East Africa (Oxford 1971) p. 104.

17) The Pioneer 27 February and The Times 27 October 1896, quoted in the German Foreign Office's Colonial Department (Potsdam) files, see Werner, op. cit., p. 296.

So desperate was the need for imported labour that the big German business concerns in East Africa and the German Government
had to think of other devices to get Indian labourers. As early as
1894 Gaertner, the German Consul General in Calcutta, suggested
that pressure tactics be applied against Great Britain by German
moves in East Asia. During 1894-1903 various agents were sent
by the Deutsch-Ostafrikanische Gesellschaft to the Indian subconti-
nent to recruit labourers illegally. (18) Success in these illegal
recruitment ventures does not seem to have been great. (19) Around
the turn of the century however, the prospects for getting Indian
families as farmer settlers in German East Africa seemed to be
brighter. In 1899 the Aga Khan, the influential religious head of
the Ismaili Muslims took an interest in the plan. He visited German East Africa that same year and was in Berlin the next. In
both places he was greeted with high honour. Out of the interest
that he showed emerged a plan for forming a settlement society
with its seat at Zanzibar to recruit Khoja agriculturists from the
Punjab for German East Africa. In February 1900, after the Aga
Khan had agreed, the German Consul General at Calcutta, Waldthausen met T.W. Holderness, Secretary to the Revenue and Agricultural Department, which was responsible for Indian emigration.
Waldthausen explained the German proposal that cultivable land
could be assigned to the Indians under advantageous terms if they
were to come to the German colony as real immigrants with a
view to settlling permanently as German subjects. (20) Waldthausen's
proposal was seriously considered by the Government Departments,
including that of Foreign Affairs, and eventually it went to the
Viceroy. Meanwhile both the Chancellor and the Kaiser were hopeful
about the settlement of Indian families in German East Africa. In
December 1900 when Bülow told the Kaiser about the progress of
the Settlement Society, the latter found the whole thing 'very pleasant' and to Bülow's sentence that the Imperial civil servants would
be instructed to become acquainted with the laws and customs of

18) See Werner, pp. 296-7.

19) For example, in 1914 the German East African railway
staff included only 25 British Indians and 17 Goans. The
other staff members were 36 Europeans and 466 Africans.
M. F. Hill, Permanent Way: Vol. II, Story of the Tanganyika
Railways (Nairobi 1957) p. 109, quoted in Gregory, op. cit.,
p. 103. Gregory quotes another source giving the German
recruitment figure in 1902-3 as 100 agricultural labourers
from Ceylon and a number of artisans from Madras.

20) Waldthausen to Holderness, 20 February 1900, cited in
Gregory, op. cit., p. 105 and n. 1.

the new immigrants the Kaiser added: "and to make efforts to be helpful and nice and not to think that they are going to deal with 'Wasserpolacken'."(21) The hopes were actually in vain. Lord Curzon who was never known to be friendly to Germany, gave his final verdict on the matter thus: "I am opposed to the entire suggestion of making German East Africa pay (which it does not now) by means of Indian labour...If A. Khan means business, he will come through the Bombay Government."(22) Within a couple of years all hope for the project had to be given up anyway, as the Aga Khan and the Colonial Department of the German Foreign Office could not agree to each other's claim for a larger influence in the direction of the proposed society. Nor could the Aga Khan agree to the German demand that the Indian immigrants renounce their British allegiance.(23)

Although the plan to bring a large-scale Indian labour force did not materialise, it did not follow that the Indians were completely unconnected with the development of German East Africa. The story of the Indian business community in German East Africa makes this clear.

There were, by 1910, 6,723 Indians in German East Africa, with a large majority of Muslims. Most of them were traders or artisans from Gujrati-speaking areas of the western coast of India and more than a quarter of them lived in Dar es-Salaam. As there had been an age-old trade connection between East Africa and India, the Indians naturally followed the German administration into the interior of the colony. Skillfully they mediated trade between the railway and the village, becoming thereby an important factor in the economy of German East Africa.(24)

The success of the Indian trading communities subjected them, however, to the instant contempt by the German settlers. As

---

21) Werner, op.cit., p.298. The word 'Wasserpolacken' is used here perhaps to mean rough, disorderly or undignified people.

22) Gregory, op.cit., p.105.

23) Werner, op.cit., p.298; Aga Khan, India in Transition (London 1918) pp.119-22.

24) See J. Iliffe, Tanganyika under German Rule 1905-1912 (Cambridge 1969) pp.93-4.

businessmen with a near monopoly over the retail of important consumer goods they were considered dangerous commercial competitors. They were, further more, labelled as dangerous supporters of local rebellion against the European communities and looked upon as racial antagonists. In 1906 the settlers' organisations unleashed an attack on the Indian community on the ground that Indian businessmen kept their accounts in Gujrati language which caused difficulties in levying taxes and facilitated fraudulent bankruptcy. (25) In subsequent years besides proscriptions on the Indians' book-keeping, the settlers demanded prohibition of Indian immigration; a limit to their basic earnings; laws prohibiting them from giving credit to the Africans; and the introduction of security measures relating to their health and possible political involvement. (26)

In the beginning the German colonial administration did not favour the settlers' opposition to the Indian businessmen and Berlin, too, followed the advice of the official Germans in the colony. When the settlers' proposed that the Indians must keep their accounts in Swahili or in a European language the newly appointed Governor of the protectorate Albert Baron von Rechenberg, who was then about to leave Berlin for East Africa, advised the Government to reject the proposal. The Colonial Secretary Bernhard Dernburg also refused legislation on the proposal. In 1908 Dernburg in the Reichstag budget debates denounced the settlers' views on the Indians very bluntly: "It is truly wonderful that the small planter should really say that the Indians extort from the blacks. What then does the small planter want? He wants to replace the Indians. "(27)

What was uppermost in the minds of those concerned with German colonial administration and colonial big business was to transform German East Africa into a viable economic entity. The Deutsch-Ostafrikanische Gesellschaft, the Deutsch-Ostafrika-Linie and other big German export-import firms which depended upon the intermediary trade of the Indians were at one with Rechenberg in valuing and supporting the Indians. Rechenberg also argued that any discriminatory legislation against the Indians would violate the Congo Act and would lead to British reprisals against German trade in India. Rechenberg undoubtedly had good relations with the Indians, speaking their language as well as Arabic and Swahili. But his main reason for supporting the Indians was economic. He expected them to stimulate trade along the railways and was satisfied with the job they were doing.

---

25) Ibid., pp. 94-5.

26) See Werner, op. cit., p. 292.

27) Iliffe, op. cit., p. 95.

Until his resignation in 1911 Rechenberg persisted supporting
the Indians. But Dernburg, faced with growing pressure from
the right, from the Colonial Society and from the settlers'
supporters in the parties of order, especially in the anti-Islamic
Zentrum, gradually gave in. After the resignation of Rechenberg,
his successor regulated Indian immigration. (28)

The venomous invectives used against the Indian petty businessmen
by the settlers and the papers siding with them were full of racial
hatred. (29) Being settlers their fear of being engulfed by non-white
people and of facing competition in their day-to-day lives was not
unusual. Even those big German business houses supporting the
Indians were not free from racial prejudice. But they as well as
the official Germans in East Africa, Berlin and India were concerned with one great fear: the damage that discriminatory legislation against the Indians in German East Africa might bring to
German trade in India. The boycott of British goods in India
during the Swadeshi Movement made the official Germans doubly
cautious. (30)

2. German Economic Interests in India

Ever since the discovery of the sea passage to India the people
of Germanic descent from Central Europe began to take an active
interest in Indian trade. As early as 1504 the first 'Indian Con-
sortium' of German merchant houses was formed with an agreement

---

28) Ibid. , pp. 95-6.

29) Some of these papers were: Deutsche Tageszeitung; Deutsch-
Ostafrikanische Zeitung; Westfälische Zeitung; Deutscher
Courier and Frankfurter Zeitung. Some of the invectives
used were: 'yellow haggler', 'unclean Indian money purse',
'black ones' etc. ; see Werner, op. cit., pp. 291-2.

30) The representatives of the German East African Company
(DOAG), German East Africa Line (DOAL) and the heads
of the firms of O'Swald and Hansing to State Secretary
(Colonial Deptt.) Dernburg, 12 March 1908; Report of
German Consul General in Calcutta to A. A. , 16 April 1908
(pointing out that German exports to India amounted to
only 6, 0 million marks); Dernburg's declaration in
Reichstag agreeing with the opinions of the big business
houses. See ibid. , pp. 293-4.

with the Portuguese. (31) The voyage of the first two young Germans to India which followed soon after did not, however, result in much trade; it only produced the first German travelogue on India printed in 1509. (32) Although the Austrian Empire and the Prussian Kingdom later sponsored many a venture in the eighteenth century and many individual Germans were employed all along in the Dutch, English and French trading establishments in India, Germany as such, did not make any headway in her Indian trade until at least the last decade of the nineteenth century.

In 1854 for the first time a Prussian trade representation (Wahlkonsulat) was established in Calcutta. The areas covered by it were the Bengal presidency, the north-west provinces, and the province of Audh, including all the native states falling with in these areas. Two years later a branch (Konsulat) appeared in Bombay. (33) As the German overseas interests slowly grew, the lack of a fully fledged official consular representation in British India was greatly felt. Consequently, on 19 January 1886 the Reichstag acceded to the demands of the Foreign Office to open in Calcutta Imperial Germany's Consulate General. As mentioned earlier, the German Consul Generals in India were mostly occupied in observing and reporting Britain's political and diplomatic situation from her most precious and yet vulnerable possession. The bulk of the trade-commercial business continued to be conducted by the Wahlkonsulat which existed until 1914. Later, special trade experts were also attached to the Consulate General.

Germany's share in Indian trade gradually increased following the establishment of the consular-diplomatic connection. In the period 1887-88 with trade valued at 123 lakhs of rupees (34) she held a very low position in Indian trade ahead only of Aden, Asiatic Turkey and Japan. These were the last three in a list of nineteen countries trading with India: The countries above her were successively Zanzibar, Arabia, Australia, Persia, Mauritius, Ceylon, Belgium, Egypt, Austria, Italy, the United States of

---

31) See Walter Leifer, India and the Germans: 500 years of Indo-German Contact (Bombay 1971) p. 26.

32) Die Merfahrt written by one of the voyagers, Balthasar Sprenger. For details see ibid., ch. II, pp. 23-35.

33) For the names of the Wahlkonsuls in Calcutta from 1854 to 1914 and the consuls in Bombay during 1856-1888 and after see appendix I.

34) 1 lakh = 100,000; 1 rupee = approx. 1.50 mark.

America, Straits Settlements, France, China, Hongkong and the Treaty Ports and finally Great Britain at the top with trade valued at 8,776 lakhs of rupees.(35) From this low position in less than a decade Germany rose to fourth. In 1894-5 with trade valued at 94.5 million rupees she took up a position after Great Britain, China including Hongkong and Treaty Ports, and France.(36) So steadfast was Germany in increasing Indian trade that in 1912-13 she held second position, although the difference between hers and British trade was still great.(37)

Statistic show that the rise of Germany was at the cost of Britain. In second half of the 70's British exports constituted 82% of all the goods imported by India, but at the turn of the century it had already sunk to 69%, and by 1914 it had decreased by a further 5%. At the end of the 80's Britain's share of Indian exports was more than 50%. In 1908 she bought only 25% of India's goods, yet 11% of that was further exported to the British colonies. As against this picture Germany's share in Indian trade increased as follows: at the beginning of the 90's Germany imported 7.5% of India's goods. In 1897/98 she imported 7.8% and in 1913 10.8%. German export figures for the same periods were 2.3% and 3.5% and 6.9% respectively. In consequence of the increasing Indian trade, British goods exported in 1890/91 increased by 31% whereas German ones increased by 222%. Goods imported from India increased in Britain by 39% but in Germany by 323%.(38) Dr. Heyer (39) who was German Consul in Bombay for the period 1909-14, wrote in a report later that in the years immediately before the War Germany imported from India raw materials worth 300 to 400 million marks annually and exported to India her manufactured products worth about 100 million marks.(40)

---

35) Deutsches Handels-Archiv, compiled by the Ministry of Interior, Berlin (hereafter cited as H.A.) 1889 II, p.607.

36) H.A. 1897 II, p.209.

37) The following are some of the countries participating in Indian trade in 1912-13 with the trade valued in million marks: Great Britain, 2231; Germany, 569; American Continent, 411; China and Hongkong, 312; Japan, 303; France, 239; Belgium, 215; See H.A. 1914 II, p.843.

38) Werner, op.cit., pp.280-281.

39) For Heyer's career see above p. 89n.

40) Heyer to A.A., Amsterdam 13 February 1918, about 'Die Aussichten für die Wirtschaftsrichtungen des Reichs mit Indien nach dem I. Weltkrieg', Bundesarchiv, Koblenz (hereafter BAK) R 85/7039.

Germany's imports from India consisted mainly of rice, raw cotton, untanned hides and skins, raw jute, shellac, oil-seed, poppy, rape, manganese ore and tea. She exported to India cotton piece goods, synthetic dyes and other chemicals, metals and metal goods and large varieties of low-priced manufactured goods. (41) Dumping and very pushing sales methods adopted by the Germans (also by Japanese and American traders) were the main reason for the gradual growth of German exports. Before the War the Germans made strenuous efforts to conquer the Indian market by introducing miscellaneous manufactured articles suited to the taste of the masses of India at a price and on terms with which the English goods could not compete. The German traders not only sold cheaper, they also gave easier credit facilities and took more trouble to study the tastes of their customers. For instance, whilst the English merchants quoted f.o.b. the Germans quoted c.i.f. prices to save their customers the trouble of calculating freightage. (42)

The importance of Indian trade for Germany can be judged from the following facts. In 1913 goods bought by her from India amounted to 5% of her total imports whereas her exports to India amounted to 1.5% of all goods exported from Germany. Inge Werner, quoting the official files at the Potsdam Archive, shows the importance of the goods imported from India by the share they held of Germany's total imports of the same goods as follows (43):

Jute	97	per cent.
rice (unpolished)	90	" "
rice (polished)	70	" "
rapes and turnips	77	" "
sesam	25	" "
peanuts	21	" "
poppy	50	" "
flax-seed	11	" "
India-rubber	23	" "
dried ox skins	30	" "
goat skins	17	" "
shellac	98	" "
manganese ore	35	" ".

41) Ibid.

42) Reports on the Conditions and Prospects of British Trade in India, 1919, quoted in V. Anstey, The Economic Development of India (4th Ed. Lond. 1952) p. 342.

43) Werner, op. cit., p. 285.

160

Germany played an outstanding role in the Indian market with
her chemical and pharmaceutical products. In the supply of
aniline dyes she almost held a monopoly position creating a
great decline of the Indigo plantations in India after 1897. (44) The British obviously looked upon this economic loss with great jealousy
and during the period of the Boer War, when Anglo-German
antagonism conducted by the press in both countries was at a
high pitch, the Germans feared the possibility of severe restrictions on the sale of German synthetic dyes in British colonies. (45)
In 1907 the Verein zur Wahrung der Interessen der chemischen Industrie Deutschlands (Association for the protection of the interest
of Germany's chemical industry) was established with a branch also
in Bombay where there were agents of three big chemical firms,
namely Farbenfabrik Bayer & Co. Ltd., Elberfeld, Berliner Anilin
Co., Frankfurt-on-Main, and Ostermayer & Co. (Badische Anilin-
und Sodafabrik). (46) Apart from chemicals Germany also tried to
sell the products of her heavy industry although her attempts to
export railway material were frustrated by Britain's almost complete
monopoly.

Just as in trade, Germany ranked second after Britain in sea traffic
to India in the years immediately before the War. And this direct
marine connection also enhanced the progress of German trade with
India. German shipping lines were run by the German Steamer
Company, Hansa, Bremen; German-East Africa Line; Hamburg-
America Line; German-Australian Steamer Company; and North
German Lloyd. In 1896 a branch of the German Asiatic Bank was
established in Calcutta and the Germans also tried to invest capital
in India.

The position that Germany achieved in her Indian trade before
the First World War was certainly not a mean one when one
considers the trying circumstances under which those involved
in it had to work. Besides the normal jealousy of the British,
Anglo-German mutual antagonism since the turn of the century
and the jingoistic and chauvinistic elements in both countries
kept German business and official circle in India in a state of

44) Anstey, op. cit., p. 288.

45) 'Ein beabsichtigter Schlag gegen den deutschen Handel',
    Calcutta correspondent's report on 8 February 1900 to
    Welt-Korrespondenz 27 February 1900. AABI 22.

46) Asiatisches Jahrbuch (Ed. Vosberg-Rekow) (Berlin 1914)
    pp. 174-6.

perpetual anxiety over it. In the early months of 1900 for example,
a nearly catastrophic situation arose when a controversial report
appeared in Berliner Neueste Nachrichten throwing doubts on the
loyalty of the Indian princes and making disparaging remarks
about those Englishmen in India who out of patriotic feelings had
joined Lumsden's Horse to participate in the South African War.
The report, written by one Dr. Noetling from Calcutta and which
had earlier appeared in Welt-Korrespondenz, came under criticism
both in The Times and the Anglo-Indian press.(47) The result was
great anti-German feeling in Calcutta: the biggest crisis, the
Austro-Hungarian Wahlkonsul told Waldthausen, that the German
community in India had faced for decades.(48) The official Germans
and the German business circle in India were very upset about
the incident fearing inevitable harm to German trade. They took
the earliest opportunity to express their regret about the report
and to contradict its views.(49) The Kaiser's Indian famine relief
gift in May 1900 which had several motives, was also especially
timed to counteract the anti-German feeling so far as it was
encouraged by the Berlin articles. The general appreciation that
the Kaiser's donation and message found in India encouraged
Waldthausen to think that it would probably wipe out the current
anti-German mood in India.(50)

As the twentieth century advanced and along with it the rivalry
between Germany and Great Britain on the one hand and the
political consciousness of the educated Indians on the other, the
German fear for the safety of their trade in India increased. In
1902, when the Anglo-German relations were at cross roads, the
Germans in India were apprehensive again of the Indian Government's

---

47) 'Gährung in Indien', Calcutta correspondent's report of 25
January 1900 in Welt-Korrespondenz, Berlin, ? February 1900,
in AABI 22; See also The Indian Daily News, Calcutta 22 February,
Englishman, Calcutta 10 March 1900. In a later issue (27 February)
Welt-Korrespondenz rebutted The Times criticism of its earlier
article and made a policy statement saying that "it is of vital importance that the people of a country with such huge world political
and world trade-political interests as the German Empire should
be given a correct picture of the conditions in overseas countries."

48) Waldthausen to Hohenlohe, Calcutta 5 March 1900, AABI 22.

49) Otto Hadenfeldt, President, German Association (Deutscher Verein)
to Lt. Col. Lumsden, Calcutta 23 February 1900; R. Schenk's
(a German broker) letter in The Indian Daily News, 24 February
1900. Ibid.

50) Waldthausen to Hohenlohe, Calcutta 18 May 1900, AABI 23.

putting obstacles in the way of trade. In particular they feared that the Government might cancel an order for forty locomotives which a German firm had agreed to supply not only at a price, £ 30,000 lower than that quoted by English manufacturers, but also with a shorter delivery period. (51)

Being ideologically opposed to the political aspirations of the educated Indians and being also true admirers of the British rule in India, the Germans in India, and particularly the official ones, had no sympathy for the Indian nationalists and even less for those with a revolutionary bent who created conditions uncongenial to economic development. Their views were the same as expressed by the Vossische Zeitung on 24 July 1908:

> "We consider the maintenance of British rule in India as great luck not only for Britain but also for all other people including Germany whose imports from there amounted to 407 million marks in 1907 and whose exports to that country amounted to 105 million marks. These figures would be considerably higher if one included the indirect imports and exports via Britain, Antwerp, Genoa, Triest. "(52)

Yet the fact that Indian revolutionaries were also operating from abroad and some of them advocating a united cause with Germany against Britain, tempting the Germans with greater economic pros- pects in an India without the British (53) made it no easier for the Germans in India to operate freely. In the years immediately before the War German consular officers in India faced restrictions on free movement in the interior of the country for business pur- pose. (54) As the War approached, the Indian Government further widened its intelligence activities.

In November 1908 Berlin as well as the Germans in India got an opportunity to show their complete disassociation with Indian unrest. In that month, quoting the London Standard the Nationalzeitung reported that the British customs in India had lately confiscated a box full of seditious oil paintings imported from Germany by an Inidan. One Abinash Chandra Chatterjee, a Bengali artist from Calcutta, got a painting of his entitled 'Blessed Oppressed' printed by the firm of Brauer & Westphal in Hamburg. The painting was no doubt political and akin to that already current in Bengal

51) See 'Anglophobia and Trade', Englishman 9 January 1902.

52) 'Der Ernst der indischen Frage für England', Vossische Zeitung 24 July 1908, quoted in Werner, op. cit., p. 275.

53) See below ch. VIII p. 185.

54) Heyer to A. A. , Amsterdam 13 February 1918, BAK 85/7039.

showing oppressed 'Mother India' calling for sacrifices from her brave sons.(55) On an elaborate enquirey from the German official side it was established beyond doubt that the Hamburg firm had absolutely no idea of any political implication of the painting.(56) The German Consul General in India gave his full co-operation to the Calcutta police in enquiring into the details of the matter and the latter expressed their full satisfaction.(57)

The prosperity of German trade in India did not, however, depend only on the good behaviour of the Germans in India. It depended largely on how much the British themselves were prepared to accomodate the Germans keeping in mind their own economic and political interests. As early as March 1900 an Anglo-Indian journal representing the views of the British commercial class there wrote:

> "The commercial progress of Germany is a thing independent of the Government. It must continue up to the time when the inevitable rupture comes - a rupture which will take one of two forms, either the closing of the doors of the British Empire to German trade, or the coming to a head of the diplomatic and racial hostility which time is steadily accentuating."(58)

---

55) Below to Bülow, Calcutta 20 January 1909, AABI 44.

56) See 'Geschäft und Politik', Hamburgischer Correspondent 17 February 1909. The Hamburg firm mentioned that not only the fact that the order came through their British agent in Calcutta but also the attainment of the certificate of merit by the painting at the Indian Industrial and Agricultural Exhibition in Calcutta in 1907 left them beyond any doubt about the merit of the painting.

57) Below to Bülow, Calcutta 20 January 1909, AABI 44.

58) 'German Expansion Vs. British Possession', Englishman 1 March 1900.

PART THREE

BERLIN'S RECONCILIATION WITH

INDIAN NATIONALISM

AUGUST - DECEMBER 1914

VIII THE BEGINNING OF BERLIN'S WAR-TIME ALLIANCE WITH INDIAN REVOLUTIONISTS

"Now our job is to show up the whole business ruthlessly
and tear away the mask of Christian peacemaking and put
the pharsical hypocrisy about peace in the pillory!!! And
our consuls in Turkey and India, agents, etc. must get
a conflagration going throughout the whole Mohamedan
world against this hated, unscrupulous, dishonest nation
of shopkeepers - since if we are going to bleed to death,
England must at least lose India."

Kaiser Wilhelm II on the night of
30 - 31 July 1914

"It is a great privilege for us Oriental revolutionists to
work in co-operation with the great and powerful German
Government..."

Har Dayal to Consul General Geißler
Geneva, 19 October 1914

1. The War and Germany's Threat-to-India Policy

We have seen (1) that ever since Germany took to the course of
Weltpolitik she had been interested in seeing Turkey's influence
in Afghanistan and among the Indian Muslims. When Anglo-German
rivalry gradually took a collision course in the early years of the
twentieth century, the Kaiser and the German Foreign Office were
happy to see Britain's deteriorating relations with Turkey with the
same object in view: the possibility of endangering British India
through the Turkey-oriented Muslims of Afghanistan and Northern
India. Until 1913 however, the official Germans in India neither
shared the belief of the Kaiser and the German Foreign Office
that British India could be dangerously threatened by a foreign
power, nor were they as optimistic as the Kaiser about the Turkey-
oriented Indian Muslims' power to endanger British India internally.
But in 1913 it was a German Consul General in India who for the
first time recommended to Berlin an active anti-British policy in
India. The growth of Pan-Islamism in India especially since 1912,
coupled with the latent terrorist movement, was responsible for
this change in the time-honoured view of official Germans in India.

---

1) See above pp. 49-57.

The hopes that the growth of Pan-Islamism in India aroused in Luxburg in 1913 (2) gave authenticity to what had already been assumed in some quarters of the German military circle. As early as October 1911 General Friedrich von Bernhardi published his much circulated book Germany and the Next War where, while pleading for a war with Britain, he tried to show how the precarious conditions prevailing for the British in India would come to German advantage. "England so far, in accordance with the principle of divide et impera has attempted to play off the Mohammedan against the Hindu population," wrote Bernhardi and added: "But now that a pronounced revolutionary and nationalist tendency shows among the latter, the danger is imminent that Pan-Islamism, thoroughly roused, should unite with the revolutionary elements of Bengal. The co-operation of these elements might create a very grave danger, capable of shaking the foundations of England's high position in the world."(3) Gradually the German newspapers began to give information about the revolutionary nationalists abroad.(4)

On the eve of the War these developments in the internal Indian scene were very reassuring to Kaiser Wilhelm II who, irrespective of the views of others, had long been convinced of Turkey's hold on the Indian Muslims and of the latters' power to bring disorder to British rule in India. Thus on the night of 30-31 July 1914 when he read a report from the German Ambassador at St. Petersburg that according to Sazonov Russian mobilisation could not be reversed and inferred therefrom that war was inevitable, he wrote the following in the excitement of the moment:

> "Now our job is to show up the whole business ruthlessly and tear away the mask of Christian peacemaking and put the pharsical hypocrisy about peace in the pillory!!! And our consuls in Turkey and India, agents, etc. must get a conflagration going throughout the whole Mohamedan world against this hated, unscrupulous, dishonest nation of shopkeepers - since if we are going to bleed to death, England must at least lose India."(5)

---

2) See above p. 90.

3) General F. von Bernhardi, Germany and the Next War (London 1911) p. 96.

4) See for example Leipziger Neueste Nachrichten 1 April 1913 (see below p. 185 and n) and Berliner Tageblatt 6 March 1914, for Dr. Johannes Tschiedel's article on 'Englands indische Sorge'.

5) Deutsche Dokumente zum Kriegsausbruch (hereafter D.D.) (1927) II no. 401, p. 120; The English version from Balfour, op.cit., pp. 351-2.

Here the Kaiser was within the concept of the German Oriental policy expressed as early as 1898 in his own famous Damascus speech. The dominant belief that guided this policy was that in case of a war against England and Russia, Germany would get the support of the Muslim people living under the subjugation of both these countries. (6)

Throughout our period of study the Kaiser took a special interest in sending copies of important political despatches from India to the German General Staff and Admiral Tirpitz. Since 1912 the General Staff's own eagerness to know the latest military and political conditions in India increased, with special reference to the mood of the Muslim population. (7) When the War ultimately came General von Moltke wrote to the German Foreign Office on 2 August 1914, the day of the treaty between Germany and Turkey, emphasising this:

> "If Britain becomes our opponent, attempts will have to
> be made to instigate a rebellion in India. The same has
> to be tried in Egypt... Persia must be called upon to
> make use of the favourable opportunity to throw off the
> Russian yoke and, if possible, to act together with
> Turkey. "(8)

In this connection the military importance of the Baghdad Railway also came to the forefront. General von der Goltz spoke forth-rightly about its connection with British India. In his view to force Britain to her knees an invasion might become necessary either in Egypt or in India, and in both cases the Baghdad line was needed. On 26 February 1915 Goltz assessed the importance of the speedy construction of the Asia-Minor Railway. A march on India, Goltz declared, was not a 'fairy tale adventure' by any

---

6) Wilhelm II, until almost the very end of the War, was looking for means of threatenning British India. On 7 June 1918 for example, he emphatically endorsed proposals for incorporating Georgia in the Reich and stressed the importance of Trans-caucasia as a bridge to Central Asia and a threat to British possessions in India. See F. Fischer, Griff nach der Weltmacht (Düsseldorf 1961) p. 732; Balfour, op. cit., p. 390.

7) Chief of the General Staff to A. A., Berlin 21 November 1912, AABI 49; Luxburg to General Staff (secret), Calcutta 15 Jan. 1914, AABI 50; Major Hochwaechter to A. A., Colombo 16 April 1914, AABI 51.

8) D. D. Vol. 3, no. 662, pp. 133-36. On 5 August Moltke repeated this request. D. D. Vol. 4, no. 876, pp. 94-5.

means; for what Shah Nadar of Persia had accomplished in the eighteenth century and others like Alexander the Great and Tamerlane before him, could certainly be done 'with the perfect means of the modern age'. Indeed, a carefully prepared campaign against India would constitute a 'worthy and decisive conclusion' to the present world conflict. (9)

Once the instigation of a revolution in the Mohamedan world became a military necessity, German diplomatic agents immediately became busy finding ways to do it. In fact it was already too late to organise a Pan-Islamic movement as the German Ambassador in Turkey, Wangenheim, was to comment towards the end of August 1914. Only by quick and determined action could Germany now, in his view, make up for the blunder of omitting such preparations in the pre-War period. (10) The man who took the lead at the beginning in organising the Pan-Islamic movement on behalf of the German Foreign Office was Baron Max von Oppenheim. (11) Oppenheim, who has been credited as the spiritual father of the Kaiser's famous

9) A.A. Türkei 152, vol. 79, quoted in U. Trumpener, Germany and the Ottoman Empire 1914-1918 (Princeton 1968) p. 291.

10) Wangenheim to A.A., Therapia 26 August 1914, telg., Auswärtiges Amt, Bonn, Weltkriegsakten (hereafter WK) vol. 1, p. 39. Wangenheim got full encouragement from the Foreign Office to go ahead with any action against British colonial possessions. Ibid., p. 40, Zimmermann's reply to Wangenheim 27 August 1914.

11) Dr. Max Adrian Simon Baron von Oppenheim (1860-1946): 1883 doctorate in Jurisprudence (Göttingen); 1896 attached to Consulate General, Cairo and extensive study tours in Islamic countries, mainly in the Arab world, emerging famous as an archaeologist through his expedition to the Chad Lake area; 1896-1910 Attaché, Consulate General Cairo; 1910 designated as 'Ministerresident' but left Foreign Office of his own wish; 1911-1913 engaged in archaeological excavations on the Hittite city of Tel Halaf; August 1914 in Foreign Office again and founded in Berlin the Nachrichtenstelle für den Orient (Information Service for the Orient); 1915 attached to Embassy in Constantinople to organise information and propaganda centre. See also W. Caskel, 'Max Freiherr von Oppenheim 1860 - 1946', Zeitschrift der Deutschen Morgenländischen Gesellschaft (Wiesbaden 1951) vol. 101; W. Treue, 'Max Freiherr von Oppenheim - der Archäologe und die Politik', Historische Zeitschrift (München 1969) vol. 209, I, pp. 37-74.

Damascus speech of 1898 (12) and who had been informing himself about the Indian Muslims for quite some time (13) wrote to the German Foreign Office on 18 August 1914 thus:

"Britain knows that once she is pushed out of India she may never get India back again. If there were deeper unrest in India Britain would be forced to send a major portion of her fleet to Indian waters to protect the numerous British interests, the British people there, and the British world position. British public opinion would also want it and thus Britain would have to conclude an early peace favourable to us..."(14)

The concrete shape of Germany's threat-to-India programme came however from an idea of Envar Pasha whose great wish it was to see a group of German military officers, dressed like Muslims, accompany a group of Turkish officers to the Amir of Afghanistan who according to Envar was only waiting for encouragement to attack India. (15) Wangenheim informed Berlin about this wish of Envar and the German Foreign Office was ready to co-operate.

---

12) See Fischer, Germany's Aims... p. 123; Prof. Wilhelm Treue who happens to be also the keeper of the Records of 'Bankhaus Oppenheim' in Cologne, refutes Fischer's assertion that Oppenheim submitted to Kaiser Wilhelm II his thesis about the world political importance of the Pan-Islamic movement. But Professor Treue does not rule out Oppenheim's indirect influence on the Kaiser's speech and he even says that Count Metternich who accompanied the Kaiser on his Orient trip might have presented to the Kaiser Oppenheim's papers (see W. Treue, op. cit.). From our study (see above pp. 49-57) it is clear, however, that the Kaiser's interest in Turkey-oriented Muslim politics in Asia for the benefit of German diplomacy dated from earlier than 1898.

13) On 20 February 1909 Oppenheim sent from Cairo to the Imperial Chancellor Bülow a report on the contemporary Indian political situation after his meeting with the Aga Khan. On 16 May the same year he submitted a report on the close relationship between the Indian Muslims and the Egyptians. AABI 44.

14) Oppenheim to Bethmann-Hollweg, Berlin 18 August 1914, W. K. 11, 1, p. 32.

15) U. Gehrke, Persien in der deutschen Orientpolitik während des I. Weltkrieges (Stuttgart 1960) p. 23, n. 8 and 9.

Oppenheim worked enthusiastically in selecting the German group
and he was able to inform Envar Pasha before the end of August
1914 that 15 people were ready to participate in the Afghan expedition. (16) Information from the Swedish explorer Sven Hedin
that the Amir of Afghanistan 'was burning with desire to attack
British India' gave impetus to the venture from the start. (17)
The preparatory work from the German side was put into the
hands of a commission. (18) On 4 September Wangenheim recorded
that in the Turkish War Ministry a central office for the Islamic
Movement had recently been formed. (19) Ali Bey Bashhamba of
this office, known as Tashkilat-i-Mukhsusa, and Fuad Bey of the
Turkish Secret Service were the contact men for the anti-British
Indian revolutionists in Turkey. In Constantinople an Indian, Abu
Said el-Arabi, was also given editorial charge of the Urdu portion
of the Pan-Islamic journal Jehan-i-Islam. (20)

2. Indian Revolutionists in Europe and North America

While such preparations for an Indian revolution were going on in
Berlin and Constantinople, some of the Indian revolutionary nationalists living abroad also seem to have agreed that their objective
would best be served by siding with the Germans in the War. But
before discussing how they came to be associated with the German
plans, a peep into their checkered lives in London, Paris and some
North American cities is essential, for in these places they had
formed their main centres of activity.

In autumn 1897, the year which saw the first act of organised
political terrorism against the British in India following the bubonic

---

16) Ibid., p. 23.

17) Reichenau to A.A., Stockholm 25 August 1914, W.K.e. 1.

18) The commission consisted of: von Holtzendorf, Director,
    Hamburg-America Line; H.R. Mannesmann, firm Mannes-
    mann-Roselius; Naval Captain Löhlein, Reichsmarineamt;
    Ministerresident Baron von Oppenheim; Dr. Ernst Jaeckh,
    Orient publicist; and Legation Secretary von Prittwitz,
    deputy of Dirigent Baron Langwerth in Foreign Office.
    Prittwitz's note on the sitting of 4 September 1914, W.K.e., 1.

19) W.K. 1, 4 September 1914, p. 64.

20) Details of the war-time activities of the Indians in Turkey
    form part of a separate work of this author on the Berlin
    India Committee.

plague in Poona that year, Shyamaji Krishnavarma (21), the wealthy would-be patron saint of the Indian revolutionaries in Europe - and indirectly in America - left India for good. He was 40 years old with a mission to preach and propagate from a safer place militant ways to end the British rule of India.

In England Shyamaji spent a long period of comparative quietness devoted mainly to the study of the works of Herbert Spencer and preparing his future political course. As his biographer tells us he devoted the period between 1897 and 1905 to cultivating personal contacts with many people of advanced views - the rationalist thinkers, Social Democrats, British Socialists and Irish Republicans - and generally those who were fighting for liberty in any part of the world. (22) But in January 1905 he issued the first number of his Indian Sociologist (23), a penny monthly as "An Organ of Freedom of Political, Social and Religious Reform." The journal, which was the first Indian extremist journal from abroad, initiated an attack both on British rule in India and its supporters - the Moderate Congressmen. Shyamaji offered six lectureships and three travelling scholarships to young Indians to enable them to go abroad to complete an education that would help them in the struggle for national independence. In February 'The Indian Home Rule Society' was formed at Shyamaji's house in Highgate, London, on the lines of the Irish Home Rule Movement, with the aims 1) to secure Home Rule for India; 2) to carry on propaganda in the United Kingdom by all practical means to attain this end; and 3) to spread amongst the people of India a knowledge of the advantages of freedom and national unity. In July of the same year a hostel for Indian students, the famous 'India House', was opened in Highgate. (24) In all these activities Shyamaji

---

21) The most authentic biography of Krishnavarma from the latter's own private papers is: Indulal Yajnik, Shyamaji Krishnavarma: Life and Times of an Indian Revolutionary (Bombay 1950).

22) Yajnik, op. cit., p. 17.

23) It appeared regularly every month until July 1914 although its centre of publication changed in 1907 to Paris and then, on the eve of the War, to Geneva. The importation of this journal to India was prohibited by a notification under the Sea Customs Act, 19 September 1907. Copies, however, continued to be sent to India in covers which were changed from time to time to escape detection. J. C. Ker, Political Trouble in India (Calcutta 1917) (A Government of India publication from the records of the Intelligence Department) p. 106.

24) Ibid., pp. 130, 141.

was inspired among others by the British Social Democratic leader
H. M. Hyndman. Due particularly to the Minto Government's concern (25), Shyamaji's propaganda activities were criticised first in
the British press led by The Times in May 1907 and later also in
Parliament. In June that year Shyamaji moved to Paris.(26)

When Shyamaji left 'India House' virtually came under the control
of one of the first holders of Shyamaji's travelling scholarships,
Vinayak Damodar Savarkar, a 22-year-old graduate from Bombay.
Savarkar was already an experienced man in revolutionary propaganda
having edited a journal, Vihari, in Bombay before coming to England
in the middle of June 1906. In England he translated Mazzini's
autobiography into Marathi, adding an introduction of his own emphasising the importance of elevating politics to the rank of a religion.
It pointed out how Mazzini relied upon the youth of the country to
attain independence. Savarkar also wrote a history of the rebellion
of 1857 entitled The Indian War of Independence which became a
bible for Indian revolutionaries. He formed his own select group
of revolutionaries known as Abhinav Bharat (Young India), with
regular weekly meetings and issued various revolutionary leaflets
from time to time, especially on the occasion of the annual 1857
rebellion celebrations which took place regularly at 'India House'.

'India House' under Savarkar became an active centre for revolutionary programmes. Buying and sending pistols to India; learning
bomb making; sending bomb making manuals to India; courses in
shooting; and formulating policy concerning political assassination
became regular occupations of the inmates and their associates.
The Indian revolutionaries who, due to their personal differences
with Shyamaji, had stayed away from the 'India House' activities
now joined Savarkar. Three of Savarkar's colleagues at this period,
whom we shall later meet also in the Berlin Committee, were
Virendranath Chattopadhyaya, M. P. T. Acharya and for a short
time Har Dayal. The most practical minded assistant was, however,
V. V. S. Aiyar.(27)

As a result of these activities several assassinations took place
in India and one in London involving 'India House' directly.
Vinayak Savarkar's brother Ganesh wrote and published two books
of songs which the Government considered seditious and he was
sentenced to transportation for life. It was alleged that Vinayak
instigated murder of Englishmen at the 'India House' meetings in

---

25) See S. R. Wasti, Lord Minto and the Indian Nationalist Move-
    ment 1905 to 1910 (London 1964) pp. 91-92.

26) Yajnik, op. cit., pp. 220-1.

27) Ibid., p. 263; Ker, op. cit., pp. 172, 175, 177-8.

revenge for this. The direct result of this was that in London on 1 July 1909 Sir William Curzon Wyllie, the Political A. D. C. at the India Office, was killed by Madan Lal Dhigra, an inmate of 'India House'. Early in February that year Vinayak had sent 20 Browning pistols to his brother, and these arrived in India at the time when Ganesh's appeal to the High Court in Bombay was dismissed on 18 November 1909. On 21 December A. M. T. Jackson, the District Magistrate of Nasik, was shot dead with one of the pistols sent from London.

As a consequence of this incident Vinayak Savarkar left London for Paris on 6 January 1910. But against Shyamaji's advice he returned to London on 13 March only to be caught by the police on his arrival. In July he was sent to India for prosecution. An important ramification of the Nasik conspiracy was traced also to Gwalior. (28)

When Vinayak Savarkar was caught the old London group was completely shattered. Neither Aiyar nor Chattopadhyaya had Vinayak's personality to command loyalty. The former, however, was more practical than Chattopadhyaya who had the greater intellectual ability. Both combined perhaps could have managed the organisation but being suspects and closely observed they soon made their way to Paris in 1910.

In Paris there was Shyamaji Krishnavarma carrying on his journalistic propaganda as vigorously as before stressing passive resistance but not failing at the same time to praise every successful violent action by the Indian revolutionists. But in Paris he was no longer considered the leader by the old London group. (29) The Paris group was under the patronage of Madame Cama and S. R. Rana. While Rana (30), a scion of a princely house in Gujarat, was

---

28) Ker, op. cit., pp. 186-7; Wasti, op. cit., p. 123.

29) See Chattopadhyaya's letter in The Times, 1 March 1909, denouncing Shyamaji, quoted in Yajnik, op. cit., pp. 263-4.

30) Born in a princely family in Kathiawar in 1878 Sardar-singhji Rewabhai Rana was educated in England. About 1899 he went to Paris to do business in pearls. However, he kept his revolutionary activities going alongside and in 1905, soon after Shyamaji's declaration of travelling scholarships, he too donated money for three such scholarships. He also associated himself with Shyamaji's 'India House Society', taking care of it after Shyamaji had left London.

mainly an able nationalist-minded businessman, Cama (31) was a
firebrand revolutionist with good contacts in socialist circles.
At the International Socialist Congress of 1907 at Stuttgart she
defied the protests of the British delegation and brought an
unofficial resolution condemning British imperialism in India. (32)
She also maintained a good relationship with the French socialist
press.

The activities of the Paris group were mainly literary although
the facility that Paris offered in procuring arms led the group
to take advantage of it. (33) Besides Hem Chandra Das who learnt
bombmaking in Paris three other young revolutionaries, formerly
of the London group, played a dominant role in the active days
of the Paris group after the autumn of 1909. They were Har Dayal,
V. V. S. Aiyer and V. Chattopadhyaya.

Born in 1884 in Delhi and a graduate of the Punjab University in
1903, Har Dayal had gone to Oxford with a government scholarship
in 1905 to study History and Economics. (34) It is said that at Oxford

---

31) Madame Bhikaiji Rustom Cama, a Parsi lady, born about 1875,
was the guiding spirit of the Paris group. She had left India
about 1902 and after travelling in Scotland, France, England
and America she settled down finally in Paris about the middle
of 1909. Madame Cama followed exactly the same line as
Vinayak Savarkar: instigating violence and terror.

32) See Internationaler Sozialisten-Kongreß Stuttgart 1907 vom
18. bis 24. August (Berlin 1907) pp. 38-9, 131.

33) The Browning pistols which Savarkar sent to India from London
were originally purchased in Paris.

34) Har Dayal was essentially a scholar. The following is an
outline of his academic and scholastic career: 1903 B. A.;
1905 M. A.; 1903-5 Aitchison Ramrattan Sanskrit scholar,
Punjab University; 1905 Lecturer in History and Economics,
St. Stephen's College, Delhi; 1905-7 Govt. of India scholar
in History and Economics, Oxford; 1907 Bowden Sanskrit
scholar, Oxford; 1907 Casberd Exhibitioner in History,
St. John's College, Oxford; 1911 lecturer in Indian Philosophy, Stanford University, California. After his revolutionary career which he practically discarded in 1916 he
took to serious scholastic life again. He got a Doctorate
in Philosophy from the University of London in 1930 for his
work on The Bodhisatta Doctrine in Buddhist Sanskrit Literature (2 Vols.). His other scholarly works are: Hints for
Self-Culture (London 1934) and Twelve Religions and Modern
Life (London 1938).

he came to believe that the English were undermining the Hindu character, that their educational policy and methods had been designed to destroy Hinduism and to perpetuate the political bondage of the Hindus by destroying their social consciousness and their national individuality. (35) Holding such views and being in constant touch with Bhai Paramanand (36) in London, who often visited 'India House, Har Dayal could not have gone for long without meeting Shyamaji who, besides being a revolutionary, was also a great Sanskrit scholar - an additional attraction for Har Dayal. Har Dayal met Shyamaji in April 1906 and during the whole year of 1907 had correspondence with him. (37) In the May 1907 issue of Shyamaji's paper Indian Sociologist Har Dayal suggested what sort of persons would be best suited for Shyamaji's proposed new organisation of political missionaries. The views expressed by Har Dayal in this article are particularly interesting because in all his later political activities, to which we shall soon come, he maintained the same uncompromisingly extreme view as maintained there. "What sort of men do we want for this society?" he asked and then answered himself: "They should love nothing more than the cause. It should be to them in the place of father, mother, brother and friend. They should reject the counsels of timid prudence, the 'false reptile prudence' anathemised by Burke, even if they come from the nearest and dearest relatives. They should undertake the task in a religious spirit; earnestness and self-denial should be their guiding principles. They should grieve like Commander Hirose of Japan that they have only one life to give to their country. If such men appeal to the down-trodden masses of India, they would conquer the hearts of the multitude of our people, who pay sincere homage to genuine character, but are not moved by mere rhetoric... "(38)

Within a few months Har Dayal renounced the government stipend; cultivated friendship with Shyamaji; and submitted elaborate schemes to him to expand the new society, 'India House' and the Indian Sociologist. In January 1908 however, he left for India with his ailing wife.

---

35) Lajpat Rai, Young India (New York 1917) p. 196.

36) Bhai Parmanand was a leading person in the Arya Samaj movement and a friend both of Lajpat Rai and Har Dayal. cf. Sedition Committee, Report, 1918, p. 100.

37) Dharm Vira, Lala Har Dayal and Revolutionary Movement of his Times (New Delhi 1970) pp. 17, 34; Yajnik, op. cit., p. 201.

38) Quoted in Yajnik, op. cit., p. 200.

Returning to India Har Dayal met Tilak for advice on his proposed future political course in the Punjab. Tilak did not fail to see the burning zeal and intelligence of Har Dayal and wrote to Shyamaji on 14 February, 1908: "I saw Mr. Har Dayal and have given him my views regarding the work to be done in the Punjab...I think he will soon develop into a strength to the Nationalist Party generally."(39) However, in the Punjab Har Dayal preached to his followers a very extreme form of passive resistance or disassociation advocating that true nationalism required that one should not help the government even by working as pleader in court. This was too much for most of his followers who were pleaders themselves and even the nationalist paper The Punjabee on 5 August 1908 repudiated Har Dayal as a 'quixotic dreamer'. In the same month he left again for Europe and after staying for a time in London went to Paris towards the end of 1909.(40)

In Paris Har Dayal took charge of the editorship of Madame Cama's Bande Mataram, 'a monthly organ of Indian Independence', the first number of which appeared on 10 September 1909. In the February 1910 issue Har Dayal held that an enslaved people must pass through three stages before it can again establish itself as a member of the community of nations: 1) moral and intellectual preparation, in which the heart of the craven people must be purified - the spirit of the slave must desappear before slavery; 2) the stage of war - the debris of the old regime must be removed by the sword; 3) the work of reconstruction and consolidation. "After Mazzini, Garibaldi; after Garibaldi, Cavour. Even so, it must be with us. Virtue and Wisdom first: then war: finally independence..."(41) During this time Har Dayal also saw the advisability of Indian revolutionaries having connections with Germany.(42) Har Dayal, however, did not stay long in Paris. In April 1910 he went to Algiers for his health and returned to Paris in July. In the following October he went to Martinique and from there to the United States of America in January 1911.

The next person, V. V. S. Aiyar from Trichinopoly and a graduate from Madras University, was more a practical than a literary man. In 1908 he went to England and became a close associate of Savarkar with whom he was one in the view that terrorism and assassination

---

39) Ibid., p. 243.

40) Ker, op. cit., p. 196.

41) Yajnik, op. cit., pp. 273-4; Ker, op. cit., p. 113.

42) Bande Mataram, February 1910.

were only the first stage of revolution and although it should be
carried on vigorously for the present they ought to keep in view
their ultimate goal, namely a final revolution and a pitched battle
with the English forces. It was necessary therefore to send men
to America or France to learn the manufacture of the latest type
of arms and ammunition and to study the essentials of military
training. The only proper limitation of terrorism or individual
assassination was collective assassination or war. (43) In October
1910 Aiyar returned to India and remained active in revolutionary
propaganda in South India. His indirect connection with the Tinnevelly murder case (44) in 1911 was detected.

The third important, young active member of the Cama-Rana group
was Virendranath Chattopadhyaya. Chatto (45), as he was generally
known, was born in 1880 in a distinguished Bengali family of
Hyderabad. He was the eldest son of Dr. Aghorenath Chattopadhyay,
who after his studies in Scotland and Germany became the Principal
and Professor of Science at the Nizam's College, Hyderabad State.
Chatto grew up with wide all-India mindedness and learning foreign
languages was one of his early interests. (46) After his graduation
from Calcutta University Chatto went to England in 1902. During
the period of Savarkar's leadership at 'India House' Chatto associated himself with the activities of the House and even supported
Savarkar's action publicly. (47) From London Chatto tried to maintain
contact with the revolutionaries of Hyderabad and Bengal and as soon
as he arrived in Paris in June 1910 he planned to send rifles to
Calcutta. This plan, however, did not succeed. (48)

Chatto's concrete work during 1909 - 1910 was his editing of the
paper The Talvar (The Sword) financed by Madame Cama. The
first issue was shown to be printed in Berlin in November 1909
although the printing was actually done in Rotterdam. Supporting
the terrorist acts which were then sporadically going on in India
and which were termed as anarchism by the Government, the
December issue of the paper wrote: "But if it is anarchism to be

---

43) Ker, op. cit. , p. 187.

44) Murder of Mr. Ashe, the District Magistrate of Tinnevelly,
    by a young man called Vanchi Aiyar on 17 June 1911.

45) This short form will be used hereafter for 'Chattopadhyaya'.

46) P. Sengupta, Sarojini Naidu (London 1966) p. 14.

47) Letter to The Times 6 July 1909, mentioned in Ker, op. cit. ,
    pp. 198-9.

48) For the details of this plan, see ibid. , pp. 199-200.

thoroughly ashamed of being ruled by a handful of vile alien vandals, if it is anarchism to wish to exterminate them with the noble desire of establishing our national freedom upon the basis of pupular sovereignty, of justice, of mercy, of righteousness, and of humanity, if it is anarchism to rise for the sanctity of our homes, the integrity of our life, and the honour of our God and our country, and to slay every individual tyrant, whether foreign or native, that continued the enslavement of the great noble people, if it is anarchism to conspire ceaselessly to take human life with the only object of emancipating our beloved motherland, then we say, cursed is the man that is not an anarchist! Cursed is the man that sleeps in his bed or carouses merrily in halls of wine, women and song, while alien parasites live and grow fat over the land and slowly, silently, and 'peacefully' draine away the very life-blood of our nation!"(49) After October 1910 Chatto was much pre-occupied with his private affairs and until the beginning of the War in 1914 he was practically lost to the revolutionary cause. The paper The Talvar consequently was fefunct. On the eve of the War Chatto was in Germany.

The difficulties caused by the departure of Har Dayal and V. V. S Aiyar and the temporary inactivity of Chatto led to the Paris group becoming virtually ineffective. The reason for all these young men leaving Paris was that they found it no longer easy to maintain contact with the revolutionists at home due to the strictures of the French Government. As early as May 1908 the Paris Police warned the Indian Government about a possible anarchist conspiracy in India with a link with the Paris group. In May 1908 Richthofen of the German Consulate General in Calcutta informed Berlin of what he had confidentially learnt about the warning from Paris which led to the discovery of the entire anarchist network in Calcutta complete with Russian literature, a bomb making workshop and smuggled a munition. (50)

Madame Cama continued her connection with the French socialist group and the Gaelic American until 1914. Cama's contact with the socialists helped the Indian revolutionaries in France. Monsieur Maître Jean Longnet, Advocat à la Cour d'Appeel de Paris, a well-known young socialist wrote frequent articles for the socialist paper l'Humanité for the Indian revolutionaries. The French socialist press and the socialist deputies led by M. Jaures also took up Vinayak Savarkar's case (51) and pressed successfully for it to be referred

---

49) Ibid., p. 118.

50) Richthofen to Bülow, Simla 7 May 1908, AABI 42.

51) Savarkar was sent to India on the P & O ship Morea for prosecution. On 8 July 1910 when the ship was calling at

to the Hague Tribunal. Similarly, George Freeman, an Irish-man and a staff member of the Gaelic American in America remained in close contact with Madame Cama who continued editing Bande Mataram until the middle of 1914.

While the Indian revolutionary nationalists were thus gradually losing their locus standi in the traditional homes for rebels in Europe, the New World seems to offer them an excellent base for their activities. The presence of a substantial number (52) of Indian workers with money and growing grievances against the British in the area between Vancouver and San Francisco, tempted many Indian revolutionists in America to create a revolutionary workshop on the Pacific coast with the ultimate aim of activiating India against the British.

The year 1906 was particularly favourable for the anti-British nationalist politics of the Indians in America. In that year the American Secretary of State and candidate for the Presidency, William Jennings Bryan, after paying a brief visit to India denounced the Government of India without reserve in his lectures and articles in the New York Sun.(53) No wonder that the first anti-British political society was formed in New York in the autumn of 1906 by Samuel Lucas Joshi, a Marathi Christian, and Mohamed Barakatullah (54) who was to associate later with the

---

Marseilles he escaped through a porthole and ran about 300 m ashore. The British guardsmen shouted and Savarkar not knowing a single word of French to explain that he was a political refugee was caught by the gendarmes and mistakenly handed over to the British guards. French socialists ultimately succeeded in sending the case to the Hague Tribunal which decided the case on 24 February 1911 in favour of the British Government. See Yajnik, op. cit., pp. 285-292.

52) According to one source the number was 30,000 by 1910. Rattan Singh, A Brief History of the Hindustan Gadar Party (Pamphlet) (San Francisco 1929) quoted in Mark Naidu, 'Propaganda of the Gadar Party' Pacific Historical Review, Vol. XX, 1959, p. 251.

53) These articles were thoroughly used by the Berlin Committee later for its propaganda. See W.J. Bryan, British Rule in India, republished without date and place by the Berlin India Committee in 1915. For the Anglo-Indian criticism of Bryan's views see Pioneer 9 August and 2 September 1906; Times of India 2 September 1906.

54) For Barakatullah's political career see below

Berlin India Committee. In October the next year Madame Cama visited New York and publicly announced her intention of "giving a thorough exposé of the British oppression which is little understood so far away and to interest the warm-hearted citizens of the great Republic in our enfranchisement."(55) As a result, much enthusiams was aroused and George Freeman helped the Indians to bring out a journal called Free Hindustan in 1908. Soon Freeman helped not only in the publication of Free Hindustan which was edited by Taraknath Das, but also in sending revolutionary literature to India.

By the end of 1910, however, New York ceased to be a centre of Indian revolutionary activities. The centre shifted to the Pacific coast where several thousand Indian labourers, mostly Sikhs from the Punjab, had been concentrating since 1905 and were gradually facing restrictive measures both from the Canadian and American governments.(56)

In 1907 one Ram Nath Puri from the Punjab who had come to America in 1906 after having already been involved in revolutionary activities at home, introduced nationalist politics among these labourers by founding an organisation called 'Hindustan Association' in San Francisco and issuing a periodical, Circular-i-Azadi (Circular of Feedom), in Urdu, the language of the immigrants. Another prominent person to work amongst the Sikhs was Taraknath Das, a future active member of the Berlin Committee. Born in Calcutta about 1884 Das had early connections with the Bengali revolutionary societies in Calcutta. He left India about 1906 proceeding to San Francisco via Japan. For a time he was a student at the University of California and in 1908 also employed at the Immigration Office at Vancouver. In April the same year he began his revolutionary activities by bringing out Free Hindustan, the August and subsequent issues of which were published in New York with the help of George Freeman.(57) Das was connected with Puri's group and he believed in open war supported by the masses and the regular army. However, he was conscious of his limitations

---

55) Quoted in Ker, op. cit., p. 219.

56) In 1910 the Indian labour population on the American Pacific coast was 5,424. The rate of growth was an increasing one: from 84 in 1902 it rose to 1,710 in 1910. This growth created feeling against the immigrants. An association called the Asiatic Exclusion League became very active and consequently the immigration officers became very strict. See R.K. Das, Hindustani Workers on the Pacific Coast (Berlin 1932) pp. 15-17.

57) See Ker, op. cit., pp. 119-122, 221.

and was hoping for a leader who could speak to the Sikhs in their own language for effective results. The vacuum was soon filled when Har Dayal plunged into the field of revolutionary propaganda amongst the Sikhs of North America in 1913.

Har Dayal who had arrived in the United States early in 1911 made his way to Berkeley, California. In the same year he was appointed a lecturer in Indian Philosophy at Stanford University. After one year of service he was dismissed from the University for a reason which has not yet been clearly elucidated. In 1913 he went on a lecture tour on the Pacific coast. To his listeners, the Sikh labourers of India, he spoke about the ruin of India through British rule and the necessity of a revolution to throw the foreigners out. In November 1913 Har Dayal and his friends in San Francisco founded the Ghadr (Rebellion) newspaper and the Yugantar Ashram, a bureau to preach and propagate revolution in India. On 26 March 1914 Har Dayal was arrested by the United States authorities for his anti-British lectures with a view to his deportation as an undesirable alien. He was released on bail but jumped bail and absconded to Switzerland before the case came up for hearing. His assistant Ram Chandra continued the activities of the Yugantar Ashram and the Ghadr newspaper which was published in several Indian languages and distributed widely among the overseas Indians.

Thus on the eve of the First World War two of the veteran Indian revolutionary propagandists outside India, Chatto and Har Dayal, were within easy reach of the Germans if wanted. Besides them and three other people who have appeared in our narrative above, namely, M. P. T. Acharya, Taraknath Das, and Ram Chandra, there were very many other Indian revolutionary nationalists with organising abilities scattered in Europe, America and West and East Asia at this time. Some of these men, like Bhupendra Nath Dutta, Heramba Lal Gupta and Chandra Kanta Chakravarti in America and Abinash Chandra Bhattacharya in Germany, remained rather quiet after their earlier Indian activities. Others, like Jodh Singh Mahajan and Ajit Singh, with less intellectual gifts but perhaps with more stamina, had been touring far and wide in Europe, South America and West Asia since 1908, suggesting to their revolutionary colleagues various plans for anti-British conspiracies from abroad. There were yet others like Sufi Amba Prasad and P. N. Dutt (Dawood Ali) who because of their presence at this time in Persia and Turkey, could hardly remain uninspired by the prospects of a joint Pan-Islamic and nationalist conspiracy against the British in India. Being in the same situation as absconders or self-exiles with uniformly bitter anti-British feelings, all these much-travelled men always maintained some contact with one another. Driving the British out of India or at least harming them in some big way being their prime political aim, nothing would be more welcome to them than a chance to co-operate with the Germans in their anti-British ventures. As a matter of fact long before the War actually came, the Indian revolutionists in Europe and America pinned their hopes on a possible war between Germany and England.

3. The Formation of the Berlin India Committee

We have already seen that as early as January 1909 George Freeman informed Professor Schiemann of the preparations by the Indian revolutionists. (58) In the February 1910 issue of Madame Cama's paper Bande Mataram the editor (Har Dayal) considered Berlin to be "the capital of the country which at present is most hostile in spirit to England" and gave his opinion that "the cultivation of friendly relations [by Indian revolutionists] with the powerful German nation will be of great advantage to the cause of Indian independence."(59) It was also in a German journal that in March 1911 Shyamaji Krishnavarma's views about Indian nationalism and unrest appeared. (60) In 1912 Mohamed Barakatullah (61), a Pan-Islamist who, however, worked hand in hand with the revolutionary nationalists, giving a glowing tribute to Kaiser Wilhelm II in his paper Islamic Fraternity remarked: "... In case there be a conference of the European powers

---

58) See above ch. III p. 82.

59) Bande Mataram, February 1910, extracts in Ker, op. cit., p. 114.

60) Yajnik, op. cit., p. 300.

61) Born about 1864, son of an employee of the Bhopal State, Mohamed Barakatullah was one of the first to start anti-British Indian propaganda in America in 1907. He also urged Hindu-Muslim unity. In early 1910 he started in Tokyo his paper The Islamic Fraternity advocating militant Pan-Islamism. In January 1915 he went to Berlin to co-operate with the Berlin Committee. The Committee sent him to Afghanistan along with Mahendra Pratap and O.W. Hentig. Jawaharlal Nehru on his European trips between 1926 - 1928 met Barakatullah in Berlin and found him "a delightful old man, very enthusiastic and very likable... rather simple, not very intelligent, but still trying to imbibe new ideas and to understand the present day world." Barakatullah died in San Francisco in 1927. See Ker, op. cit., pp. 132-5, 221, 225-227; Nehru, Autobiography (London) 1949) p. 151.

[over Tripoli] or a European war, it is the duty of the Muslims to be united, to stand by the Khalif with their life and property, and to side with Germany. Germany's word alone is reliable; while the others blow the trumpet of independence, integrity, civilization and progress, but they at the same time go marching along through bloodshed, desecration of holy places, rapine and plunder."(62) In April 1913 yet another Indian revolutionary nationalist from Europe wrote an anonymous article in the Leipziger Neueste Nachrichten inviting the Germans to take greater interest than hitherto in India in general and in Indian trade in particular. The author also assured the Germans of the great love and respect the Indians had for them.(63) Thus when the War finally broke out it was only natural that those among the Indian revolutionary nationalists in Europe who could and intended to remain active would contact the Germans and try to turn England's difficulty to their advantage. In this case it was the turn of Virendranath Chattopadhyaya (Chatto) to start a new phase of the activities of the Indian revolutionary nationalists abroad.

At the beginning of the War Chatto and Abinash Bhattacharya (64) were at Halle in Germany.(65) By the middle of August 1914 they

---

62) The ungrammatical language original. Quoted in Ker, op. cit., p. 261.

63) 'Gute Aussichten für Deutschland in Indien', Leipziger Neueste Nachrichten 1 April 1913. While forwarding a copy of the article to the German Foreign Office, the editorial office of the paper did not give the name of the author who was introduced as a member of the Indian Nationalist Party living in Europe (letter to A.A., Leipzig 4 April 1913, AABI 49). The circumstantial evidence, however, shows that it was the work of Chatto and Abinash Bhattacharya.

64) Abinash Bhattacharya (born 1883) was a friend of Aurobindo Ghose and a leading revolutionist in Bengal. He was the author of the book Bartaman Rananiti (The Modern Art of War) and was also one of the founders of the revolutionary paper Yugantar in Calcutta. He was a person who had direct experience with the terrorist and conspiratorial underground activities that had been going on in Bengal since 1907.

65) According to German police information Chatto at this time was a student in Germany. From their knowledge of German and their acquaintance with the local people Chatto and Bhattacharya seem to have stayed for quite some time at Halle, perhaps also at the time of the Leipzig article in April 1913. W.K. 11f, 2, pp. 52-55, 67.

were in touch with one Mrs. Simon, the widow of a country court
counsellor at Halle, who happened to have good relations with
Helmuth Delbrück, a nephew of Dr. C. Delbrück, the Minister for
the Interior in the Prussian Government. On 22 August Mrs. Simon
sent a cable to Stettin asking Helmuth to use all his influence to
arrange an interview for Chatto with Minister Delbrück so that the
former could make some 'important proposals' connected with the
War and India. (66) Helmuth Delbrück seems to have had earlier
contact with Bhattacharya for he wrote to his uncle immediately
introducing Bhattacharya as his friend. (67) These efforts were
successful and before long Bhattacharya was informed by Mrs.
Simon that the matter was in process. On hearing this, Bhattacharya
himself wrote to Dr. Delbrück with great excitement at the prospect
of a German victory in the War about which he had no doubts. To
him German victory meant also freedom for India. (68) As a result,
Bhattacharya and Chatto were soon in Berlin and before the month
was out their association with the existing German plans concerning
India began. (69)

In the early months of the War German patriotic feelings went hand
in hand with the patriotism of the Indian nationalists. Ex-missionaries
with past Indian experience and those who returned recently with fresh
knowledge of India at the outbreak of the War offered themselves for
propaganda work. (70) The press not only brought news of the British

---

66) W. K. 11f, 1, p. 20.

67) W. K. 11f, 1, pp. 15-16.

68) Writing in German Bhattacharya poured out his excitement
    thus: "...I am awaiting to hear any hour that Bombay and
    Calcutta are on fire and that Zeppelin 'Hansa' is planting
    bombs on London. The British, the greatest liars in the
    world must get their real punishment from Germany this
    time...I have great trust in Germany. Despite the three-
    sided battle Germany will definitely be victorious; and
    after that, will give freedom to Poland, Finland, India
    [and] Egypt. It will be written in golden letters in world
    history that Germany saved half the world from slavery
    and oppression..." Bhattacharya to Dr. Delbrück, no date;
    W. K. 11f, 1, p. 18.

69) Legation Secretary von Prittwitz's note 31 August 1914;
    W. K. 11f, 1, p. 46.

70) The earliest of these missionaries to report on India was
    one Paul Walter who had left India in 1903. He wrote to
    the German Foreign Office as early as 7 August, 1914.

Indian situation but also the expression of Indian sympathy for the Germans. (71) Those people in Germany who saw this War as one forced on them unjustly by Britain found new significance in India for Germany. A young educated man from Lüneburg - no other than the future famous philosopher Professor Fritz Heinemann - for example, wrote very enthusiastically to the Berlin police: "A little while ago German newspapers carried expressions of sympathy by the Indians for Germany. In this connection I should like to ask you to send addresses of some Indians living in Berlin or in other German towns. " The young doctor of philosophy then continued:

> "It could be of greatest importance for the development of the European situation if now India would get true news about the situation of England; the Indians are almost 300 million people and are thirsting for liberation. England would get heavy blows by difficulties in her most important colony and would soon be forced to peace with Germany. "

To emphasise the importance of the work he further added: "I should be grateful if you would answer my letter soon. Quick action is necessary and could be of great value for Germany. "(72)

The news of Envar Pasha having information about the Afghan Amir's eagerness to join any venture against England and Russia was already very inspiring. It was followed by various misguided rumours and reports about outbreaks of revolt in India and of England

---

See W.K. 11f, 1, pp. 1-3. In November came the report of the freshly returned missionary O. Schmidt-Ernsthausen who considered British India as being encircled by dangerously threatening problems. Later in 1916 through Mathias Erzberger came various other reports and suggestions from recently returned missionaries from India. They were Father Windhausen, Father Schwarz, Father Hoffmann, and Father Aßmuth. In October 1914 another missionary, Graetsch, with special abilities in Indian languages met Oppenheim and later became engaged in the Indian programme of the Foreign Office throughout the War period.

71) See for example 'Das Geheimnis der indischen Aufstandbewegung', Deutsche Montagszeitung 21 Sept. 1914, AABI 51.

72) Dr. Fritz Heinemann to the Berlin police, Berlin 31 Aug. 1914. Stress original. W.K. 11f, 1, p. 102.

seeking Japan's help at a heavy price to save India. (73) As a result of these the Berlin-sponsored programme for India acquired new dimensions. In its search for Indians in Germany, Austro-Hungarian territories, Switzerland, America, and the Ottoman Empire, the German Foreign Office could not only trace all the leading Indian nationalists in these countries but also acquired the direct assistance of many Indians in Germany and some from outside. The veterans of Indian revolutionary propaganda in Europe were however not available for active help. Shyamaji Krishnavarma who was living in Geneva at the time, showed his sympathy with the Germans but was reluctant to play any active part in any programme because of his old age. (74) The patrons of the Paris group, Madame Cama and S. R. Rana had already been interned in France. (75) Berlin was, however, successful in getting the active support of the most important one of the Indian revolutionists whose political aim co-incided with the German plan of an Indian invasion. This was Har Dayal,

---

73) On 25 August 1914 Quadt, at this time the German Minister at Athens, transmitted to Berlin the information he received from a German who had recently returned from India that India would send no more troops to Egypt for in the event of war between Turkey and England unrest among the Indian Muslims would be certain. In another report from Teheran to Wangenheim on 27 August Kardorf, the German Minister there, mentioned what he heard from British sources that the Indian expedition force was being ordered to return from Muscat because of besieging conditions prevailing in Bombay and Karachi. On 4 September the Admiral staff got news of an Indian revolt in a message from China. Six days later, via Sweden, came the news from the Washington Embassy that Japan confirmed officially to Chinese quarters the outbreak of revolution in India and that Japan was asked for military support by England which she promised under the following conditions: 1) free immigration to British possessions in the Pacific; 2) 200 million dollar loan; 3) free hand in China. See AABI 51, 25 Aug., 28 Aug., and 12 Sept. 1914; W.K. 11f, 1, p. 63, W.K. 11f, 1, p. 5. It must be pointed out, however, that the Indian revolutionists did not believe the report of the Indian outbreak to be true. Har Dayal in Constantinople considered it improbable. Wangenheim to A.A., 13 September 1914; W.K. 11f, 2, p. 33.

74) Romberg to A.A., Bern 8 Sept. 1914; W.K. 11f, 1, p. 107; See also W.K. 11f, 1, p. 117 and W.K. 11f, 6, p. 112.

75) Ker, op. cit., pp. 213-14.

'an advocate of open rebellion'. (76) Har Dayal whose early political career we have already discussed, was first mentioned in Wangenheim's report of 1 September from Constantinople. Giving Har Dayal's Geneva address where Har Dayal was staying with the Egyptian Dr. M. Rifaat, Wangenheim suggested that the Foreign Office contacted this man 'who could be of valuable service to us.' (77) On the very next day the Consul General in Geneva, Geißler, contacted Har Dayal. Geißler was impressed by the intelligence and energy of this young man of 30 years who was already experienced and influential in revolutionary activities. In order to bring about an Indian outbreak Har Dayal recommended invasion of India from Afghanistan and Beluchistan and said that he would be ready at any moment to go to Constantinople to help in preparing an Afghan expedition. (78) On the night of 5 September Har Dayal left for Constantinople as German East African merchant Romalingam Das, born in Dar es-Salaam. In Constantinople he was to stay with his friend Abu Said. (79)

The next person outside Germany who spontaneously made contact with the German Foreign Office and who extended to it his active co-operation was Champakaraman Pillai (80) in Zurich, the president

---

76) See Lajpat Rai, op. cit., p. 199. Later when Har Dayal was asked by the German Foreign Office why he wanted Indians from America to come to Constantinople instead of going straight to India which would be cheaper, Har Dayal told Wangenheim that it was not the question of sending help to India; it was the question of recruiting a good number of determined young Indians for the planned invasion of India so as to encourage rebellion in India. Wangenheim to A. A., Therapia 26 September 1914; W. K. 11f, 3, p. 24.

77) W. K. 11f, 1, p. 53.

78) Romberg to A. A., Bern 3 September 1914, enclosing Geißler's telegram; W. K. 11f, 1, p. 56.

79) Romberg to A. A., Bern 5 September 1914; W. K. 11f, 1, p. 77.

80) Champakaraman Pillai (1890-1936): Born in Trivandam this young South Indian had been brought to Europe by a very pro-Indian Englishman, Sir Walter Strickland, from the latter's journey to the East. In June 1912 Pillai formed his Pro-India Committee in Zurich, with himself as president. Edward Briess as vice-president and Sir Walter Strickland, Karl Bleibtreu and Shyamaji Krishnavarma as assessors. His inexperience and immaturity were proved by the fact that towards 1918 his vice-president Dr. Briess

of the high-sounding 'International Pro-India Committee'. (81)
Pillai was, however, not in the main stream of the Indian revolutionary nationalists abroad and except for a little contact with
Shyamaji, who was named as one of the 'assessors' of his
Committee, he does not seem to have had any other personal
contact with other Indian nationalists in Europe before going to
Berlin. (82) His only work until the outbreak of the War seems
to have been the two issues of the paper Pro-India under his
editorship. On 23 September Pillai expressed his intention to come
to Berlin at his own cost. (83) Meanwhile many other Indians had
gathered in Berlin from various parts of Germany due to the efforts
of Dr. Wilhelm Mertens and Professor Solomon in Heidelberg.
Later Chatto also made a round trip of Germany and Switzerland
to collect Indians. (84) Special care was taken not to hamper those
Indians who wanted to carry on their studies in spite of the War. (85)

---

was compelled to admit in a court case that he had cunningly
crept into the 'Pro-India movement' from its very inception
as a paid agent of the British Government. Pillai's immaturity
was detected by the veterans of the India Committee and he
was kept aside from the Committee's activities towards the end
of 1916. Pillai was then active in the German Fatherland Party.
In later years in Berlin, where he died, he was one of the very
few Indians in Germany who sympathised with the Nazis. W. K.
11f, 1, p. 95, Pillai about himself, 1 September 1914; Yajnik,
op. cit., p. 318. See also J. Nehru, op. cit., p. 153 for his des-
cription of Pillai's pomposity and personality.

81) Romberg to A. A., Bern 6 and 8 September 1914; W. K. 11f,
1, pp. 94, 116; W. K. 11f, 2, p. 104.

82) Pillai has been wrongly credited as the founder of the Berlin
Committee in most of the accounts so far published about the
Berlin Indians. This was perhaps due to Edward Briess's
endeavour to magnifiy his own achievement in the records of
the British Intelligence, which have often been unquestioningly
used by the scholars as the main source for the Indian revolutionists.

83) Romberg to A. A., Bern 23 Sept., 1914; W. K. 11f, 2, p. 124.

84) W. K. 11f, 1, pp. 44, 120; W. K. 11f, 3, p. 17; W. K. 11f, 6, p. 89.

85) Oppenheim's note on 31 Oct. 1914, W. K. 11f, 1, p. 2; see
also Zimmermann to D. Dr. Rudolf Otto, Professor, Göttingen, Berlin 13 Nov. 1914, W. K. 11f, 5, p. 65. It is because
of this special favour that Messrs. Vasanji P. Dalal,
Satyabodha Hadilkar and Jamshedji Maneckji Unvala could

Among the Indians from Germany, Switzerland, and America who had already established direct contact with the Berlin-oriented programmes before the end of the year and those Indians who were to do so or arrive in Berlin before long were: Virendranath Chattopadhyaya, Abinash Chandra Bhattacharya, Safia Caderwail, Har Dayal, Abdur Rahman, A.S. Siddiqui, Dr. Mansur Ahmed, Debendra Bose, Satish Chandra Roy, Ramana Pillai, Sarat Dutta, Dr. J.C. Dasgupta, Narayan Marathe, K.S. Rao, Gopal Paranjpy, Hormaz Kersasp, Satyendranath Sen, Professor Joshi, Dhirendra Sarkar, V.G. Pingley, M. Barakatullah, Heramba Lal Gupta, Akhil C. Chakravarty, S.C. Mukherjee, Champakaraman Pillai, M.P.T. Acharya, Maharaj Narain Kaul, Dr. M. Prabhakar, Taraknath Das, J.N. Lahiri, B.N. Dasgupta, L.P. Varma, Kedarnath, Basant Singh, Rishi Kesh Latta, Chet Singh, A.C. (Chaudhuri) Sharma, P. Khankoje, Shiv Dev Singh Ahluvalia, V. Joshi, K.K. Naik, Tarachand Roy, Dr. Abdul Hafiz, Mahendra Pratap, Harish Chandra, Bhupendra Nath Dutta, Sardar Umrao Singh, and Jodh Singh. (86) Besides, information about two Muslim brothers from Delhi, Abdul Jabbar and Abdus Sattar Khairi, who had been living for a long time in the Ottoman Empire, was also collected and they were being contacted from the Constantinople end. (87)

Baron Oppenheim was the chief adviser and supervisor of the Indian work. The three other persons who also acted as links between the Indians and the Foreign Office were Ernst Jaeckh (88), H.K. Regendanz (89), and Herbert Mueller (90). Once the Afghan

---

continue their studies in Heidelberg inspite of their being British subjects. W.K. 11f, 5, p. 92.

86) W.K. 11f, 1, pp. 26, 60, 114; 2, pp. 52-57, 79, 153-154; 3, pp. 17, 100; 5, pp. 29, 79, 113, 117-8; 6, pp. 118, 153-154; 9, pp. 27, 87, 107, 135, 170-75; 11, p. 50; 47, no page number, see the entry of 7 April 1919.

87) W.K. 11f, 2, p. 79; W.K. 11f, 4, p. 63.

88) About Jaeckh's importance and influence during the War in Germany see F. Fischer, Germany's Aims... p. 124.

89) Regendanz was the liaison-man in general between the Imperial Colonial Office and the banks, and the chief mover behind the scenes of policy in Morocco. It was Regendanz who as early as August 1914 devised an ingenious plan of sending a mixed group of three persons - a German, an Italian and an American - with Naval Captain Loehlein to India as travelling salesman in the luxury goods of an American firm. In this plan, while the last mentioned

expedition commission selected the German team for it, Oppenheim did not have much to do with the conduct of the expedition which, in any case, was to be carried out from Constantinople. As a member of the commission and as the expert on the Muslim world he was to choose appropriate Indians to taking part in the expedition from Berlin. (91). It was also Oppenheim's official duty to coordinate and conduct the activities of the Indians in Berlin. The propaganda work proposed amongst the Indian soldiers recently taken by the British to Egypt; propaganda amongst the Indian prisoners of war; finding ways to send money to Indian revolutionaries at home and in America; receiving Indians and attending to their problems; collecting authentic information about the situation in India; sending true War news from Europe to be circulated among the Indians in India; arranging contact-men in various parts of the world for Indian work; purchasing, collecting and sending weapons and explosives to India; collecting articles, translations etc. from the Indians to be used by the 'Information Service for the Orient' - all these activities came under the general supervision of Oppenheim. In the middle of September 1914 Oppenheim opened an office for Indian activities at Friedenau, Meinauer Straße 2, with Dr. H. Mueller as the manager. (92) On 16 September Oppenheim asked the Foreign Office to pass on to Constantinople the information that a Committee for Indian work was founded in Berlin out of the best Indians from Germany and Switzerland. (93)

The opening of a separate office for Indians' activities signified the importance given to the Indian work. But when everything seemed to have gone well with the Indian programme both in Constantinople and in Berlin - both sides exchanging enthusiastic

---

one (the American) was to remain unaware of the ulterior motive, the first two were to act as political agents and meet the native princes and help in preparing proclamations to be circulated amongst the local people. See Regendanz to Langwerth, 20 August 1914, W.K. 11f, 1, pp. 9-12.

90) Dr. Herbert Mueller, later a sinologist and journalist, was soon to be the treasurer (from the official side) of the Berlin Committee. See also H. von Glasenapp, Meine Lebensreise (Wiesbaden 1964) p. 71.

91) He selected Dr. Mansur Ahmed for this expedition in September 1914. W.K. 11e, 2, pp. 125-128.

92) W.K. 11f, 2, p. 58.

93) Ibid., p. 67; W.K. 11f, 3, p. 32.

and encouraging news (94) - on 15 October came abruptly the
news of Har Dayal's sudden departure from Constantinople to
Geneva. He took a Turkish passport as Ismail Hakki Hassan and
left Constantinople without even consulting or bidding farewell to
Wangenheim. (95) The reason of Har Dayal's sudden leaving was
suspected by Wangenheim to be Hindu-Muslim animosity. (96) In
a belated clarification Har Dayal, however, had different reasons
to give.

The whole plan for Har Dayal's to go to Constantinople had
originated out of his meeting with Geißler in Geneva on 2 September 1914. On the same day Har Dayal handed over to Geißler a
project in his capacity as the 'General Secretary of the Hindustan
Gadar Party. U.S.A.'. (97) This was a project for bringing about
a general uprising in India by an invasion of the country from
Afghanistan. "As India is a vast plain, and England holds the
seas, and the semi-independent Indian states have no modern
armies," Har Dayal suggested that "an effective military movement
against England can be started only with the help of Afghanistan,
a mountainous country of brave soldiers, numbering 5,000,000,
who hate England and Russia." Har Dayal also suggested how
to set about it. A non-official Turkish group of priests and notables,
bearing letters from the Shaikh-ul-Islam (Head of Islam) at Con-

---

94) In one of Wangenheim's reports of this period a draft
    telegram from Har Dayal to be sent to New York was en-
    closed wherein Har Dayal asked Chakravarti to send "largest
    possible number of Hindu boys from California for work in
    Constantinople." Har Dayal also added that they should
    come on their own and with six months expenses with them.
    Wangenheim to A.A., Therapia 21 September 1914; W.K. 11f,
    2, p.117. From the Berlin side Oppenheim was planning to
    send Chatto to Constantinople where he was to join Har
    Dayal for the onward journey to Afghanistan and Baluchi-
    stan where they would make preliminary preparations for
    the military invasion of India. Oppenheim's draft telegram
    to Constantinople, 16 September 1914; W.K. 11f, 2, p.67.

95) Wangenheim to A.A., Therapia 15 October 1914; W.K. 11f,
    4, p.21.

96) Ibid.

97) Har Dayal to the German Consul General in Geneva, Geneva
    2 September 1914; W.K. 11f, 5, p.44; Geißler, however,
    did not send this letter to A.A. until 2 November 1914
    along with Har Dayal's subsequent letters to him.

stantinople should visit Kabul and persuade the Court at Kabul to attack the British forces in Baluchistan. Besides this he recommended attempts to organise the tribes in Southern Persia and also in Baluchistan where according to him only a few British regiments were stationed. (98)

While the arrangements for an invasion would go on as described, the 'Indian Nationalist Party' would concentrate its whole strength on the state of Kashmir. Kashmir according to Har Dayal had only a few irregular troops and they could probably be won over. Kashmir being a mountainous region, Har Dayal thought that the Nationalist Party would be able to resist the British forces for a long time. He emphasised that initial success was indispensable for such a movement in India. He expected of course that Germany would help Afghanistan, Southern Persia, and the Indian Nationalist Party with officers, arms, ammunitions, bombs, aeroplanes and wireless apparatus. (99) The optimism for success in Kashmir was derived from this: "Apart from the general unrest in India among all classes," Har Dayal wrote, "we have 10,000 Hindus in the United States and Canada and about 100,000 in China and the Malay Peninsula. The nationalist paper Gadar (Rebellion) circulates among them, and they are just now very much agitated over the Indian question in British Columbia. At least a few thousand will respond to an appeal for immediate action, if German support is assured. They came from the Punjab, the province adjacent to Kashmir. Many of them have been soldiers in the army."(100)

Har Dayal's scheme included also deeds of terrorism to be accomplished in other parts of India to produce effect. He wrote: "We have young men ready for any sacrifice." The success of the invasion, he visualised, would let loose the forces of revolt all over India, especially in the states of Hyderabad and Nepal. He also stressed the necessity of establishing communication by cable letter or messenger with the Hindus in China, the United States and East Africa. Offering himself to the cause of his project Har Dayal wrote: "I shall be successively at Constantinople, Mecca, Baghdad and Kabul to help the execution of this project, if it is accepted."(101)

---

98) Ibid.

99) Ibid.

100) Ibid.

101) Ibid.

Geißler at that time did not send Har Dayal's complete letter to the Foreign Office but only the gist of it. (102) He later denied that he had told Har Dayal of Berlin's acceptance of his (Har Dayal's) plan in its entirety. According to Geißler he had only informed Har Dayal of Berlin's great interest in his plan. (103)

Justifying suddenly leaving Constantinople, Har Dayal said that he had gone to Constantinople with a twofold object in view: propaganda among the Indians living in Turkey and Persia and the establishment of a revolutionary centre at Kabul with German co-operation. (104) He said he failed to achieve his object for four reasons: First, the Germans in Constantinople did not wish to spend money; secondly, the Germans did not know how to deal with men; thirdly, the Germans did not trust the Indians; and fourthly, the Germans did not wish to encourage his independent initiatives. (105) To prove his points Har Dayal gave examples. Regarding German parsimony he mentioned that when he told Wassmuss that several thousand Indians could be brought from the U.S.A. with proper encouragement, Wassmuss to his (Har Dayal's) surprise enquired whether they could come on their own. Similarly, when the first batch of the expedition had left for Aleppo it failed to take the most experienced Indian, Dawood Ali (real name P.N. Dutta) on financial grounds although he would have been the only Indian. Even when he persuaded Dawood Ali to volunteer on his own in the service of the cause Dawood was not allowed to take part in the first batch of the expedition. As to his second charge, Har Dayal complained that Wassmuss did not treat him as a responsible and trustworthy colleague. As an example of his third charge, Har Dayal said that while he was organising the Indian group he was kept utterly in the dark about the other acitivities of the expedition, so much so that he did not know even when the first batch of the Turco-German expedition had left Constantinople. Moreover, when he asked to send information to Berlin about the need for Indian helpers the matter was treated in a half-hearted manner. Lastly, Har Dayal objected to Dr. Weber's and Wassmuss's insistence on their own ideas and not allowing any initiative on his part. (106)

---

102) As Geißler wrote to A.A. on 2 November 1914; W.K. 11f, 5, pp. 42-43.

103) Ibid.

104) Har Dayal to Geißler, Geneva 2 November 1914; W.K. 11f, 5, pp. 42-43

105) Ibid.

106) Ibid.

Wassmuss, who seems to have annoyed Har Dayal most, was the leader of the German contingent of the Turco-German expedition of Afghanistan according to the earliest plan. Compared to the rest of the group of utterly inexperienced Germans whom he was to lead, Wassmuss alone - having hitherto been posted at Bushir as German Chargé d'Affaires - had some knowledge and personal experience of that part of Persia through which the expedition was to march. Yet accounts of the ill-fated Turco-German expedition and its German participants reveal that due to his fanciful and visionary character, Wassmuss was unable to fill his subordinates with trust and respect and that he had difficulties with the Turks as well.(107) That Wassmuss was not free from having his own egotistic plans, untenable by reason, is also admitted by his sympathetic English biographer.(108) Dr. Weber who also came in for Har Dayal's criticism was connected with this expedition being the dragoman in the German Embassy at Constantinople.

When the complete story of the Berlin Committee is told, which we propose to do in a later work, it will be revealed that Har Dayal as a leader had similar limitations to those seen in Wassmuss. Like Wassmuss, Har Dayal was given to egotistical assertions and was consequently disliked by his colleagues and followers. Besides, Har Dayal had other limitations as a leader, the greatest of them being his lack of tenacity of purpose in which Wassmuss triumphed. In the present case however, Har Dayal based his charges on the violation of the alleged conditions under which his services were accepted by Geißler as representative of the German Foreign Office. It is quite likely, and also natural, that Geißler had assured Har Dayal of the co-operation of the German leadership in the Turco-German expedition, in organising the Indian group for it and making preparations for the final part of the expedition. It is also true that in the midst of multifarious initial problems with the inapt German contingent (109) there was hardly any time at this stage for the German leaders to give thought to the ultimate aim of the expedition i.e. the invasion of and rebellion in India. In any case there was no strong refutation of Har Dayal's charges from the official side, except on the question of money. On getting Har Dayal's charges from the Foreign Office Wangenheim wrote back on 27 November:

107) U. Gehrke, op. cit., p. 25 n. 27.

108) C. Sykes, Wassmuss; The German Lawrence (Leipzig 1937) pp. 42-44, 66.

109) See Gehrke, op. cit., p. 24, n. 22.

"You will not mind if I do not refer in detail to the four accusations against the German Civil Service. They are mainly based on wrong understanding and conclusions and most of them could have been solved satisfactorily here had Har Dayal spoken out more precisely. So in particular the money question which has now become a matter of complaint, arose only because Har Dayal himself declined to accept any means when asked. According to Har Dayal's own instructions the Indians who were to be called from the United States were to have sufficient money with them. His plans could have been supported financially from here if they were initiated. But instead, Har Dayal suddenly left Constantinople thereby causing - particularly among the competent Turkish quarters - the suspicion that he might be a traitor. "(110)

Wangenheim persisted in what he had earlier said to be the reason for Har Dayal's departure: "In reality, however, I think that Har Dayal's main reason was the fear that because of the Turkish-Islamic character of the propaganda initiated here with German support the Hindu element would be neglected and that he himself would not play the role he had hoped for. "(111)

That Har Dayal much resented being allowed to play only second fiddle in Constantinople there was no doubt. He himself made it clear in the latter quoted before. Referring to Weber's and Wassmuss's treatment of him he wrote:

"They knew that I had asked Indian colleagues to come from Berlin, London and America and yet they would ask me to leave Constantinople as an ordinary member of the party. They did not seem to understand that I had come to Constantinople to organise action on behalf of the Indians, that I had a definite plan of work, and that I did not need their advice but co-operation. "(112)

If the ultimate purpose of an Afghan mission was to bring about revolution in India then the Indian element should be sufficiently represented in it, Har Dayal argued. "The whole object of the mission would be frustrated, " he wrote, "if a few Indians

---

110) Wangenheim to A.A., Therapia 27 Nov. 1914; W.K. 11f, 6, p. 59.

111) Ibid.

112) Har Dayal to Geißler, Geneva 2 Nov. 1914, W.K. 11f, 5, in packet.

accompanied a large expedition as ordinary members, without any
position or authority formally recognized by the German or Turkish
government."(113) Har Dayal thought he was invited to fill this gap:
"I was appointed to organize the movement for India and the Indians:
other men did not know the situation of our party and could not
judge what should have been done."(114)

The Har Dayal issue actually brought the whole question of Indo-
German co-operation into question both amongst the Indians and
also at Foreign Office level. The whole co-operation seemed to
have been based on shaky foundations in the first place. Indians
in Berlin were not happy to work under the direction of Baron
Oppenheim. Although they were yet to meet the Foreign Office
personnel directly they seem to have already conveyed to them
their dissatisfaction with Oppenheim through some channel. There
were many influential men outside who had their own schemes for
an Indian revolt and who met the Indians privately to this end.
With one of these men, Professor Rudolf Otto of Göttingen, who
himself disliked Oppenheim, some of the leading Indians had very
good relations and they discussed their working problems with
him.(115) The problem they faced particularly was that they were not

---

113) Ibid.

114) Ibid. By 'our party' Har Dayal meant his Gadar Party in
America - as general secretary of which he signed this
letter to Geißler on 2 November 1914. It was expected of
him to bring Indians from America to Constantinople or
to India for revolutionary purposes.

115) The fact that Chatto and Kersasp wrote to Professor Otto
on the very next day (8 December) after having their first
talk with the German Foreign Office personnel, in which
they complained about Oppenheim's control over them,
reveals that the Indians had discussed their grievances
with Otto before having direct contact with the German
Foreign Office. It was because of his prior knowledge of
Oppenheim's methods of working with the Indians that Otto
had, while submitting his own scheme of Indian work to
the Foreign Office on 8 November, put the following
condition: "I would be ready to work in co-operation with
Herr Baron von Oppenheim, provided there shall be complete
mutual frankness and co-operation, but not under his direction." It is also clear that when Oppenheim insisted on the
Indians' not meeting any private persons other than those
to whom they were entrusted, he had men like Otto in mind.
Later Oppenheim resented (for reasons of maintaining secrecy)

able to guide their own policies concerning matters which touched them primarily. The Har Dayal issue showed this problem in yet another dimension: What would be the position of the Indian revolutionists, co-operating with the German Government, if at any point they and their cause were to be suddenly discarded by the German Government? This question seemed to have been left out in the beginning, obviously because the Indians had no bargaining strength at that time. Har Dayal's support with all his rich American connections was not counted upon confidently by Chatto and his friends in the initial stages of collaboration.(116)

By the end of October Chatto and Siddiqui were in Switzerland to meet Har Dayal. It was during their stay in Geneva that Har Dayal wrote on 2 November his strong report detailing all his experiences in Constantinople and giving his four reasons for abruptly leaving Constantinople. The letter was handed to Geißler by Siddiqui.(117) Prior to this Har Dayal had already written two letters to Geißler on 19 and 24 October but in neither of them did he use such strong language. In answer to Geißler's persuation(118)

Otto's giving a public lecture on 'Indian behaviour in the present War' as announced in the evening edition of Vossische Zeitung of 2 February 1915. Chatto and Kersasp to Otto, Berlin 8 December 1914, W.K. 11f, 7, pp.5-7; Otto to Zimmermann, 8 November 1914, W.K. 11f, 5, pp.52-53; Zimmermann to Otto, 13 November 1914, ibid., p.65; Har Dayal to A.A., 4 February 1915, W.K. 11f, 9, p.36; Oppenheim to Zimmermann, 3 February 1915, ibid., p.39.

116) Har Dayal himself was not introduced to the German Foreign Office by Chatto; nor did Har Dayal name Chatto in his list of Indian revolutionary nationalists in Europe.

117) Geißler to A.A., Geneva 2 November 1914, W.K. 11f, 5.

118) From the very moment the German Foreign Office came to know of Har Dayal's sudden return to Geneva it constantly asked Geißler to persuade Har Dayal to come to Berlin. The fear that Har Dayal might divulge the German conspiracy had gone after Wangenheim's report that the original Turkish suspicion of betrayal on Har Dayal's part was utterly baseless, and lately the Foreign Office also came to realise the importance and influence of Har Dayal among the revolutionary Indian nationals in America, some of whom had already arrived in Berlin. After Har Dayal's letter of 2 November some annoyance was shown by Geißler who wrote to the Foreign Office that in case Har Dayal's further usefulness was not under consideration his letter should be returned to him as unacceptable for its

to go to Berlin or return to Constantinople Har Dayal had previously very politely rejected the idea only by pointing out the
ineffectiveness of the existing plan. He then wrote: "It is a great
privilege for us Oriental revolutionists to work in co-operation
with the great and powerful German Government, but I am afraid
that the ideas according to which this part of the work is being
carried on will lead only to failure and my visit will not change
matters. I am rather sad, but I must state the situation as I see
it in the light of my judgement."(119) He was a bit sharper in his
next letter of 24 October in which he said: "I also notice that while
you and the authorities in Berlin wish me to follow your plan in
every particular, you do not wish to accede to my requests in any
matter...I therefore desire to be excused from repeating the experiences of Constantinople."(120) According to Har Dayal the only
practical and mutually helpful undertaking was a mission to Afghanistan
and until he met Chatto and Siddiqui at the turn of the month - when
he probably also discussed the future organisation of the Berlin
Committee with them - he had no respect for the work that was
being done by the Indians in Berlin. As postscript to the letter just
quoted Har Dayal mentioned. : "I have no desire to go to Berlin for
the petty and unimportant work that is being done there by the
Indians. My presence is not necessary for such work."(121)

At their meeting in Geneva Chatto and Har Dayal seem to have
compared notes about the conditions of work for the Indians in
Constantinople and Berlin. They seem to have also settled their
old personal differences and agreed to a joint effort if Chatto could
secure better working conditions and terms from the German Foreign
Office. As Chatto was not able to make any headway in this direction
Har Dayal gave no final answer to Geißler about coming to Berlin.
On 17 November Geißler wrote to Berlin that "after getting a letter
from Chatto, Har Dayal wrote to me that neither now nor ever after
is he going to come to Germany. I have a feeling that he does not
think the Berlin job to be fitting for his ambition."(122) It is difficult

---

'improper form'. The German Foreign Office, however, did
not intend to blow up the incident and considered it still safer
and even useful to have Har Dayal in Berlin. Ibid., and A.A.'s
comment on it, W.K. 11f, 4, pp.63, 76-78.

119) Har Dayal to Geißler, Geneva 19 October 1914, W.K. 11f, 5.

120) Har Dayal to Geißler, Geneva 24 October 1914, ibid.

121) Ibid.

122) Geißler to A.A., Geneva 17 Nov.1914; W.K. 11f, 5, p.87.

to say what exactly was the content of the letter from Chatto but circumstantial evidence shows that Chatto may have written about the same sort of difficulties which he was soon to bring to the notice of the Foreign Office.

On 7 December Chatto, Dr. Mansur Ahmed and Kersasp met the Legation Secretary von Wesendonk (123) at the Foreign Office. The purpose of the visit was to submit a plan of action proposed by them and to know whether they could in future meet and work with the Foreign Office directly instead of being linked with it through liaison men like Baron von Oppenheim, Dr. Müller or Dr. Jaeckh. According to the Indians these liaison men were not well informed about the Indian condition and Indian people and therefore there was the possibility of their being engaged in unnecessary and fruitless activities under the guidance of such people. (124) As in any case all the active stimulation of Indian propaganda had so far been made by them, they saw no reason why they should not contact the Foreign Office directly. They emphasised that as far as Indian conditions and people were concerned they were better informed than any European. (125)

---

123) Dr. Otto Günther von Wesendonk (1885-1933): 1903-1908 studied in Bonn, Berlin and Heidelberg (Dr. jur.); 1908 joined Foreign Service and was attached to German Embassy, London; 1910 a short spell each at Brussels and Constantinople; 1911 at Berlin; 1913 Legation Secretary at Tangiers and another Doctorate in Politics from Würzburg; January 1914 had to leave Foreign Service for having married a Portuguese; 10 August 1914 called back to the Foreign Office; August 1914 - April 1919 at Berlin, attached to the Political Department; 1922 Consul General, Tiflis, also Dr. phil. from Bonn; 1927 (over and above the Foreign Office assignment) General Secretary of the International Elbe Commission at Dresden.

124) As examples of their difficulties they mentioned Oppenheim's demanding from them a report about the Hindu-Muslim relations in India and Dr. Jaeckh's taking an uneducated Indian, (Caderwail [+]), to Constantinople to take the leadership in the Indian propaganda activities there. Wesendonk's official note on the meeting of 7 December 1914, W.K. 11f, 6, pp. 44-45.

[+]Sofia Caderwail was born in Colombo in 1880. In June 1912 he was registered with the police in Hamburg. Between 1913 and July 1914 he was in Silesia as a seaman. Then he was a salesman in a tea stall. In India he had been a personal servant of some highly placed personage. W.K. 11f, 1, p. 26.

125) Wesendonk's note 7 December 1914, W.K. 11f, 6, pp. 44-45.

The plan that Chatto and his company brought gave a very rosy picture of the prospects of an Indian revolution. They said that almost since the beginning of the War an organisation of Indian nationalists in Germany and Switzerland had been functioning in Berlin to bring about a great uprising in India with the help of the German authorities. They mentioned that their Committee had sent about twelve of its members to India to get in touch with the leaders of the various secret and other organisations to explain their plans personally. These members from Berlin were all trained in the production and use of explosives and they in turn would select in India several intelligent people to whom to pass their training. Moreover, they would give exact instructions to all their friends and the leaders of the revulutionary organisations so that when the Amir of Afghanistan declared war on Britain troops all over India would be mobilised at the borders to stage a great urpising immediately, to destroy all telegraph and railway connections, blow up bridges and monuments and attack and destroy the British everywhere. (126)

Their plan also included propaganda in India during December when there would be great activity among the political and social organisations at their annual meetings. They mentioned particularly the Indian National Congress, Indian Industrial Conference, Indian Social Conference, Indian Educational Conference, and All India Muslim League. (127)

They were hopeful of success particularly because of the discontent prevalent among Indians overseas particularly in America, Canada and South Africa which had already stirred up the public in India. As an example they mentioned the incident of Koma Gata Maru (128)

---

126) W.K. 11f, 6, pp.48-49.

127) Ibid., p.50.

128) Koma Gata Maru was a ship chartered in Hongkong from a Japanese firm by one Gurdit Singh, a Sikh from the Punjab, to take Indians intending to emigrate to Canada. The purpose was to challenge the recent immigration restrictions brought especially against the Asiatics. On 4 April 1914 the ship sailed with 165 Punjabis from Hongkong; when it arrived at Vancouver on 23 May there were 375 Punjabis on board including 25 Muslims. They were, however, not allowed to disembark and were compelled to return. The British authorities brought the ship back to Calcutta where it was moored at Budge-Budge on the Hoogly river on 29 September. The passengers were directed to disembark and proceed to the special train which was to take them straight to the

that year, as a result of which they said 300 to 400 people were killed. Pointing to the plight of the Indians in Canada they said that already some 3-4,000 emigrants and workers had returned to India through whom it would be easy to influence the masses and soldiers.(129)

The memorandum by Chatto and his friends mentioned also organisations like Gadar and Hindustan Association in America which stoked the anti-British mood outside India. It also stated that some eight weeks before the Berlin Committee had sent two of their number to America who in turn sent from there five very well chosen Indians and encouraged others also to come to Berlin. Two of these gentlemen from America would be sent back again to inform various organisations there about the Berlin Committee. These two gentlemen would also deal with two further questions: 1) the establishment of a revolutionary centre in Shanghai from where true War news, appeals and weapons would be smuggled into India by means of agents, and 2) the establishment of a similar centre in Java (Batavia). According to the memorandum the men for Shanghai and Batavia were already selected. On the importance of Batavia it said that there were always sailing boats running between Batavia and India which carried sugar and that several thousand Indians, mainly workers and merchants, lived there.(130)

The momorandum pointed out the great importance of weapons for revolution in India. The problems over this were: how should they be brought to shore and who should receive them. To solve these problems two members would soon be sent to India to negotiate with the leaders of the revolutionary parties. After fixing the exact place and recipients they would send an agent to Shanghai and one to Batavia who would deliver the message orally.(131)

The plan of the Chatto party included propaganda among the Indian pilgrims to Mecca; winning the minds of Indian soldiers, some

---

Punjab. The Sikhs, however, decided to march to Calcutta, 15 miles away, and on their way encountered European police. A riot between them broke out resulting in indiscriminate firing with 22 casualties. See Ker, op.cit., pp.239-245; Sedition Committee Report pp.103-104.

129) W.K. 11f, 6, pp.50-51.

130) Ibid., p.53.

131) Ibid.

15,000 of whom were said to be in South Persia, Basra and the Persian Gulf; revolutionary propaganda among the Indians of Afghanistan and the transmission of messages through them; trying to get news from Indian students in London and especially trying to bring Indian nationalists from there to Berlin; and finding ways of sending some members to spread anti-British propaganda among Indian soldiers in France. (132)

Forwarding the complaints and the Indians' plan of action to Zimmermann, the Under Secretary of State for Foreign Affairs, Wesendonk asked what reply he should give to the Indians as to their desire to work directly with the Foreign Office. Zimmermann said he had no objection to Wesendonk's negotiating directly with the Indians. (133) Wesendonk who was in charge of propaganda among the suppressed nationalities of the Russian and British Empires, seemed to have understood the difficulties of the Indians in having to work through the mediation of persons who had little understanding of the Indian situation. Energetic and professionally ambitious as he was (134), it is quite probable that he wished to handle and direct the course of Indian activities himself. This was a time when so much was heard about India being ripe for

---

132) Ibid., pp. 54-55.

133) Ibid., p. 45.

134) The fact that Wesendonk personally looked into each and every aspect of the Berlin-sponsored programme for helping the various nationalities of vast areas under Russian and British subjugation to revolt against their foreign masters show how tremendously energetic and enthusiastic he was. So far as the Indian part of his work was concerned, whatever may have been the original motive behind the German sponsorship of the Indian freedom struggle, the records clearly show Wesendonk's genuine sympathy for the Indians. As his understanding of Indian politics grew in the course of time he knew that a revolution in India was a far cry and the Indian freedom struggle must be a long-drawn out one. In his limited capacity he tried, in the later period of the Berlin Committee, to harmonise the Hindu-Muslim differences which, he thought, was the necessary first step towards a national struggle for freedom. Wesendonk's role in the field of the suppressed nationalities of the British Empire - especially in India - has been hitherto largely unknown. But to his stupendous work in the Russian sphere of influence the following fact remains an eloquent testimony:

revolution. The latest of the inspiring firsthand reports about India came from Vienna. It was a report which Count Thurn, the erstwhile Austrian Consul General in Calcutta who had left India on 3 October 1914, had submitted to Count Berchtold. (135) Thurn described the condition of India at the outbreak of the War, which he had seen for himself, mentioned also the Indian revolutionary organisations in Europe and America. He was optimistic and saw every advantage for the Central Powers in aiding the preparations for revolution in India. (136) There is no doubt that all these factors encouraged the youthful Wesendonk who, at 29, was still a year younger than Chatto, the leader of the Indian group.

As a result of this successful meeting between the Indians and the Foreign Office, Oppenheim's India Committee came under the complete control of the Indians. In the beginning Oppenheim was not aware of the change of policy at the Foreign Office and he considered the latters' frequent visits there more an unfortunate aberration than a rule. As the work of his Nachrichtenstelle für den Orient (137) frequently overlapped with the India Committee

---

the Baltic Baron Uexküll, whom the Foreign Ministry had commissioned to organise the 'League of Russia's Foreign Peoples' said in a letter of thanks to Wesendonk on 8 May 1916 that the German Reich ought to erect two monuments in recognition of his services: one on the northernmost point of Finland, the other on the southernmost point of the Caucasus. See F. Fischer, Germany's Aims... p. 125, also pp. 145, 558-9 for Wesendonk's work in the Russian borderland.

135) Thurn to Berchtold, 5 December 1914, in Tschirschky to Bethmann-Hollweg, Vienna 20 December 1914, W. K. 11f, 6, pp. 136-42.

136) Thurn said that India without the British would most probably be divided into small states and the Austrians and Germans would share the most important concessions for mining and industry in that richest country of the world. Thurn argued that in aiding a big revolution in India the Central Powers could gain also in a different way: the fear of losing India would force Britain to withdraw troops from European theatres. Ibid.

137) Nachrichtenstelle für den Orient which was founded by Oppenheim in the middle of August 1914 and was renamed after the War as Deutsches Orient-Institut, collected valuable news about the countries of the Middle East and the Far East to use them for propaganda purposes. It also looked after the Orientals living in Berlin. Besides Germans, it had co-workers from various countries,

work, news and reports concerning Indian activities continued to come to him while he remained in Berlin. But at the beginning of 1915 he was transferred to Constantinople and the India Committee established itself firmly under Indian leadership and also acquired, an office of its own at Berlin-Charlottenburg, Wielandstraße 38. The Indians were happy to work under friendly Wesendonk.(138) In the middle of January 1915 Chatto met Har Dayal in Geneva again and as a result of this Har Dayal came to Berlin on 27 January 1915 to join the India Committee's leadership.(139) On a visit to Berlin in February 1915, Oppenheim saw the change in the method of working with the Indians and warned Zimmermann that in the interest of both the Indians and Germany direct contact by the Foreign Office with the Indians should be avoided and in this respect the Foreign Office should revert to the policy maintained by him December 1914.(140) The Foreign Office apparently took no notice of this.

---

although they were forever changing. It issued a prisoners newspaper in the various languages of the prisoners of war after due censure by Wesendonk of the Foreign Office and Capt. Nadolny of the General Staff. It also gave out frequent bulletins which were periodically compiled into a quarterly called Der Neue Orient. Among its German co-workers were Dr. Herbert Mueller; Heinrich Jacoby, General Secretary of ' Persische Teppich-Gesellschaft AG' ; Ferdinand Graetsch, a missionary with Indian experience; Professor Eugen Mittwoch, orientalist; and the young indologist Dr. Helmut von Glasenapp. See H. v. Glasenapp, Meine Lebensreise, ch. IV.

138) The documents of the four years of the War period which are under our investigation show clearly the extremely good relations that existed between Wesendonk and the Indians throughout the War period. The Indians were also invited to private parties at Wesendonk's house.

139) Romberg to A.A., Bern 13 and 26 January 1915; W.K. 11f, 7, p. 81; W.K. 11f, 8, p. 110.

140) Oppenheim's emphasis on secrecy is understandable. Har Dayal, too, never ceased to emphasise this. But Oppenheim certainly went too far in his bureaucratic methods which the Indians, if nothing else, found time consuming. The following is the procedure that Oppenheim laid down for the Indians if they had anything to convey to the Foreign Office: "The decisions or requests which the Committee would like to submit to the Foreign Office are to be addressed to Herr von Wesendonk and deposited with the porters of the Foreign Office in written form with dates

It does not come within the scope of the present work to discuss the work and activities of the Berlin India Committee during the four years of its existence nor do we propose to assess its merits and demerits here. But as the preference given to the Chatto plan meant the virtual elimination of other plans preceeding it, i. e. those of Oppenheim (141) and Har Dayal the significance of Chatto's success may be noted here.

In his Indian work Oppenheim took into account primarily Muslim factors. So far as the Afghan expedition was concerned the idea was that Afghanistan should be persuaded by Turkey to attack India. It was expected that the pro-Turkish Indian Muslims, especially of north and north-west India would revolt being aroused by Pan-Islamism and thereby cause concern for the British in India, who consequently would sue for peace with Germany. In this Machiavellian scheme there was no ultimate concern for the Indians, neither Muslims nor Hindus, although the formers' pro-Turkish bias was counted upon and the latters' political unrest was taken as a helping factor. The participation of Indians - who were mostly

---

and numbers and signed by two gentlemen (preferably always the same ones). Only in urgent cases the written messages should be handed over directly to Herr Wesendonk. In order to avoid drawing attention the submission of messages etc. it be best done by a German, perhaps by the servant of Nachrichtenstelle für den Orient which is housed opposite Reichskolonialamt, entrance Mauerstraße 45/56 and not Wilhelmstraße..." Oppenheim also said that in his time he had made the Indians realise that they were living in a war-time situation and were therefore not free to meet any people they liked. According to Oppenheim his old policy was more fruitful and bore better results. Oppenheim to Zimmermann, Berlin 25 Feb. 1915, W. K. 11f, 10, pp. 55-57.

141) It was Oppenheim's policy rather than his plan which was discontinued as a result of the acceptance of the Chatto plan, for both the Turco-Afghan expedition plan into which Oppenheim's ideas fitted neatly and Oppenheim's other works to bring about a connection between the Indian revolutionists abroad and their counterparts at home formed, more or less, parts of the Chatto programme. But although many Indians later joined different German expedition groups in Persia, the Turco-German Afghan expedition as such could not operate due to the lack of co-operation between the Turks and the Germans and also due to the disunity among the German members themselves. The uncertainty of that expedition was very clear to the German Foreign Office by the time Chatto and his party met Wesendonk.

Hindus - in this plan would have been embarrassing both for the Indians and the Germans.

Parallel to this plan but with different emphasis was Har Dayal's plan. His was also basically a military plan. He conceived two military undertakings in fact. One was an Afghan attack on India, the other was the anexation of the State of Kashmir by the Indian nationalists by force of arms. Both the undertakings were to be performed with the help of German 'officers, arms, ammunitions, bombs, aeroplanes, and wireless'. The success of these two endeavours, Har Dayal visualised, would bring about a revolt all over India and especially in Hyderabad and Nepal. It would suit the needs of the Germans and the Indian nationalists alike.

To keep the revolutionary situation alive in India both Oppenheim and Har Dayal also accepted measures for encouraging unrest in India.

In contrast to these two primarily military schemes (142) the Chatto scheme completely left out military aspects. Chatto aimed, first and foremost, at measures which would bring all the Indian revolutionary elements in India and abroad under the united front

---

142) Originally there was one more scheme with a military aspect among the various devices of propaganda in India. This, the so-called Brun or Brun-Mannesman plan, was submitted to the German Foreign Office in the autumn of 1914 in the form of a memorandum by one 29 year old Swiss national Edgar Brun, who had earlier come in touch with Count Witte in Russia while serving in St. Petersburg as an official of the Russian Asiatic Bank and who presently claimed to have the sympathy, though not active help, of Krishnavarma for his proposed Indian venture. This scheme, which aimed at the formation of an independent United States of India, at the cost of Britain and with economic connection with Germany, Russia and Austria, was, however, not considered apt for the existing war-time situation by the German Foreign Office. Har Dayal considered Brun's suggestions of no practical value and Chatto and Kersasp even warned the A.A. against Brun who was suspected to be working in the Russian interest. Oppenheim, too, was against Brun's venture. As a result Brun's plan was abandoned in early February 1915. See W.K. 11f, 5, pp. 126-7, 134-5, 142-3, 166; 6, pp. 4, 41-42, 64; pp. 94-100, 101[a].

of an Indian National(ist) Party (143) with German financial and other assistance.

Chatto also planned to build up public opinion against British rule in India both in India and in the world at large. The most important programme included in this scheme was the buying of arms and ammunitions and sending them to India. They were to be stored in safe places by the chosen revolutionists until the inevitable advent of a general revolt.

This elastic, propaganda-based plan of action to bring about an Indian revolution was, in a way, a clever device on the part of Chatto to bind the Germans to the Indian cause on a long-term basis. The defence of India's north-west frontier being, in fact, the defence of India itself, the British frontier experts with direct knowledge of it and the whole of Central Asia were not sleeping over the issue. A cursory glance at the Proceedings of the Central Asian Society, London, for the pre-War years would prove this point. The Indian revolutionists could of course reap a fine harvest in the event of an invasion of India provided they were united and active, but they were hardly people with the ability to plan, guide or control such an invasion. In fact none of them, including Har Dayal, betrayed any scientific knowledge of the north-west frontier or of the British imperial defence mechanism. Har Dayal himself, while advocating an invasion, leaned heavily on his own idealised picture of an all-pervading 'Indian Nationalist Party' active in India. Such a thing, of course, did not exist. Moreover, far from having the ability to harness a foreign invasion to their advantage and to the detriment of the British, the militant nationalists' own house was not in order. Among their various groups there were strong differences based on principles (144) and personal likes and

---

143) In the scheme submitted to Wesendonk on 7 December 1914 the unity of the various secret groups under one body was stressed but the name Indian Nationalist Party was not mentioned. In other correspondence, including those of Har Dayal, the concept of an Indian Nationalist Party - meaning thereby a party of all the militant nationalists of India who parted from the Indian National Congress in 1907 - was, however, always present. The Berlin Committee's early propaganda material was issued under this name. See for example A manifesto of the Indian National Party, W.K. 11f, 18, pp. 21-22.

144) For example, Lajpat Rai, a leading Indian extremist nationalist, remained in the U.S.A throughout the War and inspite of long endeavours on the part of the Berlin Com-

dislikes. (145) The Indian revolutionists in Europe and America
never had any mass base in India and whatever contacts they
had in India on a personal level were all swept away by the
repressive measures introduced by the Government at the outbreak of the War. (146) Chatto's plan was, therefore, an endeavour
to revive with German help the latent Indian disaffection towards
British rule. The same was also the object of many measures
taken during August and December 1914 under the leadership of

---

mittee he refused to join the Committee on the principle of
not taking foreign help for India's struggle for freedom and
not using violent means for it. Har Dayal differed from
other revolutionary nationalists in that he believed in
organised, open rebellion. Then again, in 1914 after release
from imprisonment even Tilak disclaimed all hostility to
the British Government and repudiated acts of violence.
For the characteristics of the various groups of Indian
nationalists see Lajpat Rai, op. cit., ch. V. 'Types of
Nationalists'.

145) We have already mentioned the differences of various Indian
revolutionary nationalists with Shyamaji Krishnavarma. That
the relation between Chatto and Har Dayal was also not very
amicable at the earliest stage of the Berlin Committee is
clear from the fact that inspite of Chatto's presence in Berlin
the German Foreign Office had to learn about Har Dayal from
Wangenheim in Constantinople. Again when Har Dayal named
Krishnavarma as one of the important members of the nationalist party and later the Turks wanted to have him in Constantinople Oppenheim had to warn the Foreign Office thus:
"My Indians, who know Krishnavarma very well warn against
him saying that he is a cowardly man of low mentality and
is concerned about his own material and personal benefit and
would never take part in revolutionary activity. No Indian
nationalist would like to have anything to do with him as he
has till now only discredited the nationalists and through his
indiscretion in many ways damaged the nationalist cause..."
Oppenheim to A.A., 21 November 1914, W.K. 11f, 4, p. 104.

146) For example, 'The Ingress into India Ordinance 1914' introducing severe control of persons entering British India by
sea or land; 'The Foreigners Ordinance 1914'; 'The Defence
of India (Criminal Law Amendment) Act 1915' etc. See
Government of India, Legislation and Orders relating to the
War (Calcutta 1918) pp. 2-13, 51-52.

Baron Oppenheim (147); but Oppenheim was too authoritarian and with him the Indians had little chance to plan anything which did not directly and primarily benefit the German cause. Moreover, Oppenheim was concerned more with the Muslim factors whereas the revolutionary elements in India were to be found mostly among the Hindus. Under such circumstances there was no certainty of long standing Indo-German co-operation, for at any moment - and certainly in the case of the Indians' failing to deliver the goods - the bond of union could abruptly be snapped. By achieving control over the whole Indian programme and by establishing a lasting understanding with youthful and friendly Wesendonk, who, to the great advantage of the Indians, remained in the same job in Berlin throughout the War period, Chatto got rid of the twin danger to the Indians of either being exploited or discarded. Later, when the primary action of invasion from Afghanistan failed it was the subsidiary activities of Chatto on which the German Foreign Office hopefully depended.

The Berlin India Committee during its four years of existence took up a wide range of programmes in America, the Middle East, the Far East, South East Asia, Afghanistan and India itself during the First World War which were to bring mutually helpful results for both the Germans and the Indians. These programmes, however, did not ultimately succeed in their main objectives. The lack of a common programme and mass base on the part of the Indian militant nationalists; unflinching loyalty of the Indian princes to the British throughout the War period; the strict neutrality of the Afghan Amir; the severe measures adopted by the British to stamp out Indian sedition and treason; the superiority of British Intelligence; the immaturity, pretentiousness, rivalry, jealousy, and Hindu-Muslim mutual distrust among the Indians in Berlin and Constantinople; the easy availability of any quantity of money encouraging vague, expensive, and not infrequently fraudulent projects (not from the Indians alone) - all these factors separately and collectively sapped the original revolutionary urge and purity of purpose of the Berlin Indians and made their Committee ineffective in so far as its original aims were concerned. But as the culmination of nearly thirty years of Indo-German official contact, with which we are concerned in this study, the

147) All the activities in Chatto's memorandum, shown to have been carried out by the Indians until early December 1914 were those undertaken with Oppenheim's approval and mediation.

Berlin Committee's significance lies elsewhere. Quite contrary to
the account so far given of the downright exploitive nature of Germany's promotion of revolution among the suppressed nations,
here, at least from the end of 1916, we find a different picture.
The failure of the Indian collaborators to bring about a revolution
in India was very clear by then and yet a genuine endeavour
persisted on the part of those concerned at the German Foreign
Office and at the Nachrichtenstelle für den Orient to understand
those complexities of the Indian situation which hindered the Berlin
Committee's efforts and to help the Committee plan for the future. (148) Still remarkable is it that permission and finance were
granted to the Berlin Committee from the middle of 1917 to start
broadcasting India's case for freedom to the world at large from
a neutral country - Sweden - which later resulted in contact with
the European socialists and the Bolsheviks.

It was of course necessary in Germany's own interest as well to
counteract 'the fear of German despotism' in neutral countries
which, as historian Hans Delbrück considered, was "one of the
most effective facts and strongest factors in favour of the enemy"(149).
The very successful propaganda of the Stockholm branch of the
Berlin India Committee against British wrongdoings in India seemed
to have fulfilled this task to some extent. Chatto in Stockholm won
the co-operation of many of the newspapers and his ceaseless and
systematic propaganda drove Britain to make counter-propaganda
there against the Berlin Committee Indians. (150) But the change

148) Thus Ludwig Dehio is quite right in saying that "to speak
of pure cynicism" about Germany's concern for those in
the shade "would certainly be an unjustified over-simpli-
fication." See L. Dehio, Germany and World Politics in
the Twentieth Century (Tr. D. Pevsner London 1959) pp. 88-9.

149) Delbrück quoted in H. Kohn, The Mind of Germany: The
Education of a Nation (New York 1960) p. 302.

150) Professor Gilbert Murray had already started defending
Britain in India in the Swedish press a little before it
was flooded by Indian propaganda (see Dagens Nyheter
10 July 1916). Later the British sent Professor Yusuf
Ali to Stockholm to make counter-propaganda against the
Berlin Committee Indians (see Afton Tidningen 4 and 9
May 1918 and Stockholms Tidningen 11 May 1918). One
of the British propaganda publications of this time, German Judgements on British Politics included passages
of pre-War German praise for British rule in India.

that came over Germany's attitude towards the Indian freedom movement during the War was not a temporary one; it was to outlive the War and bring a broad and liberal understanding of the subject in the Germany of the Weimar Republic. As a result, the popular Indian image of Germany as a sympathetic country with respect for indology remained intact; the old contempt for a socialist association with India's anti-colonialism was gone; and the subject of the Indian Muslims began to be treated in the inner context of Indian history rather than of Pan-Islamism. (151)

151) Some of the old participants in the War-time India programme of the German Foreign Office also helped bring about this climate of understanding. As witness Helmuth von Glasenapp's interest in the Indian freedom movement side by side with his serious research in ancient Indian religion and philosophy, Werner-Otto von Hentig's translation of H. M. Hyndman's The Awakening of Asia (Der Aufstieg des Morgenlandes, Leipzig 1921, translator's preface pp. 239-245) and Joseph Horovitz's Indien unter britischer Herrschaft (Leipzig 1928) can be cited. (Glasenapp had been associated with the Indian propaganda of the Nachrichtenstelle für den Orient; Hentig had been the leader of the Berlin Committee's Afghan Mission; Horovitz had often been consulted by the German Foreign Office during War-time on the question of Indian Muslims for his pre-War personal knowledge in Aligarh.) A study on German interest in the Indian freedom struggle after the First World War is still wanting. For a list - by no means a detailed one - of some German titles on the subject of the Indian freedom movement in the Weimer period see W. Leifer, op. cit. , p. 228.

SOME CONCLUDING REFLECTIONS

In the foregoing pages we have tried to discuss in historical perspective official Germany's attitude towards India during a period of nearly thirty years ending at the outbreak of the First World War. The drive for imperialism and a power-state in Germany, and the rise of nationalism in India being the two most significant political developments in the two respective countries during this period, this study, within its own limitation and emphases, has concerned itself primarily with these two main political currents. The topics and trend of this study have also been determined by the nature of the basic source material consulted for the purpose, namely, the foreign-political documents of the German Foreign Office at the time.

We have suggested here that in 1886 when Bismarck established consular relations with British India, his prime motive was to keep a watch on Britain's strength and weaknesses in India for diplomatic reasons. He was conscious of the fact that British foreign policy depended to a large extent of the 'defence of India' question. Bismarck was convinced that to protect India from external danger Britain would, sooner or later, feel the necessity of a German alliance. He was in favour of such an alliance but perhaps not until the chances of a British clash with Russia in Central Asia diminished. By maintaining a tie with Russia Bismarck kept Britain in need of Germany.

The German assessment of the British Indian situation towards the close of the Bismarckian period revealed something very significant for the Germany of Kaiser Wilhelm II. As the latter's imperialism and navy implied an ultimate enmity with Britain, it was no wonder that the belief that an uprising would inevitably occur against the British in India in the event of a British reverse in a major war, constantly inspired, intrigued and solaced Wilhelmian Germany throughout the years leading to the First World War. Wilhelm II showed a keen interest in Indian developments by personally vetting most of the political despatches concerning India and commenting upon them. The official Germans in India while truthfully reporting the fears and forebodings of the Anglo-Indians never failed to see the realities of the situation which always remained in favour of the British. Nevertheless, the Kaiser and to some extent the Foreign Office in Berlin came to hold an exaggerated notion of British India's insecurity from various angles such as the possibility of a Russian invasion, the internal disaffection of the Indians, the Turkish influence on the Indian Muslims and Japanese imperialism. (1) At first Berlin hoped that

---

1) India does not seem to be the only area about which Berlin,

these potential dangers to British India would act in Germany's favour in exacting concessions from Britain. But the conviction that Anglo-Russian reconciliation was impossible and the caution imposed by the so-called danger period before the navy was built seem to have led Berlin merely to expect things to turn in its favour without evolving a policy either alone or in conjunction with Russia to profit from Britain's Russophobia in India. As a result in 1907 the era of this Russophobia ended without any German diplomatic advantage therefrom. Germany's pro-British neutrality in the Boer War did not either result in any benefits for her in the field of economic expansion as she had expected from reciprocal British good-will. Curzon, then Viceroy of India, was responsible, directly or indirectly, for thwarting some German hopes in this direction. Even immediately after the Anglo-Russian Convention of 1907 there was an opportunity for Germany to hinder the growth of Anglo-Russian friendship by taking advantage of dissatisfaction in Russia about the limitation which this Asiatic settlement placed upon further Russian expansion in Central Asia and about Britain's getting the best of the bargain. But Germany failed to comprehend this and thereby "the easiest way by which Great Britain and Russia could be kept apart was ignored."(2)

In the post-1907 period, when German world-power policy was heading for a collision with Britain, which now was no longer suffering a Russian 'pressure on India', the Kaiser and the German Foreign Office seem to have counted upon anti-British Indian revolutionary elements as a possible ally in case of a final clash with Britain. Some evidence of 1909 shows how Professor Schiemann, the influential commentator of the Kreuz-Zeitung, had been regularly fed with exaggerated news of Indian revolutionary preparations by George Freeman, an Irish Sinn Fein leader in America, connected with the Indian revolutionary nationalists abroad. Such news seem to have convinced Berlin of an inevitable anti-British uprising in India in case Britain engaged herself in a war with Germany. "The British should be aware" wrote the Kaiser, "that war with Germany would mean the loss of India and thus the loss of their world power."

Having missed an earlier opportunity to profit from Britain's Russophobia regarding India, it was natural that Berlin would be watching for Britain's other weak spots. But while discovering

---

in the pre-War years, held a different opinion from the authentic judgement of its accredited agents. cf. Sir H. Nicolson, Diplomacy (3d ed. London 1963) pp. 148-9.

2) R. P. Churchill, op. cit., pp. 343-4.

one in the extremist elements of Indian nationalism, Berlin failed
to evolve a cautious, compromising policy based on it so as to
make sure of Britain's doom in India, as revealed in the Kaiser's
words. It would have been only logical for Germany to establish
at least some contact with the Indian nationalist movement if she
really expected an Indian uprising to coincide with her impending
war with Britain. But this was not to happen. The burden of the
whole social-political tradition of Imperial Germany stood in its
way. The political education of the Indian nationalists ran counter
to that of the official Germans. Anti-parliamentarism, hostility
to Western liberalism, disregard of the modern importance of the
fundamental rights of man, and the consideration of aristocracy
as a superior socio-political system over democracy were some
of the chief characteristics of the German conservative tradition (3)
to which the official Germans belonged. Even the German liberals
of the time were not concerned so much with the individual rights
of man; they were votaries of the German power-state for the sake
of which they readily accepted social Darwinism and 'illiberal imperialism' (4). The influence of Gladstonian liberalism among some
of the British officials in India, the Indians' agitation for decentralisation, representative government, and the rights of man based
on the principle of equality, were the subjects of perpetual condemnation by the pre-War Germans in India. In them the impact of
racialism was also profound. In the post-1907 period, at a time
when political terrorism was quickenning the tempo of Indian natioalism, the sympathy of some liberal and socialist politicians in
England for some of the political aspirations of the Indians was
enough to enrage the Kaiser and the official Germans. Political
terrorism was also no help to German commerce in India. Under
such circumstances there could hardly be any thought of mutual
understanding between the Indians and Germans on a politico-con-
spiratorial level.

With the political agitations of one section of the Indian people
- the Indian Muslims - the official Germans had, however, no

---

3)   cf. H. Kohn, op. cit., pp. 273, 277.

4)   Discussing two leading German liberals of the time Hans
     Kohn points out the impact of social Darwinism on Max
     Weber who countered an attack on Prussia's policy against
     her Poles by saying: "We alone made out of the Poles
     human beings." Similarly, in Friedrich Naumann's eyes
     Karl Peters' inhumanity was insignificant compared to
     his services to German expansion. See ibid., pp. 283, 288.
     For Weber, see also R. Dahrendorf, op. cit., p. 57.

quarrel. There were two main reasons for this. First, being under the spiritual influence of Turkey, the Indian Muslims formed a part of the so-called German Orient policy. Germany counted upon their support in any policy undertaken jointly with Turkey. Secondly, the Indian Muslims, frightened at the possibility of being submerged under Hindu domination in case of a full parliamentary democracy in India, remained mostly outside the pale of the primarily Hindu-directed reform-cum-liberation movement. So the politics of the Indian Muslims was not ideologically repugnant to the Germans. Besides, the Turkey-oriented aspect of it, it was thought, could only be an asset to the German power-state policy. Naturally, after the Balkan wars when the traditional Muslim support for the British was eroding in India, the official Germans, at the threshold of a war with Britain, pondered whether it was not time to activate the traditional tacit German interest in the Indian Muslims by egging them on against the British. To this thinking Enver Pasha's idea of a Turco-German Pan-Islamic expedition to Afghanistan to induce her to invade India came as a most welcome suggestion to Berlin at the outbreak of War.

While plans for the Afghan expedition and other measures to bring about a revolution in India - purely as a war strategy - were gradually advancing in the autumn of 1914, one event suddenly broadened the base and purpose of this planning before the year ended. A fruitful personal meeting of some leading Indian revolutionary nationalists with the German Foreign Office resulted in the foundation of an organisation, the Berlin India Committee (5), and Germany's declaring the independence of India as one of her War-time objectives. Entirely financed by the German Government and yet largely under the control of the Indians themselves, the India Committee took both conspiratorial and propaganda means to achieve its declared object. Thus with the hope of a prompt success in revolutionising India against the British Berlin abandoned its hostility to Indian nationalism.

This accidental change in the German attitude towards Indian natioalism, irrespective of its original motive, is highly significant for future relations between Germany and the Indians' India. First of all, if Germany had gone ahead with the plan for a Pan-Islamic invasion of India in its original form, it would have shattered the century-old image of Germany, firmly imprinted on the Hindu mind, that there was a home of indology with great love for things Indian. It is, however, not suggested that the fact of the German

---

5) For the various names under which this organisation
    functioned in different areas see Appendix III.

Government supporting the Berlin India Committee automatically raised either that Committee or the German Government high in the estimation of the Indians in general including the nationalists of all kinds. But - and this is our second and more important point - the Berlin India Committee by making Indian independence one of Germany's War-time missions abroad and by achieving the sustained efforts of the German Government for it, created a climate of good-will in Germany for the Indians in general and their political aspirations which was to outlive the War. Many Germans who at this time either actively participated in the German Foreign Office-sponsored programmes involving India or were otherwise influenced by the climate created by these programmes, helped replace the old arrogant, indifferent, or hostile attitude of Germany towards Indian nationalism and anti-imperialist struggle by a sympathetic approach to understanding the problems of the Indians.

APPENDIX I

OFFICIAL GERMANS IN INDIA 1854 - 1914

A. 'Wahlkonsuls' at Calcutta (1)

1854 - 1869	Ed. Dunbar Hilburn
1870 - 1876	Johann Smidt
1877 - 1882	P. F. Eisenlohr
1883 - 1893	Wilhelm Bleeck
1893 - 1898	O. Schmidt-Ernsthausen
1899 - 1910	William Bleeck
1911	unoccupied
1912 - 1914	Hans R. Schuler

When five years after the end of the First World War the German
official connection with India was reestablished the post of the
'Wahlkonsul' at Calcutta was abolished.

B. Consul Generals at Calcutta

March 1886 - August 1889	Dr. Hermann Gerlich
Jan. 1890 - Jan. 1894	Dr. Edmund Baron von Heyking (later Minister at Peking, Mexico and Belgrad)
April 1894 - Dec. 1895	Günther Baron von Gaertner-Griebenow (later Minister at Teheran)
March 1896 - Jan. 1901	Dr. Julius von Waldthausen (later Minister at Buenos Aires, Copenhagen, and Bukharest)
Jan. 1901 - June 1903	Hermann Baron Speck von Sternburg (later Ambassador at Washington)
Feb. 1904 - Jan. 1908	Albert Count von Quadt-Wykradt-Isny (later Minister at Teheran and Athens)
July 1908 - Nov. 1910	Claus von Below-Saleske (later Minister at Sofia and Brussels)

---

1) Areas of operation: Bengal, the United Province of Agra
    and Audh and the native states falling in these areas.

Nov. 1910 - July 1912	Heinrich XXXI Prince Reuss J.L. (later Minister at Teheran)
Nov. 1912 - Aug. 1914	Karl Ludwig Count von Luxburg (later Minister at Buenos Aires)

C. Vice-Consuls at the Consulate General, Calcutta

1901 - 1904	Dr. Ernst Voretzsch (later Ambassador at Tokyo)
1905 - 1908	Dr. Friedrich von Keller (later Ambassador at Ankara)
1909 - 1912	Dr. Erwin Remy (later Consul General at Canton)
1913 - 1914	Dr. Erich Baron von Rosen (showed disinterest for higher consular career)

D. Secretaries at the Consulate General, Calcutta

1887	Dr. Rudolf Eiswaldt
1888	Fritz Wegener
1889	unoccupied
1890	Dr. Wilhelm Solf
1891 - 1892	unoccupied
1893 - 1904	Theodor Rathsam
1905 - 1908	Michael Noculak
1909 - 1912	Karl-Josef Menne
1913 - 1914	Fritz Grimm

E. Military and other experts attached to the Consulate General at Calcutta

1899 - 1900 von Stumm	Royal Prussian First Lieutenant of the 15th Hanoverian Hussar Regiment
1901 - 1902 Bramsch	First Lieutenant of the 18th Royal Saxonian Lancers
1903 - 1905 Walter	Royal Prussian Lieutenant 53rd Pomeranian Field Artillery Regiment

1905	-	1906	Waetjen	Royal Prussian Lieutenant of the 6th Thuringian Lancers

1905 - 1906 Waetjen   Royal Prussian Lieutenant of
the 6th Thuringian Lancers

1907 - 1908 von Brüning   Royal Prussian First Lieutenant
of the 3rd Brandenburgian
Hussar Regiment

1908 - 1909 Herbert Baron von Richthofen   with a desig-
(later Minister at Copenhagen,   nation of Le-
Brussels and Sofia)   gation Secretary

1906 - 1914 Fritz Gösling as trade expert

F.   Prussian and later German Consuls at Bombay

1856 - 1861   F. Matthey
1862 - 1871   A.C. Gumpert
1872   unoccupied
1873 - 1874   O. Nölke
1875 - 1876   unoccupied
1877 - 1886   Carl Kapp
1887 - 1888   Heinrich Bartels
1889 - 1895   Friedrich von Syburg
              (later Consul General at Yokohama
              and Minister at Addis Abeba)
1896 - 1898   Max Biermann
1898 - 1903   Markus Count Pfeil
1903 - 1908   Eduard Hopmann
1909 - 1914   Dr. Friedrich Heyer

G.   Other German official representatives in different parts
of India between 1912-14 preoccupied mainly with
German trade-commercial interests

Karachi   (operating areas: the pro-   Consul A. Thöle
          vinces of Sind and the   (1912)
          Punjab, the nearby native
          states, the state of Cutch,   Consul E. Neuenhofer
          and north-west frontier   (1914)
          areas)

Madras   (operating areas: Coroman-   Consul Max. Miersch
          del Coast from Madras to   (1912 - 1914)
          Cape Comorin excluding the
          French colony of Pondi-
          cherry and Karikal)

| Cochin | (operating areas: native states of Cochin and Travancore, district of Malabar and Laccadive Islands) | Consul Adolf Bueler (1912 - 1914) |

APPENDIX II

GERMAN COMMERCIAL AND INDUSTRIAL FIRMS IN INDIA IN 1914 (1)

In Bombay: Import houses: dyeing factories Bayer & Co., Ltd.
(Elberfeld); Berlin Anilin Co., Ltd.; Meister, Jucius & Brüning,
Ltd. (Höchst-on-Main); Cassella & Co. (Frankfurt-on-Main);
Ostermayer & Co. (Badische Anilin and Soda Company); Bauer &
Krause (Leipzig); Blum, Josef; Blascheck & Co, (Frankfurt-on-
Main); Blume & Reif (Hamburg); Flor & Co. (Leipzig); Grimm &
Bendien; Orenstein & Koppel (representative, Killick Nixon & Co.,
Ltd.); G.A. Schlechtendahl & Co. (Barmen); Schroeder, Smidt &
Co.; Steffens & Nölle (Berlin); Strandes & Co. (representative of
East Africa Line); Wörmann & Co. (Hamburg).
Export houses: Bauer & Krause (seeds); A. Blascheck & Co.
(seeds, cotton); Dreyfus & Co., Paris (seeds, wheat); Brothers
Salomon, Hanover (cotton, cotton by-products); Wolf & Sons, Stutt-
gart (cotton by-products); C. Schultz (photographer); An association
dedicated to the service of needy Germans; A German Association
and Reading Club.

In Calcutta: German-Asiatic Bank; Import-export-houses: Hadenfeldt
& Co.; Smidt, Sanders & Co.; Schroeder, Smidt & Co.; A. Menges
& Co.; Wörmann & Co.; Schache & Co.; Export houses: Moll,
Schütte & Co.; F. Ad. Aßmann & Co.; Wuetow, Gutmann & Co.;
O. Boyes & Co.; Import houses: Orenstein & Koppel; Meyer,
Soetbeer & Co.; F. Schonert & Co.; Dr. C. Schulten & Co.
(chemical study laboratory); Wm. O. Boeckel (agency).

In Cochin (Feroke, Malabar district): Henke's Tile works.

In Madras: C. Simon's Sons (branch of C. Simon & Sons, leather
factory, Kirn-on-Nahe. Export of tanned and raw hides, indigo,
tannery, representative of North-German Lloyd, insurance); Badische Company, Ltd. (Badische Anilin and Soda Company); Wiele
& Klein (photography, agency).

In Karachi: Wichers, Kaiser & Levy Ltd. (import & export).

---

1) See Asiatisches Jahrbuch 1914, pp. 174-176.

APPENDIX III

A NOTE ON THE NOMENCLATURAL, FUNCTIONAL AND LEADERSHIP CHANGES OF THE BERLIN INDIA COMMITTEE 1914 - 1918

In its earliest form the Berlin India Committee (I. C.) was known as Oppenheim's India Committee, having been founded by Baron Max von Oppenheim in the middle of September 1914 and being completely under his supervision. The ultimate aim of Oppenheim's Committee was to help in producing a revolutionary situation in India so as to divert British attention from European theatres of war and compel Britain to sue for peace. Naturally, in this scheme there was no promise of help for Indian liberation. Oppenheim stressed keeping the Committee a secret one and its Indian participants, whom, with a mixture of authoritarianism and paternalism he called 'my Indians', under strict control. The Indians under his management had no direct contact with the German Foreign Office (A. A.)

At the beginning of 1915 the Committee came under Indian leadership but with regular direct contact with and financial support from the A. A. V. Chattopadhyaya (Chatto) and Har Dayal were the leaders and so as to attract the Indian princes they extracted from the A. A. a written declaration that Germany had no selfish designs on India in helping the Indian liberation struggle. The same old conspiratorial and propagandist methods were used for the same old goal of bringing about an anti-British revolution in India, but now the policy-making of the Committee was entirely left to the Indian leaders.

When in April 1915 Har Dayal arrived in Constantinople to guide from there the I. C. activities in Mesopotamia and Syria he named the I. C. 's Constantinople office 'The Office of the Indian Nationalist Party' whose French rendering was, however, Bureau du Parti National Hindou. By the end of August 1915 Har Dayal left Turkey with the I. C. 's work there in a moribund state. In November the Committee sent a new team to Constantinople with emphasis on Muslim membership. With Dr. Hafis as President the new group formed the Young Hindustan Association in Constantinople. This completely useless body was officially dissolved in September 1916 and was replaced by the Indian National Party with Champakaraman Pillai, M. P. T. Acharya and L. P. Varma - the first being nominated as leader. The chief undertaking now was propaganda among the Indian prisoners in Turkey and taking care of them. In December the same year the I. C. withdrew completely from Turkey and Acharya was charged with the business of liquidation.

Towards the later half of 1915 Har Dayal was practically out of
the Berlin Committee and B. N. Dutta, a veteran Bengal revolutionary but a newcomer to Berlin from America (he arrived in Berlin
in early May 1915 via Athens and Constantinople), was mostly
dealing with the routine official correspondence of the I. C. The
name Indian Independence Committee appeared for the first time on the
the top left of the letters, now neatly typed in English, sent by the
India Committee to the A. A. The Committee seems to have had a
loose working constitution at this time to govern its internal matters.
The verdict of the 'General Body' was the deciding factor in the
question of personal conduct by the Committee members. (Har
Dayal's conduct was censured by this body.) There was no permanent executive committee as such, with designations such as
president or secretary, although to give the stamp of formality
and authority some correspondence with the A. A. went under the
name of the General Secretary. In the earlier period Chattopadhyaya
adjoined this designation to his signature in some of his letters to
the A. A. dealing with important and controversial subjects where
the authority or the policy of the I. C. needed to be asserted. At
a later period when he was mostly away in Stockholm and Dutta
was merely running the routine work of the Berlin office, Dutta,
too, used the designation of secretary in some correspondence of
minor importance. But Chatto remained head of the I. C. throughout and without his approval the A. A. did nothing concerning India
or the Indians. The propaganda material published by the I. C.
often bore the name Indian National Party.

In May 1917 a branch of the India Committee was founded by
Chattopadhyaya and Acharya in Stockholm. Named the European
Central Committee of the Indian Nationalists this organisation
aimed mainly at propaganda amongst socialist circles and later
at establishing contact with the Bolsheviks. The Stockholm branch's
name was taken by the Berlin office alternatively during the later
half of 1917 and in 1918.

SELECT BIBLIOGRAPHY [+)]

I MANUSCRIPT SOURCES

A AT THE POLITISCHES ARCHIV, AUSWÄRTIGES AMT, BONN

1. Englische Besitzungen in Asien 2,
   Britisch Indien   Vols. 1-58   (Oct. 1884-March 1920)

2. ...do. ...Militaria   Vols. 1-18   (Nov. 1885-June 1919)

3. ...do. ...Personalien indischer
   Fürsten   Vol. 1   (May 1887-April 1914)

4. Preussen I. Nr. 1g. Nr. 2.
   Reise Sr. K. u. K. Hoheit des Kronprinzen
   nach Indien   Vols. 1-10   (June 1910-April 1911)

5. ...do. ...Secr. ...   Vol. 1   (1911)

6. Weltkrieg Nr. 11e. Unternehmungen und
   Aufwiegelungen gegen unsere Feinde
   in Afghanistan und Persien
       Vols. 1-10   (Aug. 1914-March 1915)

7. Weltkrieg Nr. 11e   Entwürfe
   von Randschreiben an den Emir
   von Afghanistan u. indische Fürsten
       Vol. 1   (March 1915-May 1918)

8. Weltkrieg Nr. 11f.   Unternehmungen
   und Aufwiegelungen gegen unsere
   Feinde in Indien   Vols. 1-48   (Aug. 1914-April 1920)

9. Akten von der Deutschen
   Botschaft London   178-182   (Feb. 1888-Dec. 1909)
                           360 (1) (2)   (Jan. 1910-Jan. 1912)

+) This bibliography omits some other sources (including our personal interviews and correspondence) consulted in Germany, Switzerland, Sweden, and England to trace the activities of some of the important Berlin Committee Indians in the later part of the World War I and in the post-War years as our story of the Committee here stops at the beginning of 1915.

B AT THE BUNDESARCHIV, KOBLENZ

1. R 85/158   Die Indischen Eisenbahnen

2. R 85/665   Postverbindung nach Indien 1913-1915

3. R 85/720   Telegraphenverhältnisse
                   in Indien 1912-1920

4. R 85/773-776   Telegraphenwesen in Indien 1914-1917

5. R 85/6604   Waffenhandel 1911-1914

6. R 85/7039   Die Aussichten für die Wirtschafts-
                   richtungen des Reichs mit Indien
                   nach dem I. Weltkrieg von
                   Konsul Heyer, Amsterdam 13 Feb.1918

C AT THE INDIA OFFICE LIBRARY, LONDON

Mss. Eur. F 111/158-161, 221   Curzon Papers

Mss. Eur. C 125/1-3, C 126/1-3   Hamilton Papers

Mss. Eur. C 138   Trial of Ghadr Party Conspirators
                       1917-1918, Reporter's Transcript
                       Vols. 1-75

Mss. Eur. F 288/1-4   Catalogue and Abstracts of Hostile
                       Oriental Propaganda Pamphlets,
                       Old and New Series and Trans-
                       lations of the 'Ghadr'

II PRINTED SOURCES

1. Die große Politik der europäischen Kabinette 1871-1914,
   Sammlung der diplomatischen Akten des Auswärtigen
   Amtes (edited by Lepsius, J., Bartholdy, A.M., and
   Thimme, F.) (Berlin 1922-1927) Vols. IV, XII, XVII,
   XIX, XXI 2, XXIV, XXV 1

2. Deutsche Dokumente zum Kriegsausbruch
   (edited by Montgelas, Graf M. and Schücking, W.)
   (Berlin 1927) Vol. II

3. British Documents on the Origin of the War 1898-1914 (edited by Gooch, G. P. and Temperley, H.) (London 1927) Vol. I

4. Deutsches Handels-Archiv (compiled by the Ministry of Interior, Berlin) Vols. 1889 II, 1893 II, 1896 II, 1897 II, 1914 II

5. Berichte über Handel und Industrie (compiled by the Ministry of Interior, Berlin) Vol. XX 6 (Berlin Sept. 1913)

6. Letters from the Kaiser to the Czar (edited by Levin, I. D.) (New York 1920)

7. The Letters of Queen Victoria (edited by Buckle, G. E.) Series 3, Vol. III (London 1932)

8. Political Trouble in India 1907-1917 (written by J. C. Ker of the Indian Criminal Intelligence Department, summarising the information at the disposal of this Department on the political and revolutionary agitations of the time and published by the Government of India) (Calcutta 1917)

9. Sedition Committee (1918) Report (published by the Government of India) (Calcutta 1918)

III CONTEMPORARY JOURNALS AND NEWSPAPERS

Afton Tidningen (Stockholm)

Asiatisches Jahrbuch

Berliner Lokal-Anzeiger

Berliner Neueste Nachrichten

Berliner Tageblatt

The Bombay Chronicle

Civil and Military Gazette (Lahore)

The Daily Telegraph

Dagens Nyheter (Stockholm)

L'Eclair

The Englishman (Calcutta)

Free Hindusthan (New York)

Hamburgischer Correspondent

The Hindu (Madras)

Justice

Kölnische Zeitung

Leipziger Neueste Nachrichten

Le Moniteur de Rome

Münchener Neueste Nachrichten

Novoye Vremya

Pall Mall Gazette

The Pioneer (Allahabad)

Proceedings of the Central Asian Society

St. James's Gazette

Saturday Review

The Spectator

The Statesman (Calcutta)

Stockholms Tidningen

The Times

The Times of India (Bombay)

Vossische Zeitung

Welt-Korrespondenz

IV OTHER WORKS

Alder, G. J.   British India's Northern Frontier
                      1865-1895 (London 1963)

Anderson, P. R.   The Background of Anti-English Feeling
                      in Germany 1890 - 1902 (Washington 1939)

Anstey, V. The Economic Development of India (4 ed. London 1952)

Balfour, M. The Kaiser and His Times (London 1964)

Bernhardi, F. von Germany and the Next War (London 1911)

Bolt, C. Victorian Attitude to Race (London 1971)

Bongard, O. Die Reise des deutschen Kronprinzen durch Ceylon und Indien (Berlin 1911)

Bracher, K. D. 'Kaiser Wilhelm's Germany' in J. M. Roberts (ed.) Europe in the 20th Century Vol. 1, 1900-14 (London 1970)

Bramsted, E. K. Aristocracy and the Middle Classes in Germany (Chicago-London 1964)

Bülow, B. Denkwürdigkeiten I-II (Berlin 1930)

Carroll, E. M. Germany and the Great Powers 1866-1914: a Study in Public Opinion and Foreign Policy (2d ed. Hamden, Conn. 1966)

Caskel, W. 'Max Freiherr von Oppenheim' in Zeitschrift der Deutschen Morgenländischen Gesellschaft Bd. 101, Neue Folge Bd. 26 (Wiesbaden 1951)

Chapman, M. K. Great Britain and the Bagdad Railway (Northampton 1948)

Chirol, V. The Middle Eastern Question or Some Political Problems of Indian Defence (London 1905)

--- 'Pan-Islamism' in Proceedings of the Central Asian Society (London 1906)

--- Indian Unrest (London 1910)

--- Fifty Years in Changing World (London 1927)

233

Churchill, R. P.   The Anglo-Russian Convention of 1907 (Iowa 1939)

Collen, Sir, E. H. H.   'The Defence of India' in Proceedings of the Central Asian Society (London 1906)

Curtin, P. D. (ed.)   Imperialism (New York 1971)

Curzon, G. N.   Persia and the Persian Question, II (London 1892)

Dahrendorf, R.   Society and Democracy in Germany (New York 1967)

Das, R. K.   Hindustani Workers on the Pacific Coast (Berlin 1923)

Davies, C. C.   The Problem of the North-West Frontier 1890-1908 (London 1932)

Dawson, W. H.   The German Empire 1867-1914 and the Unity Movement, II (2d ed. London 1966)

Dehio, L.   Germany and World Politics in the Twentieth Century (London 1959)

Dutta, B. N.   Aprakashita Rajnaitik Itihas, II (in Bengali) (2d ed. Calcutta, no date)

Earle, E. M.   Turkey, the Great Powers and the Baghdad Railway (London-New York 1923)

Edwardes, M.   High Noon of Empire: India under Curzon (London 1965)

---   A History of India (Mentor, London 1967)

Emerson, R.   From Empire to Nation. The Rise to Selfassertion of Asian and African Peoples (Cambridge, Mass. 1960)

Farnie, D.   East and West of Suez: The Suez Canal in History 1854-1956 (Oxford 1969)

Farquhar, J. N.   Modern Religious Movements in India
                       (New York 1918)

Fischer, F.   Griff nach der Weltmacht
                       (Düsseldorf 1961)

---   Germany's Aims in the First World War
                       (New York 1967)

Fraser, L.   India Under Curzon and After
                       (London 1911)

Fraser-Tytler, Sir W. K.   Afghanistan: A Study of Political
                       Developments in Central Asia (2d ed.
                       London 1953)

Gallagher J., and Robinson, R.   Africa and the Victorians
                       (London 1961)

Gehrke, U.   Persien in der deutschen Orientpolitik
                       während des I. Weltkrieges (Stuttgart
                       1960)

Glasenapp, H. von   'England und Indien' in Lebensfragen
                       des Britischen Weltreiches (Berlin 1921)

---   Britisch Indien und Ceylon
                       (Berlin 1929)

---   'Britische Herrschaft und nationale
                       Bewegung in Indien' in Auslandsstudien
                       Bd. 5 (Königsberg 1930)

---   Meine Lebensreise (Wiesbaden 1964)

Gopal, R.   Indian Muslims: A Political History
                       (London 1959)

Gollwitzer, H.   .   Die gelbe Gefahr (Göttingen 1962)

---   Europe in the Age of Imperialism
                       1880-1914 (London 1969)

Gore, J.   King George V: A Personal Memoir
                       (London 1941)

Greaves, R. L. Persia and the Defence of India 1884-1892: A Study in the Foreign Policy of the Third Marquis of Salisbury (London 1959)

Gregory, R. G. India and East Africa (Oxford 1971)

Grenville, J. A. S. Lord Salisbury and Foreign Policy: The Close of the Nineteenth Century (London 1964)

Griesinger, W. German Intrigues in Persia: The Diary of a German Agent (published by the British, London u. d.)

Haldane, Viscount Before the War (London 1920)

A Handbook of German East Africa (London 1920)

Hardie, J. Keir India: Impressions and Suggestions (London 1909)

Hardinge of Penshurst Old Diplomacy (London 1947)

--- My Indian Years 1910-1916 (London 1948)

Hentig, O. W. von Der Aufstieg des Morgenlandes (Translation of H. M. Hyndman's Awakening of Asia with translators's preface) (Leipzig 1921)

--- Mein Leben eine Dienstreise (Göttingen 1962)

Heyking, E. von Tagebücher aus vier Erdteilen (Leipzig 1926)

Hoffmann, R. J. Sch. Great Britain and the German Trade Rivalry 1875-1914 (Philadelphia 1933)

Hollingsworth, L. W.   Asians of East Africa (London 1960)

Horovitz, J.   Indien unter britischer Herrschaft (Leipzig-Berlin 1928)

Hughes, E.   Keir Hardie (London 1956)

Iliffe, J.   Tanganyika Under German Rule 1905-1912 (Cambridge 1969)

Internationaler Sozialisten-Kongress, Stuttgart 1907 (Berlin 1907)

Jaeckh, E.   Deutschland im Orient nach dem Balkankrieg (München 1913)

Ker, J. C.   Political Trouble in India (Calcutta 1917)

Khan, The Aga   India in Transition (London 1918)

Kipling, R.   Departmental Detties, etc. (London & New York 1925   ed.)

Kohn, H.   The Mind of Germany (New York 1960)

Krieger, L.   The German Idea of Freedom (Boston 1957)

Kumar, R.   India and the Persian Gulf Region 1858-1905 (London 1965)

Langer, W. L.   The Diplomacy of Imperialism (New York 1956)

Legislation and Orders Relating to the War (Calcutta 1918)

Leifer, W.   India and the Germans: 500 Years of Indo-German Contact (Bombay 1971)

Lewis, S. E.   'Anglo-German diplomatic Relations 1898-1902'. Summary of a M. A. thesis, in Bulletin of the Institute of Historical Research 9 (London 1931)

Louis, W.R.   Great Britain and Germany's Lost
                               Colonies 1914-1919 (Oxford 1967)

Lowe, C.J.   The Reluctant Imperialists: British
                               Foreign Policy 1878-1902
                               (London 1967)

Lowe, C.J. and Dockrill, M.L.   British Foreign Policy
                               Vol.I 1902-1914 (London 1972)

Lowie, R.H.   Toward Understanding Germany
                               (Chicago 1954)

Maccoby, S.   English Radicalism 1886-1914
                               (London 1953)

MacDonald, J.R.   The Awakening of India
                               (London 1910)

MacDowell, R.B.   British Conservatism 1832-1914
                               (London 1959)

MacMunn, G.   Turmoil and Tragedy in India
                               1914 and After (London 1935)

Mangat, J.S.   History of the Asians in East Africa,
                               c. 1885 to 1945 (Oxford 1969)

Mansergh, N.   The Coming of the First World War:
                               A Study in the European Balance
                               1878-1914 (London 1948)

Marder, A.J. (ed.)   Fear God and Dread Nought: The
                               Correspondence of Admiral of the
                               Fleet Lord Fisher of Kilberstone II
                               (London 1956)

Martin, B.   New India 1885: British Official Policy
                               and the Emergence of the Indian National
                               Congress (Berkeley 1969)

Medlicott, W.N.   Bismarck, Gladstone and the Concert
                               of Europe (London 1956)

Mehrotra, S. R.	India and the Commonwealth 1885-1929 (London 1965)

Military Operations on the North West Frontier of India
Vol. II (London 1898)

Minogue, K. R.	Nationalism (London 1967)
Monger, G.	The End of Isolation: British Foreign Policy 1900-1907 (London 1963)
Morley, J.	Recollections II (London 1918)
Morrow, I. F. D.	'The Foreign Policy of Prince von Bülow 1898-1909' in Cambridge Historical Journal 4 (1932-34)
Muncy, L. W.	The Junker in the Prussian Administration Under William II 1888-1914 (2d ed. Rhode Island 1970)
Nadel, G. H. and Curtis, P.	Imperialism and Colonialism (New York 1964)
Nehru, J.	An Autobiography (London 1949)
Newton, Lord	Lord Lansdowne: A Biography (London 1929)
Nicolson, Sir H.	Diplomacy (3d ed. London 1963)
O'Dwyer, M.	India as I knew it 1885-1925 (London 1925)
Oncken, H.	Die Sicherheit Indiens (Berlin 1937)
Pillai, A. R.	Deutschland: Indiens Hoffnung (Rede) (Göttingen 1914)
Rai, L.	Young India (New York 1917)
Reventlow, Graf E. zu	Indien - Seine Bedeutung für Großbritannien, Deutschland und die Zukunft der Welt (Berlin 1917)

239

Rich, N. and Fisher, M.H. (ed.) The Holstein Papers I,
Memoirs (Cambridge 1955)

Rolo, P.J.V.   Entente Cordiale: The Origin and
                                Negotiations of the Anglo-French
                                Agreements of 8 April 1904
                                (London 1969)

Rose, K.   Superior Person: A Portrait of Curzon
                                and His Circles in Late Victorian
                                England (London 1969)

Sengupta, P.   Sarojini Naidu, a Biography
                                (London 1966)

Singh, H.L.   Problems and Policies of the
                                British in India 1885-1898
                                (London 1963)

Sontag, R.J.   Germany and England: Background
                                of Conflict 1848-1894
                                (New York 1938)

Sumner, B.H.   Tsardom and Imperialism in the
                                Far East and the Middle East
                                1880-1914 (Reprint 1968 without
                                place name)

Sykes, C.   Wassmuss, 'the German Lawrence'
                                (Leipzig 1937)

Taylor, A.J.P.   Germany's First Bid for Colonies
                                1884-1885: A Move in Bismarck's
                                European Policy (Reprint 1967
                                without place name)

---   The Struggle for Mastery in Europe
                                1848-1918 (Oxford 1954)

Thornton, A.P.   The Imperial Idea and its Enemies:
                                A Study in British Power
                                (London 1959)

Treue, W.   'Max Freiherr von Oppenheim der
                                Archäologe und die Politik', in
                                Historische Zeitschrift Vol. 209, I
                                (München 1969)

Trumpener, U.	Germany and the Ottoman Empire 1914-1918 (Princeton 1968)
Tschiedel, J.	'Englands indische Sorge' in Berliner Tageblatt 6 March 1914
Ullman, R. H.	Intervention and the War (Princeton 1961)
Viator, A. K.	Deutschlands Anteil an Indiens Schicksal (Leipzig 1918)
Vira, D.	Lala Har Dayal and Revolutionary Movement of his Time (New Delhi 1970)
Wasti, S. R.	Lord Minto and the Indian Nationalist Movement 1905 to 1910 (London 1964)
Wegener, G.	Das heutige Indien (Berlin 1912)
Werner, I.	'Zur Indienpolitik des deutschen Imperialismus seit dem Ende des 19. Jahrhunderts bis zum Ausbruch des I. Weltkrieges' in Zeitschrift für Geschichtswissenschaft, Sonderheft zur Geschichte des Kolonialismus und der nationalen Befreiung Bd. IX (Berlin 1961)
Windelband, W.	Bismarck und die Europäischen Großmächte 1879-1885 (Essen 1940)
Wright, H. M. (ed.)	The 'New Imperialism' (Lexington 1961)
Yajnik, I.	Shyamaji Krishnavarma: Life and Times of an Indian Revolutionary (Bombay 1950)
Zache, H.	Die Ausbildung der Kolonialbeamten (Berlin 1912)
Zugmayer, E.	'Die nationalistische Bewegung in Indien' in Vosberg-Rekow (ed.) Asiatisches Jahrbuch (Berlin 1912)

241

INDEX

(The abbreviation 'n' means 'footnote')

of India's problem, 23, 27;
Britain desires help from,
24-5; consulted by Britain
on Persian question, 26; and
Bulgarian crisis, 39; and
Russia, 39

Björkoe, 75

'Blessed Oppressed', 163

Bolsheviks, 212, 228

Bombay Chronicle,The, 136n, 146

Bose, Devendra, 191

Brodrick, William St. J. , 47n, 111

Brun, Edgar, 208n

Bryan, W. J. , 181

Bülow, Bernhard Count von, 16, 32,
39, 51-2; on security of British
India, 32-3, 75;on Indian immigrant
labour for German East-Africa, 154

Bulgarian Crisis, 30, 35n, 39

Caderwail, Safia, 191, 201n

Caine, W. S. , 129

Cama, Madam B. R. , 175, 176 and n,
178, 179, 180-1, 182, 184, 188

Central Asian Society, the Proceedings of, 209

Chakravarti, A. C. , 183

Chandra, Harish, 191

Chandra, Ram, 183

Charter Act, of 1833, 95, 122

Chatterjee, Abinash C. , 163

Chattopadhyaya (Chatto), V. , and
India House, London, 174; joins
the Paris group of Indian
revolutionists, 176; edits the
Talvar, 179-80; at Halle, 185;
comes to Berlin, 186; collects
Indians in Berlin, 190;becomes
leading member of Oppenheim's
India Committee, 191;prepares
for direct connection with
German Foreign Office, 198;meets
Har Dayal at Geneva, 199-200;
meets Wesendonk for the first
time, 201; offers the German
the plan of revolutionising
India, 201-4;comes to control
Oppenheim's India Committee,
205;his success with the German
Foreign Office, 207-11;dislikes
Krishnavarma, 210n;his relation
with Har Dayal, 210n;forms 'European Central Committee of the
Indian Nationalists', 228

Chirol, C. , 74n, 77n, 122n, 126

Churchill,Lord Randolf, 34

Circular-i-Azadi, 182

Civil & Military Gazette, 52n, 55n

Congress, Indian National, 93, 95, 98,
202

Constantinople (see Turkey)

Cotton,Sir Henry, 130

Council Act, Indian, of 1892, 99-101;
of 1909, 122
Crete, 50
Cross, 28
Currie, Sir Philip, 25-6
Curzon, Lady, 109, 135
Curzon, Lord, 11, 60, gets rebuff
from the German Kaiser, 61
and n, thanks the Kaiser for
his donation to India, 65-6;
opposes Baghdad Railway
project, 66-71; opines on the
German Kaiser, 67;against
Britain joining Triple Alliance,
70;opposes Russia in Persia,
70-1;against Indian nationalism,
107, 119-20;undermines Western-
educated Indians, 107, 119-20;
German diplomats in India
appreciate, 108-11;against Indian
immigrant labour for German
East-Africa, 155
Curzon Wyllie, Sir W. H. , 123

Daily Graphic, 136
Daily Telegraph, The, 64
Das, Hem Chandra, 176
Das, Taraknath, 182, 183, 191
Dasgupta, B. N. , 191
Dasgupta, J. C. , 191
Dawood Ali (P. N. Dutta), 183, 195

Dayal, Har, 167; and 'India House'
London, 174, 176-8;essentially a
scholar, 176n;in Paris as editor
of Bande Mataram, 178;in America,
183-4; Wangenheim from Turkey
informs about, 189; Geißler in
Geneva meets, 189, 193-5; as
Romalingam Das to Constantinople,
189; leaves Turkey for Geneva,
193 and n;and Wassmuss, 175-6;
his rift with the Constantinople-
based German officials, 195-8,
200;met by Chatto in Geneva,
199-200;comes to Berlin, 206;
differs from other Indian
revolutionary nationalists,
209-10n;leads Berlin Committee
with Chatto, 227; visits Constantinople second time as
Berlin Committee leader, 227
Dalal, V. P. , 190n
Delbrück, C. , 186
Delbrück, Hans, 63, 212
Delbrück, Helmuth, 168
Delhi Bomb Outrage, 90
Delhi Durbar, 74 and n, 134
Dernburg, B. , 165, 157
Deutsch-Ostafrica-Linie, 156
Deutsch-Ostafrikanische Gesell-
schaft, 154, 156
Dhingra, Madanlal, 175

Graeco-Turkish war, 50

Graetsch, F. , 187n

Gujaratis (language and people), in
    German East-Africa, 155-7

Gupta, H. L. , 183

Hadilkar, S. , 190n

Hafiz, A. , 191

Haldane, Viscount, 80

Hamburgischer Correspondent, 164n

Hamilton, Lord, 65, 68

Hardie, Keir J., 119,124n,130,131 and n

Hardinge, Lord, 85, 110, 127

Harmand, Jules, 135

Hatzfeld-Wildenburg, Count Paul, 33
    and n, 34

Hedin, Sven, 172

Heinemann, Fritz, 187

Heligoland-Zanzibar, the agreement of,
    39

Hentig, W-O von, 184n, 213n

Herat, 25

Heyer, Friedrich, 89 and n, 159 n

Heyking, Edmund Baron von, diplomatic
    career of, 40n; arrives in India,
    40;reports on the North-west
    frontier of India, 41-3;on Britain's
    Russophobia in India, 43-4; keeps
    good relations with Indian official
    circle, 98;his low opinion of Indian
    press and Congress leaders, 98;
    reports on Indian Council Act of
    1892, 99-101

Heyking, Elisabeth von, 40, 98, 102

Hewett, Sir John, 127

Hindu, The, 146

Hitler, A. , 146

Hoffmann, Father, 187n

Holderness, T. W. , 154

Holstein, Friedrich von, 31 and n

'Home Churges', 94, 130

Home Rule, Irish, 93, 173

Hyndman, H. M. , 132,133,174, 213n

Illbert Bill, 29 and n

imperialism, the diplomacy of, 11-2

Indian Home Rule Society, 132, 173

Indian Muslims, Prince Bismarck's
    comment on, 23;Holstein's comm-
    ent on, 31, Turkey-oriented
    attitude of, 53-4, 87-90;of north-
    west frontier revolt, 54-6;Kaiser
    Wilhelm II's comments on the
    importance of, 55, 168;in German
    East-Africa, 155;German war-time
    policy based on, 167-72, 184-206

Indian nationalism (see also Indian
    unrest), German views of, 81, 123-
    42;factors leading to, 120;extr-
    emist groups of, 120-22, 209n

Indian revolutionary nationalists,
    172-84

Indian Sociologist, 173, 177

Indian Unrest, German diplomats
    give the causes of, 123-6;

247

Kühlmann, Richard von, 119, 132 and n

Kuropatkin, General, 53, 56

Kuweit, 60, 70, 72, 73, 211

L-Eclair, 81n

l' Humanite, 180

Lahiri, J. N. , 191

Lansdowne, Lord, 71, 73, 99

Lancers, the 9th, 134-5

Latta, Rishi Kesh, 191

Le Moniteur de Rome, 32

Leipzig mission, 153

Leipziger Neueste Nachrichten, 168n, 185 and n

Lynden, Count, 97

Leyds, W. J. , 62

liberalism, of the British in India, 96-97, 129-30;official Germans opposed to, 96-101, 144-5

Lloyd George, David, 81

Lockhurst, Sir Willium, 152

Löhlein, Capt. , 172n

Longet, M. J. , 180

Luxburg, Karl-Ludwig Count von, 59, 88 and n, 89-90

Lyall, Sir Alfred, 46, 47

Macaulay, Sir Thomas, 95

MacDonald, R. , 130n, 131

Mc Mahon, Sir Henry, 78

Malcolm, Jan, 110

Malumat, 55

Mannesmann, H. R. , 172n, 208n

Marathe, Narayan, 191

Meinicke, G. , 153

Mertens, Wilhelm, 190

Metternich, Count Paul Wolff von, diplomatic career of, 33n; reports on Britain' s position in India, 33-4, 36-8; advises Berlin British friendship, 81; accompanies the Kaiser in his Orient trip, 171n

Minto, Lord, 122, 138, 174

Miquel von, 76

miscegenetion, 115-17

Mittwoch, Eugen, 206n

Modern Review, 142

Morley, Lord, 77-8, 120, 133

Morley-Minto Reforms, 122, 126

Morning Post, 142

Münchener Neueste Nachrichten, 127n

Müller, F. Max, 143, 144

Mueller, Herbert, 191, 192 and n, 206

Mukherjee, S. C. , 191

Muzaffarpur, 122

Nachrichtenstelle für den Orient, 170n, 205 and n, 212

Nadolny, Capt. , 206n

Naik, K. K. , 191

Naoroji, Dadabhai, 99, 100

Narayan, J. P. , 131n

National Review, 71

Nationalism(see under Indian
   nationalism)

Nationalzeitung, 163

Nazis, and the Hindu Mahasabha,
   144-5, 145n

Nehru, J. , 145n, 180n, 190n

Neue Orient,der, 206n

New York Sun, The, 181

Nicholas II, 14, 50, 137

Neneteenth Century and After, the,
   146

Noetling, Dr. , 162

Norddeutsche Allgemeine Zeitung,
   49

Novoye Vremya, 23n, 77

Okuma,Count, 140

Oppenheim, Baron Max von,the career
   of, 170;in charge of German
   Foreign Office organised Pan-
   Islamic movement, 170-2; and the
   Kaiser's Damascus speech of 1898,
   171;advises and supervises Berlin
   Indians, 191;opens office for Indian
   activities, 192; the Berlin Indians'
   resentment with, 198 and n;
   establishes die Nachrichtenstelle

für den Orient, 205; opposes
   Berlin Indians direct contact
   with the German Foreign Office,
   206, 207 and n;his Indian plan
   compared with that of Chatto's,
   207

Otto, Prof. R. , 198 and n

Pal, B. C. , 133

Pall Mall Gazette, 32

Pan-Islamism, 77, 87-90

Paramanand, Bhai, 177

Paranpy, Gopal, 191

Penjdeh, 25 and n

Peters, Karl, 152

Pillai, Champakaraman, 189, 190
   and n, 191, 227

Pillai, Ramana, 191

Pingley, V. G. , 191

Pioneer, The, 47, 52n, 151, 153

Polovtsov, Capt. , 78

Prabhakar, M. , 191

Prasad, Sufi Amba, 183

Pratap, M. , 184, 191

Prince of Wales, 138

Prittwitz, von, 172

Pro-India, 189n, 190

Punch, 132n

Punjabee, The, 178

Puri, R. N. , 182

Quadt, Count von, diplomatic career of, 79n;reports on British suspicion of the Germans in India, 79; on British maltreatment of the Indians, 123;reports Indian enthusiasm for Japan, 137-8, talks with Kitchener, 138-9

Queen's proclamation, 122

Raci(ali)sm(see also 'white man's superiority), 116-7, 137

Rahman, Abdur, 191

Rai, Lala Lajpat, 145n, 189n, 210n

Rana, S. R., 175 and n, 179, 188

Rand, W. C., 103

Rao, K. S., 191

Rathsam, Theodor, 47

Rech, 77

Rechenberg, Albert Baron von, 156, 157

Rechtstaat, 131 and n

Red Crescent, Society and movement, 87, 88

Regendanz, H. K., 191 and n

Reichstag, 128, 156, 158

Reinsurance Treaty, 39

Remy, Erwin, 79

Reuß, Prince Heinrich VII, 23

Reuß, Prince Heinrich XXXI, diplomatic career of, 79n;reports on Triple Entente powers' amity in India, 79-80;reports on German Crown Prince's Indian visit, 84-5;on Indians' estimation of Germany, 85;admires Lord Curzon, 110, 127;explains Indian unrest, 125-6;against Morley-Minto reforms, 126-8; likes partion of Bengal and Bomfylde Fuller, 127

Reveliotty, 80

Reventlow, Ernst Count zu, 82

Review of Religion, 138

Richthofen, Baron Herbert von, diplomatic career of, 122n; reports on terrorism in India, 122; on British MPs in India, 130

Rifaat, M., 189

Ripon, Lord, 32, 96

Roberts, General, 25

Radolin, 53

Roos-Koppel, George, 134

Rosebery, 5th Earl of, 44

Ross, 103

Roy, Satish Chandra, 191

Roy, Tarachand, 191

Sabah, 55

Salisbury, Lord, 24, 98 and n

Sarker, Dhirendra, 191

Saturday Review, The, 46

Saurma, Baron von, 55 and n

Dayal's sudden departure from
Turkey, 197
Wassmuss, 195, 196
Watan, 138
Webb, A. , 129
Weber, Dr. , 196
Wedderburn, W. , 102 and n, 129
Wegener, G. , 135-6, 146, 150
Welt-Korrespondenz, 162 and n
Weltpolitik, 16, 57ff, 167
Wesendonk, Otto Günther von, career
of, 201n; receives Chatto at the
German Foreign Office, 201;his
relations with the Berlin Indians,
204n;issues Der Neue Orient, 206n
White, General, 49
whiteman's supremacy, 133-7
Wilhelm II(see also under Curzon
and Indian Muslims), earliest
actions as emperor, 39;and the
Siam crisis, 44; and the Graeco-
Turkish war, 50-1;follows Muslim
unrest in India, 52-7;reacts to
hostile Anglo-Indian press, 62-3;
donates to Indian famine relief,
64-5;relations with the Czar, 74-5;
on Baghdad Railway, 80;on India's
importance to Britain, 81, 167, 168;
writes to George V on his son's
visit to India, 83;shows satisfaction
at British India's welcome to his son,

84, 86;approves Voretzsch's
idea of British royal line in
India, 118;on whiteman's
supremacy, 119;137;understands
Indian unrest, 124;hates socialism,
133, takes interest in military
matters (including Indian),
135, 152;fears Japanese aggression
in India, 137-42;praises British
administration in India, 151;on
Indian settlement in German
East-Africa, 154-5 and n;
approves Berlin's war-time
threat-to-India policy, 167-169
and n
Windhausen, Father, 187 n
Witte, Count, 76, 208

'yellow peri', 137 and n
Yugantar Ashram, 183

Zache, Hans, 150
Zamindar, 89
Zanzibar, 154
Zentrum party, 157
Zimmermann, Arthur, 204

EUROPÄISCHE HOCHSCHULSCHRIFTEN

Reihe III Geschichte und ihre Hilfswissenschaften

Nr. 1 Horst Zimmermann, Bern: Die Schweiz und Österreichs Anschluss an die Weimarer Republik. 253 S. 1967. (Vergriffen)

Nr. 2 Urs Brand, Bern: Die schweizerisch-französischen Unterhandlungen über einen Handelsvertrag und der Abschluss des Vertragswerkes von 1864. 332 S. 1968.

Nr. 3 N. von Preradovich, Bensheim: Die Wilhelmstrasse und der Anschluss Österreichs 1918–1933. 400 S. 1971.

Nr. 4 Erwin Bischof, Bern: Rheinischer Separatismus 1918–1924. Hans Adam Dortens Rheinstaatbestrebungen. 152 S. 1969.

Nr. 5 Walter Schümperli, Basel: Die Vereinten Nationen und die Dekolonisation. 160 S. 1970.

Nr. 6 Fritz Koenig, Bern: Die Verhandlungen über die internationale Rheinregulierung im st. gallisch-vorarlbergischen Rheintal von den Anfängen bis zum schweizerisch-österreichischen Staatsvertrag von 1892. 240 S. 1971.

Nr. 7 Rolf Darmstadt, Frankfurt: Der Deutsche Bund in der zeitgenössischen Publizistik. 242 S. 1971.

Nr. 8 Otto Marchi, Zürich: Der erste Freischarenzug. 216 S. 1971.

Nr. 9 Eva Mohr, Frankfurt a.M.: Fénelon und der Staat. 176 S. 1971.

Nr. 10 Jürg Wegmüller, Bern: Das Experiment der Volksfront. Untersuchungen zur Taktik der Kommunistischen Internationale der Jahre 1934 bis 1938. 164 S. 1972.

Nr. 11 Barbara Schnetzler, Zürich: Die frühe amerikanische Frauenbewegung und ihre Kontakte mit Europa (1836–1869). 148 S. 1971.

Nr. 12 Ursula Krattiger, Bern: Mündigkeit. Ein Fragenkomplex in der schweizerischen Diskussion im 19. Jahrhundert, vor allem zur Zeit der Armennot von 1840 bis 1860. 220 S. 1972.

Nr. 13 Jost Nikolaus Willi, Basel: Der Fall Jacob-Wesemann (1935/1936). Ein Beitrag zur Geschichte der Schweiz in der Zwischenkriegszeit. 468 S. 1972.

Nr. 14 Peter Eggenberger, Zürich: Bundesrat Emil Welti. Sein Einfluss auf die Bundesverfassungsrevision von 1874. 208 S. 1972.

Nr. 15 Peter Grupp, Tübingen: Theorie der Kolonialexpansion und Methoden der imperialistischen Aussenpolitik bei Gabriel Hanotaux. 218 S. 1972.

Nr. 16 Rudolf Gerber, Zürich: Johann Rudolf Sulzer 1749–1828. Biographische Untersuchung zur Entstehung der Mediationsverfassung. 168 S. 1972.

Nr. 17 Michel Hammer, Genève: L'entente des trois empereurs: Recherches sur les méthodes et l'orientation de la politique extérieure russe entre 1879 et 1881. 184 p. 1973.

Nr. 18 Wolfgang Miege, Mainz: Das Dritte Reich und die Deutsche Volksgruppe in Rumänien 1933–38. Ein Beitrag zur nationalsozialistischen Volkstumspolitik. 350 S. 1972.

Nr. 19 Jürg Schoch, Zürich: Die Oberstenaffäre – eine innenpolitische Krise (1915/1916). 172 S. 1972.

Nr. 20 Markus Leimgruber, Basel: Politischer Liberalismus als Bildungserlebnis bei Augustin Keller. 136 S. 1973.

Nr. 21 Ania Peter, Zürich: William E. Rappard und der Völkerbund. / Ein Schweizer Pionier der Internationalen Verständigung. 186 S. 1973.

Nr. 22 Charles Spillmann, Zürich: Otto Lang 1863–1936. Sozialismus und Individuum. 140 S. 1973.

Nr. 23 Gerlind Nasarski, Köln: Osteuropavorstellungen in der konservativ-revolutionären Publizistik. Analyse der Zeitschrift "Deutsches Volkstum" 1917–1941.

Nr. 47   Samir Girgis, Zürich: The Predominance of the Islamic Tradition of Leadership in Egypt during Bonaparte's Expedition. 138 p. 1975.

Nr. 48   Werner Meyer, Basel: Demokratie und Cäsarismus. Konservatives Denken in der Schweiz zur Zeit Napoleons III. 149 S. 1975.

Nr. 49   Kurt Meyer, Zürich: Die Gestaltung der Luzerner Volksschule von 1848–1910. 156 S. 1975.

Nr. 50   Christoph Pfister, Freiburg i.Ue.: Die Publizistik Karl Ludwig von Hallers in der Frühzeit 1791–1815. 210 S. 1975.

Nr. 51   Otto Becker, Tübingen: Kaiserwahl, deutsche Königswahl und Legitimitäts-prinzip in der Auffassung der späten Staufer und ihres Umkreises. Mit einem Exkurs über das Weiterwirken der Arengentradition Friedrich II unter seinen Nachkommen und den Angiovinen.

Nr. 52   Ahmad Mahrad, Hamburg: Dokumentation über die persisch-deutschen Beziehungen von 1918–1933. (Ergänzung zu Band Nr. 37).

Nr. 53   Jochen Grube, Tübingen: Bismarcks Politik in Europa und Übersee. Seine "Annäherung" an Frankreich im Urteil der Pariser Presse. 286 S. 1975.

Nr. 54   Joyce Schober, München: Die deutsche Spätaufklärung. 310 S. 1975.

Nr. 55   Brigitte Ahlers, Tübingen: Die ältere Fassung der Vita Radbodi.

Nr. 56   Wolfram Siemann, Tübingen: 'Volksgeist' und Verfassungsgebung. Die Bedeu-tung der Juristendominanz in den Verfassungsverhandlungen der Frankfurter Nationalversammlung 1848/49 für eine Entscheidung zwischen konservativer Reform und demokratischem Liberalismus.

Nr. 57   Hans-Wolfgang Wetzel, Tübingen: Presseinnenpolitik im Bismarckreich (1874–1890). Das Problem der Repression oppositioneller Zeitungen. 365 S. 1975.

Nr. 58   Max Madörin, Basel: Die Septembermassaker von 1792 im Urteil der französischen Revolutionshistoriographie 1792–1840. 1975.

Nr. 59   Hartmut Müller-Kinet, Heidelberg: Die höchste Gerichtsbarkeit im Deutschen Staatenbund 1806–1866. 257 S. 1975.

Nr. 60   Hans-Alois Weber, Köln: Herodots Verständnis von Historie. Untersuchungen zur Methodologie und Argumentationsweise Herodots. 1975.

Nr. 61   Karl-Heinz Wyss, Zürich: Leo Jud – Seine Entwicklung zum Reformator 1519–1523. 263 S. 1976.

ISBN 3 261 02102 0